The Legacy of Second-Wave Feminism in American Politics

Angie Maxwell · Todd Shields
Editors

The Legacy of Second-Wave Feminism in American Politics

palgrave
macmillan

Editors
Angie Maxwell
University of Arkansas
Fayetteville, AR, USA

Todd Shields
University of Arkansas
Fayetteville, AR, USA

ISBN 978-3-030-09670-0   ISBN 978-3-319-62117-3 (eBook)
https://doi.org/10.1007/978-3-319-62117-3

© The Editor(s) (if applicable) and The Author(s) 2018, corrected publication 2018
Softcover re-print of the Hardcover 1st edition 2018
This work is subject to copyright. All rights are solely and exclusively licensed by the Publisher, whether the whole or part of the material is concerned, specifically the rights of translation, reprinting, reuse of illustrations, recitation, broadcasting, reproduction on microfilms or in any other physical way, and transmission or information storage and retrieval, electronic adaptation, computer software, or by similar or dissimilar methodology now known or hereafter developed.
The use of general descriptive names, registered names, trademarks, service marks, etc. in this publication does not imply, even in the absence of a specific statement, that such names are exempt from the relevant protective laws and regulations and therefore free for general use.
The publisher, the authors and the editors are safe to assume that the advice and information in this book are believed to be true and accurate at the date of publication. Neither the publisher nor the authors or the editors give a warranty, express or implied, with respect to the material contained herein or for any errors or omissions that may have been made. The publisher remains neutral with regard to jurisdictional claims in published maps and institutional affiliations.

Cover illustration: © The Photo Access/Alamy Stock Photo

Printed on acid-free paper

This Palgrave Macmillan imprint is published by the registered company Springer International Publishing AG part of Springer Nature
The registered company address is: Gewerbestrasse 11, 6330 Cham, Switzerland

The original version of the book was revised: Final corrections have been incorporated. The Erratum to the book is available at https://doi.org/10.1007/978-3-319-62117-3_11

Contents

1 Introduction: Toward a New Understanding of Second-Wave Feminism 1
Angie Maxwell and Todd Shields

2 Generations Later, Retelling the Story 19
Sara M. Evans

3 Feminism, Anti-Feminism, and The Rise of a New Southern Strategy in the 1970s 39
Marjorie J. Spruill

4 "No More Silence!": Feminist Activism and Religion in the Second Wave 71
Laura Foxworth

5 Feminist Economics: Second Wave, Tidal Wave, or Barely a Ripple? 97
Cecilia Conrad

6 The Gender Gap as a Tool for Women's Political Empowerment: The Formative Years, 1980–1984 135
Susan J. Carroll

7   Latina Mobilization: A Strategy for Increasing
    the Political Participation of Latino Families   165
    Christina E. Bejarano and Valerie Martinez-Ebers

8   Black Women Lawmakers and Second-Wave Feminism:
    An Intersectional Analysis on Generational Cohorts
    Within Southern State Legislatures from 1990 to 2014   179
    Nadia E. Brown, Guillermo Caballero, Fernando Tormos,
    Allison Wong and Sharonda Woodford

9   Not in Conflict, But in Coalition: Imagining Lesbians at
    the Center of the Second Wave   205
    Claire Bond Potter

10 Conclusion: Assessing Second-Wave Historiography   231
    Lisa Corrigan

Erratum to: The Legacy of Second-Wave Feminism
in American Politics   E1
Angie Maxwell and Todd Shields

Editors and Contributors

About the Editors

Dr. Angie Maxwell is the Director of the Diane Blair Center of Southern Politics and Society and is the Diane D. Blair Associate Professor of Southern Studies in the political science department at the University of Arkansas. She is the author of *The Indicted South: Public Criticism, Southern Inferiority, and the Politics of Whiteness* (2014) which won the V. O. Key award for best book in Southern Politics and the C. Hugh Holman honorable mention for the best book in Southern Literary Criticism. She is also the co-editor of *Unlocking V. O. Key, Jr.: Southern Politics for the Twenty-first Century* (2011) and *The Ongoing Burden of Southern History: Politics and Identity in the Twenty-first Century South* (2012), and the editor of the new edition of Ralph McGill's *A Church, A School* (2012).

Dr. Todd Shields is the Dean of the J. William Fulbright College of Arts and Sciences and professor of political science at the University of Arkansas. He is the co-author of *The Persuadable Voter: Wedge Issues in Presidential Campaign* (2008) which was the winner of the Robert E. Lane award for the best book in Political Psychology. He is also the co-author of *Money Matters: The Effects of Campaign Finance Reform on Congressional Elections* (1999) and the co-editor of *The Clinton Riddle: Interdisciplinary Perspectives of the 42nd President* (2004), *New Voices in the Old South: How Women and Minorities Influence Southern Politics* (2008), *Unlocking V. O. Key, Jr.: Southern Politics for the Twenty-first*

Century (2011), *The Ongoing Burden of Southern History: Politics and Identity in the Twenty-first Century South* (2012), *and Taking the Measure: The Presidency of George W. Bush* (2013).

Contributors

Dr. Christina E. Bejarano is an associate professor of political science at the University of Kansas. Her research and teaching interests are in American politics, particularly in the areas of gender, race/ethnicity, and political behavior. She focuses on Latino political candidates and voters in US electoral politics. She is the author of *The Latina Advantage: Gender, Race, and Political Success* (2013) and *The Latino Gender Gap in US Politics* (2014).

Dr. Nadia E. Brown is an associate professor of political science and African-American studies at Purdue University. Her research interests lie broadly in American politics, but she has a particular interest in the politics of African-Americans and women. She is the author of a *Sisters in the Statehouse: Black Women and Legislative Decision Making* (2014), and she is the author of numerous articles focusing on black women's politics.

Guillermo Caballero is a second-year doctoral student in the Department of Political Science at Purdue University. Guillermo studies American politics, policy, and social movements. Guillermo's specific research interests are the legislative influence and representation of Black women and Latinas in the state legislatures.

Dr. Susan J. Carroll is professor of political science and women's and gender studies at Rutgers University and Senior Scholar at the Center for American Women and Politics (CAWP) of the Eagleton Institute of Politics. She is co-author of *More Women Can Run: Gender and Pathways to State Legislatures* (2013, with Kira Sanbonmatsu) and co-editor of *Gender and Elections: Shaping the Future of American Politics* (Third Edition 2014, with Richard L. Fox). Earlier books include *Women as Candidates in American Politics* (Second Edition 1994); *Women and American Politics: New Questions, New Directions* (2003); and *The Impact of Women in Public Office* (2001). Carroll also has published numerous journal articles and book chapters focusing on women candidates, voters, elected officials, and political appointees in the USA.

Dr. Cecilia Conrad is emeritus professor at Pomona College where she was the Stedman-Sumner Professor of Economics. She served two terms on the American Economic Association's Committee on the Status of Women in Economics Profession and is a past President of the International Association of Feminist Economics. Her scholarship focuses on effects of race and gender on economic status and economic thought. She is a past editor of the journal *The Review of Black Political Economy* and past associate editor of the journal *Feminist Economics* and co-editor of the *Aids, Gender, Sexuality and Development* (2011), *African Americans in the US Economy* (2005), and *Building Skills for Black Workers* (2004).

Dr. Lisa Corrigan is an associate professor of communication and the Director of the Gender Studies Program at the University of Arkansas, where she is also a faculty affiliate of the African and African-American Studies Program and the Latin American Studies Program. She is a feminist rhetorical scholar who researches and teaches in the areas of social movement studies, the Black Power and civil rights movement, prison studies, political communication, and the history of the Cold War. Her new book, *Prison Power: How Prison Influenced the Movement for Black Liberation (2016)*, examines the role of prison in shaping the Civil Rights and Black Power movements.

Dr. Sara M. Evans is Regents Professor Emerita at the University of Minnesota where she chaired the history department and served as director of the Center for Advanced Feminist Studies. In addition to serving on the editorial board for *Feminist Studies*, Evans is the author of seven books, including *Personal Politics: The Roots of Women's Liberation in the Civil Rights Movement and the New Left* (1980); *Born for Liberty: A History of Women in America* (1997); *Tidal Wave: How Women Changed America at Century's End* (2004), and she edited *Journeys that Opened Up the World: Women, Student Christian Movements, and Social Justice, 1955–1970* (2003).

Dr. Laura Foxworth is a visiting assistant professor in the Women's Leadership Program at Clemson University. She received her PhD from the University of South Carolina where she studied the women's movement, the American South, and changing religious institutions in the USA. Her dissertation, "The Spiritual is Political: The Modern Women's Movement and the Transformation of the Southern Baptist Convention," was supported by the Sallie Bingham Center for Women's

History and Culture at Duke University, the Gerald R. Ford Presidential Library, and the Southern Baptist Historical Library and Archives in Nashville, Tennessee. Dr. Foxworth has presented research at meetings for the Organization for American Historians, Southern Historical Association, Southern Association for Women Historians, and National Council on Public Historians. She currently serves as Managing Editor of *French Historical Studies*.

Dr. Valerie Martinez-Ebers is a University Distinguished Research professor of political science at the University of North Texas and former editor of the *American Political Science Review*, the flagship journal of the discipline. Dr. Martinez-Ebers has published widely on education policy, Latino/a politics, women in politics, and methods of survey research in outlets such as *American Political Science Review, American Journal of Political Science, Journal of Politics* and *Political Research Quarterly*. She is co-author of *Politicas: Latina Public Officials in Texas* (2008), *Latino Lives in America: Making It Home* (2010), and *Latinos in the New Millennium: An Almanac of Opinion, Behavior and Policy Preferences* (2012). She also edited *Perspectives on Race, Ethnicity and Religion: Identity Politics in America* (2009) and is one of the principal investigators for the Latino National Survey, an 8,600-respondent survey funded by the Ford, Carnegie, Russell Sage, Hewlett, Joyce, and National Science Foundations.

Dr. Claire Bond Potter is professor of history and Director of the Digital Humanities Initiative at The New School. She also serves as co-director of OutHistory.org, an LGBT digital history project, as a Distinguished Lecturer for the Organization of American Historians, and as a member of the Schlesinger Library Council at the Radcliffe Institute, Harvard University. From 2006 to 2015, she blogged at *Tenured Radical*, carried by the *Chronicle of Higher Education*. She is the author of the forthcoming *Digital U: Why Crowdsourcing, Social Media, Word Press and Google Hangouts Could Save the Humanities* (2018) and a history of feminist anti-violence politics, *Beyond Pornography: Susan Brownmiller, Andrea Dworkin, Catharine MacKinnon and the Campaign to End Violence Against Women*, 1968–2000.

Dr. Marjorie J. Spruill is Distinguished Professor Emerita of history at the University of South Carolina and is the author of *Divided We Stand: The Battle over Women's Rights and Family Values that Polarized*

American Politics (2017), *New Women of the New South: The Leaders of the Woman Suffrage Movement in the Southern States* (1993), and the editor of *One Woman, One Vote: Rediscovering the Woman Suffrage Movement* (1995) and *VOTES FOR WOMEN! The Woman Suffrage Movement in Tennessee, the South, and the Nation* (1995). She is also co-editor of *The South in the History of the Nation: A Reader* (1999); the three-volume anthology *South Carolina Women: Their Lives and Times* (2009; 2010; 2012), and the two-volume *Mississippi Women: Their Histories, Their Lives* (2002; 2010).

Dr. Fernando Tormos-Aponte received his PhD from the department of political science at Purdue University. He specializes in social movements, social policy, and the politics of diversity and inclusion. His research focuses on how social movements sustain mobilization and enhance their political influence. He has developed mixed-method research on the survival and political influence of social movements, including labor, environmental, human rights, student, and civil rights movements.

Allison Wong graduated from Purdue University majoring in history and philosophy. During her time at Purdue, she worked on projects relating to environmental policy and Asian American history. She currently serves as the District Scheduler for the Office of Congressman Eric Swalwell. Allison aspires to attend law school and focus on public interest law.

Sharonda Woodford is a fourth-year PhD candidate in the department of political science at Purdue University. Sharonda's research interest examines the intersection of race, sex, gender identity/expression, and sexual orientation. Sharonda is currently examining how the stigmatization of Black masculinities, shape Black male and female citizenship as marginalized constituents. Sharonda received her BA and MA from Jackson State University.

List of Figures

Fig. 5.1	Button Worn in 1980 Equal Rights Amendment March in Chicago, IL	100
Fig. 5.2	Median Earnings of Women as Percent of Median Earnings of Men, Year-round, Full-time Workers, 1960–2012	101
Fig. 5.3	Percentage of Women Employed as Private Household Workers by Race, 1960–2000	102
Fig. 5.4	Percentage of Women Employed as Clerical Workers by Race, 1960–2010	103
Fig. 5.5	Ratio of Black to White Median Earnings for Full-time, Year-round, Female Workers, 1955–2011	104
Fig. 5.6	Labor Force Participation Rate of Married Women, 1960–2010	104
Fig. 5.7	Labor Force Participation Rate of Married Women by Race, 1920–1970	106
Fig. 5.8	Feminization of Poverty, 1950–2012	106
Fig. 6.1	Number of Gender Gap Articles Published by Year, 1980–1984	138
Fig. 8.1	All Southern Legislators by Race and Gender, 1990–2014	181
Fig. 8.2	Alabama State Legislature, 1990–2014: Race and Gender by Date of Birth	188
Fig. 8.3	Florida State Legislature, 1990–2014: Race and Gender by Date of Birth	189
Fig. 8.4	Maryland State Legislature, 1990–2014: Race and Gender by Date of Birth	190

Fig. 8.5	Tennessee State Legislature, 1990–2014: Race and Gender by Date of Birth	191
Fig. 8.6	Texas State Legislature, 1990–2014: Race and Gender by Date of Birth	192
Fig. 8.7	Southern State Legislatures, 1990–2014: Black Women by Date of Birth	193
Fig. 8.8	Southern State Legislatures, 1990–2014: Black and Gender by Date of Birth	194
Fig. 8.9	Southern State Legislatures, 1990–2014: Race and Women by Date of Birth	194
Fig. 8.10	Southern State Legislatures, 1990–2014: Black Females and White Males by Date of Birth	195

CHAPTER 1

Introduction: Toward a New Understanding of Second-Wave Feminism

Angie Maxwell and Todd Shields

Abstract In this introductory chapter, Angie Maxwell and Todd Shields claim that the need to mark beginnings and endings of social movements, the over-reliance on popular, yet limited voices, the fact that feminism is not immune to white privilege, and the pain associated with lost battles for women's rights have all contributed to obscuring the true legacy of the Second-Wave feminist movement. They contend that existing narratives have inordinately focused on the media-appointed "leaders" of the movement, who were almost exclusively white, heterosexual, well-educated women who overshadowed the multi-racial, grassroots cast of hundreds of thousands of women in America and around the globe. While Third-Wave feminists drew attention to these omissions and recovered the history of overshadowed communities, the time has come to reconcile both waves and re-examine the legacy of Second-Wave Feminism in American politics. This reassessment shows that the Second Wave was comprised of a heterogeneous army of women who, though

---

The original version of the book was revised: Final corrections have been incorporated. The erratum to this chapter is available at https://doi.org/10.1007/978-3-319-62117-3_11

A. Maxwell (✉) · T. Shields
University of Arkansas, Fayetteville, USA

© The Author(s) 2018
A. Maxwell and T. Shields (eds.), *The Legacy of Second-Wave Feminism in American Politics*, https://doi.org/10.1007/978-3-319-62117-3_1

often divided, still significantly influenced economics, theology, political activism, electoral success, attitudes toward homosexuality, and support for gay marriage. In fact, in many ways they were so successful that they were blind to the anti-feminist counterattack forming across the country. This introduction highlights the feminist historians, political scientists, gender studies scholars, and economists who are placing women's activism at the center of our political landscape in their contributing chapters.

In her edited collection, *Feminist Coalitions: Historical Perspectives on Second-Wave Feminism in the United States*, Stephanie Gilmore speaks to the scholarly paralysis that has tempered our understanding of both the accomplishments and the failures, and of the structure and impact, of Second-Wave Feminism. Depicted most often as an offshoot of the Civil Rights Movement, Second-Wave feminists "are suspended in historical—or rather, ahistorical—amber, unable to move or be moved."[1] Gilmore's volume and its contributors did much to resurrect this debate. The paralysis, however, is not limited to the way in which the movement is conceived as branching from the larger fight for African-American rights, but also, as Sara M. Evans contends in Chap. 2, to our proclivity to periodization. The need to mark a beginning and an end to what has been a sustained and constant effort for women's equality—the need even to describe such periods as distinct "waves"—obscures much of the labor. And it obscures the laborers, many of whom remain absent from our narratives. Only popular leaders, or those leaders recognized by the media, present at key events highlighted by this periodization, remain in the public consciousness. Those leaders are almost exclusively privileged, white, and well-educated and function as the feature players overshadowing a multiracial, grassroots cast of hundreds of thousands of women in America and across the globe. And the movement itself, as the passage of a half-century has shown, lost control of the debate over women's rights as the individual became more powerful than the collective. And so the united front needed to brace against the titanic backlash proved elusive. The consciousness-raising opened women's eyes to their individual oppression, but not enough saw their own individual experience as part of a systemic and structural oppression for which political, collective, unified action remains the only antidote. Because the conservative backlash was so powerful, because the unity, despite the best efforts, was too fragile, because of our need to superficially mark beginnings and endings of social movements, because of our over-reliance on popular, yet limited voices, because feminism is not immune to white privilege, and because the losses were so painful for so many activists, we still struggle to understand what it all meant then and what it means for all of us now.

THE SECOND WAVE RECONSIDERED

To be fair, how the movement was portrayed in its time and how it has been remembered have drawn sharp criticism. For example, Charlotte Krolokke and Anne Scott Sorensen argue, "Second Wave feminism has come under attack from other marginalized groups, such as African American women and lesbians, for not including them." Furthermore, they assert "in the context of the complex power relationships of a postcolonial, but still imperial and capitalist world, [critics of Second-Wave Feminism] questioned what they saw as a predominantly white, middle-class, and heterosexual feminist agenda and raised the issue of a differentiated-identity politics based on the contingent and diversified but no less divisive intersections of gender, class, race/ethnicity, and sexuality."[2] The tendency, particularly in the initial scholarship on and retelling of the movement to describe a "hegemonic feminism," which "treats sexism as the ultimate oppression,"[3] disconnected from other bases of prejudice and discrimination, ignores the "double marginalization" of black women, as noted by Nadia E. Brown and her co-authors in Chap. 8 of this volume—not to mention the marginal role to which lesbian activists have been relegated, a historical correction that Claire Bond Potter boldly makes in Chap. 9. Essentialism, Krolokke and Sorensen contend— or "the tendency to assume a unitary notion of women," not only downplays African-American and Latino activism, but it prioritizes the needs of white women which are falsely assumed to be universal. Even believing in a kind of essential womanhood, promoted, for example, in Robin Morgan's *Sisterhood is Powerful* (1970)[4], is based on "unarticulated premises"[5] of some sort of common understanding of gender. Moreover, it even assumes universal motivation, as Christina E. Bejarano and Valerie Martinez-Ebers demonstrate in Chap. 7 in which they show how Latina women are transforming their leadership within the family into their electoral success as candidates. Such a tendency, Lisa Corrigan warns in Chap. 10 of this collection, threatened to "collapse the Second Wave into whiteness."

The examples of multiracial activism should have been apparent, even in the cherry-picked media coverage of the public protests and Equal Rights Amendment (ERA) marches, because, as Becky Thompson has shown, women of color not only participated in "white-dominated" feminist groups, but also in "mixed-gendered women's caucuses" and in "autonomous Black, Latina, Native American, and Asian feminist organizations."[3] The National Organization of Women (NOW), itself, was a mixed race organization with African American leaders such as attorneys Flo Kennedy and Pauli Murray.[6] Latina activists Aileen Hernandez succeeded Betty Friedan as president. And women of color were more supportive of the movement as a whole, with roughly 2/3 of those polled reporting sympathy to the cause, compared to only 1/3 of white women.[7] Thirty-five percent of the delegates to the 1977 Women's Convention in Houston with its record-setting attendance were women of color, and roughly 1/5 of the women in attendance were classified as low income.[8]

Despite the interracial nature of some women's organizations, Benita Roth has argued that early activist efforts were divided along racial and ethnic lines, but they existed alongside each other, paving many paths to Houston or "separate roads to Feminism."[9] Groups such as the Black Women's Alliance which expanded to become the Third World Women's Alliance and their journal *Triple Jeopardy*, "an antisexist, antiracist, anti-imperialist newspaper for women of color" and the fact that it criticized the Miss Black America pageant as putting "black women on the auction block again," and embraced the global struggles of African American, Native American, and Latina women,[10] gets wiped from historical memory.[11] The whitewashing of the story of Second-Wave Feminism too often also excludes the stories of theological and religious feminists, such as Catholics for the ERA, as pointed to by Laura Foxworth in Chap. 4 and has been characterized as "overly puritanical when it came to sexuality," an issue addressed by Claire Bond Potter in Chap. 9. Yet, the early histories of the Second Wave, rather than recognizing these distinct roads and analyzing where and how and when and why they intersected with each other, focused on elite white women (often WASPS, despite the fact that most of the white leaders in NOW were actually from the Midwest)[12] and on the more esoteric or philosophical competing types of feminism—liberationists versus socialists versus cultural versus radical feminists, for example.[13] It took the persistent activism of what we now label, Third-Wave Feminism, and the vocal critiques of black feminists in particular, to render the white privilege of our memory of Second-Wave Feminism visible.

The Combahee River Collective's "A Black Feminist Statement" frames gender and blackness as "interlocking oppressions"[14] that in many ways cannot be separated. Building on this image, Third-Wave Feminism advocates for widespread social justice and champions feminism "grounded in intersectional analysis." Lesbian and Jewish women have also shined a critical spotlight on whiteness within the activism and coverage of the movement, pointing to the "white woman's position as both oppressed and oppressor."[15] Still, as Corrigan summarizes in Chap. 10, "we aren't even close to producing collective, inclusive histories," and there are several reasons why.

One of the academic ripple effects of Second-Wave Feminism was a new commitment to and interest in women's history. Evans contends that the unintended consequence of this scholarly shift was that historians ignored the movement because they were engaged in the tedious work of recovering women's history. Even as early as 1979 at an academic symposium, writer Audre Lorde insisted that scholars were arrogantly ignoring the voices of "poor women, black and third-world women, and lesbians."[16] Assessments made by the media and/or on the basis of popular culture resulted in an inaccurate depiction of the Second Wave, crafted from cherry-picked events and focused on activist celebrities. Though these waves have no definitive beginning or end, events such as the 1968 Miss America pageant, as noted by Dorothy Sue Cobble, Linda Gordon, and Astrid Henry,[17] offer a well-known opening anecdote to the story of the movement, and the defeat of the ERA in 1982 is too often presented as the finale.[18] Such set points—1968 was also the year that Martha Weinman Lear penned "The Second Feminist Wave" in the *New York Times Magazine*, coining the phrase[19]—similar to the way in which Civil Rights history has had to be reconceived of as the Long Civil Rights Movement, obscure the work of countless women who labored long before the media noticed (the publication of Simone De Beauvoir's *The Second Sex*, in the USA in 1953, is sometimes considered the catalyst for feminist consciousness).[20] Moreover, as Roth argues, this timeline too often portrays Black and Chicana feminism as derivative of white feminism, as opposed to developing simultaneously as the historical record clearly indicates.[21] The same is true of Asian American and Native American organizations.

If this chosen timeline distorts our image of Second-Wave Feminism, then the preferred spokespersons who became the media-appointed "leaders" and "faces," further whitewashed the Second Wave, which, otherwise, was a heterogeneous, divided, and even unorganized movement. Women like Gloria Steinem were sought after by journalists and news outlets because of their popular writings, their intelligence, and their physical appearance. These media-appointed leaders are chosen for reasons that help media ratings, not because of reasons that help the movement, or because members of the movement have elected or chosen these individuals to be their representatives. It is important to note also that such representatives can be exploited against their own cause. Foxworth argues in Chap. 4 that these chosen celebrities—Steinem along with Betty Friedan—became targets when Christian anti-feminists pointed to these spokeswomen as evidence that feminism was a Jewish conspiracy. With a manufactured timeline and a limited cast of characters, it is not surprising that much of what was written about the movement also misrepresented its intentions and key messages. The sex wars dominated headlines, with feminists portrayed as anti-men, taking the movement's focus off gender equity in class, race, and the economic system.[22] The lack of attention specifically to economics, contends Cecilia Conrad in Chap. 5, actually drove many women of this generation into this academic field, not only developing a new subfield of feminist economics, but also establishing both the "discrimination" and "perfect market" theories that locate obstructions both inside and outside of the market to women's advancement.

The linear, singular storyline, perhaps most significantly, destroys our understanding of and appreciation for intersectionality. People's lives cross circles, Gilmore insists.[23] Their politics and interests are overdetermined and complex. Women of color, lesbians, religious women, and poor women fought multiple battles concurrently, an experience that privileged white women, nor the media, nor the first generation of scholars writing about the movement, could fully appreciate. Third-Wave feminists challenged this mythology effectively, though at times while condemning the movement whole cloth. They are not wrong. The feminist ideology of the 1970s was based on an "ethos of organizing one's own… actually recruiting large groups of women for coordinating activism across racial/ethnic lines was not prioritized," contends Roth.[24] Progress was made in the shadows, so to speak, but Second-Wave feminists did not all have equal voices, nor was everyone even given a chance to speak. There were, in reality, many different members and groups in the Second Wave who played important roles, in different places, in different times, and for different reasons.[25] According to Julia Wood, "Second wave feminism is not one, but many … and the question may not be whether you are a feminist, but which kind of feminist you are."[26] Similarly, Roth, in her book *Separate Roads to Feminism: Black, Chicana and White Feminists Movements in America's Second Wave*, argues that scholars should not consider the Second-Wave movement a single organization, but rather a mix of many separate feminist movements all pushing for different priorities and ideals, but all focused on the rights of women.

Yet if so many separate movements worked in tandem toward a collective goal of women's equality, then why were there so many failures, like the ERA? And why do so many inequities between men and women persist? In 1972, Gloria Steinem defined sisterhood in the first issue of *Ms. Magazine* as the "deep personal connection of women," which, she argued, "often ignores barriers of age, economics, worldly experience, race, culture..."[27] But this "fiction of unity"[28] seemed to dissolve within a decade. In her 1982 essay "Voices from a Postfeminist Generation," which appeared on the cover of the *New York Times Magazine*, Susan Bolotin alluded to the answer. Bolotin pointed to the divide between women's collective consciousness and their individual experiences. "Not one woman I spoke to," Bolotin wrote, "believes that women receive equal pay for comparable work, but it does not occur to most of them to use the power of the feminist movement to improve their position."[29] This disconnect may have resulted from feminist efforts to personalize the discrimination that women faced. Even Betty Friedan's *The Feminine Mystique*, credited with catalyzing women's consciousness, can be viewed as focused on "individual autonomy" and "the right to self-determination,"[30] implying that "personal transformation is a means to bring about social change."[31]

These consciousness-raising sessions, organized throughout the country, allowed women to discuss their personal experiences and come to grips with the way in which gender shapes expectations regarding housework, sexual pleasure, and their treatment as consumers. "The media treated women as mindless sex objects to sell otherwise unappealing products," notes Nancy MacLean.[32] The consciousness-raising method was a necessary step in awakening women to their specific relationship to gender oppression, but many turned a critical eye on the self, rather than uncovering the institutional embeddedness of sexism. Similarly, the mantra "the personal is political," initiated by activists in the Civil Rights Movement, such as Anne Braden, and repeated both by the New Left and many Second-Wave feminist organizations,[33] was intended to enlighten women to the way in which socially constructed gender roles affected their lives and to expose the way in which issues often considered personal and private—abortion, domestic violence, unemployment, etc.—were deeply political. In many ways, the success of this consciousness-raising resulted in specific efforts to address inequity, which in turn allowed women to focus on their individual gains. Their success unraveled any attempts at unity, so much so that, as Susan Carroll contends in Chap. 6, by 1984 it was debatable as to whether Geraldine Ferraro's nomination as Democratic-hopeful Walter Mondale's running mate would even entice more women to vote.

When women grew increasingly aware of the institutional sexism affecting them directly, they initiated campaigns to address their individual repression. In Chap. 2, Evans mentions the SEARS campaign as emblematic of this fundamental shift in the movement. The Chicago branch of NOW launched a campaign against retail giant Sears based on its refusal to promote women to higher-paying positions. Rather than focusing efforts on the ERA, this initiative prioritized the advancement of individuals. Though surely important in the overall efforts of Second-Wave feminists to secure economic power for women, the SEARS initiative and others like it altered the meaning of the "personal is political," with political protests now seen as an avenue to individual improvement. Third-Wave feminists—or those who the media has called on to speak for the Third Wave—such as Naomi Wolf and Rene Denfeld[34]—have continued to offer solutions based on not only women's needs, but also the needs of separate communities of women based on class and race and sexuality. The post-1990s feminists have been criticized by the generation that preceded them for being "all style, no substance,"[35] but many in the Third Wave continue to dispel the mythology of the Second Wave and its efforts to raise a universal women's consciousness.

The Second-Wave movement itself (its rhetoric and its success) and the Third-Wave movement gave rise to and fueled this shift to individualism, and there are advantages and disadvantages to such a shift. The Third Wave has the added difficulty of functioning in a "cultural climate hostile to feminism"[36]—not that the Second Wave didn't encounter opposition, but the real backlash surged in the wake of the 1970s movement. And that damage came at the hands of anti-feminists who also twisted the "personal is political" to fit their own cause. Phyllis Schlafly's STOP ERA movement stood for "Stop Taking our Privileges," and her rhetoric and the rhetoric of her followers convinced many women that the ERA would damage their individual lives. They would be expected to get jobs, enter the draft—"foxholes are bad enough for men, but they certainly are not a place for women"[37]—and put their children in government-run day cares, anti-feminists warned. Calling the feminist movement "a delusion," Moral Majority leader, Jerry Falwell, who praised Schlafly, employed the same technique, cautioning women about the way in which the ERA would impact their individual lives—their custody arrangements, their protection from military service, etc.[38] As Marjorie J. Spruill clearly shows in Chap. 3, the anti-feminist movement portrayed the Second Wave as a personal threat and an insult to who they were as women.

The GOP took notice too, realizing that anti-feminism, and its corollary, the "family values" movement, could pay huge political dividends if they invested in this reactionary style of identity politics. As Carroll notes in Chap. 6, Reagan's administration pointed to the individual successes of women to deny the ongoing structural sexism in America. Similarly, Susan Faludi summarizes in her book, *Backlash: The Undeclared War Against American Women*, the Reagan era gave rise to "a powerful counterassault on women's rights, a backlash, an attempt to retract the handful of small and hard-won victories that the feminist movement did manage to win for women."[39] And it wasn't just about promoting traditional gender roles; the negative attacks were so intense and so damaging as to render the feminist label wholly unpopular. The anti-ERA forces started the demonization, with members of groups such as Happiness of Womanhood (HOW) calling feminists "profane," "nihilistic," and "women but not ladies."[40] In fact, by 1992, a Time/CNN poll found that while close to 80% of college women believe that the Second Wave had improved the lot of women, only 33% were willing to call themselves feminists.[41] Moreover, by the 1990s the energy of the feminist movement seemed depleted by this backlash, resulting—most notably in the culture industry—in the closing of "feminist presses, publications, record labels, and bookstores."[42] Third-Wave activists resurrected feminist arts as explained in "Riot Grrrl Manifesto," authored by Kathleen Hanna of the band Bikini Kill, and saw them as a means to confront the family values backlash through their individual art. "We seek," she declared, "to create revolution in our own lives every single day by envisioning and creating alternatives to the bullshit Christian capitalist way of doing things."[43]

The accomplishments and methods of the prior generation, however, were not lost on this new cohort of activists. Rachel Walker, for example, creator of the Third Wave Foundation, organized youth voter registration drives and invested in women's political initiatives. Motivated by the Anita Hill interrogation by the Senate Judiciary committee in 1992, Walker (daughter of writer Alice Walker) attempted to resurrect the common bond of women in the service of activism. "To be a feminist," Walker announced, "is to integrate an ideology of equality and female empowerment into the very fiber of my life. It is to search for personal clarity in the midst of systematic destruction, to join in sisterhood with women when often we are divided, to understand power structures with the intention of challenging them."[44] The ongoing dance between this conservative backlash, between the cohorts of the Second and Third Waves, and among scholars about what the movement did or did not accomplish, deserves greater attention. When there was synergy, progress was made, though sometimes in ways that can only be seen now, long after the Second Wave has receded and after the Third Wave has forcefully crested.

Ruth Rosen notes in her landmark work, *The World Split Open*, that "each generation of women activists leaves an unfinished agenda for the next generation."[45] Whatever the criticisms may be in retrospect—even of the "wave" concept itself[46]—the legacy of the movement warrants recovery and understanding. The strength of this collaboration is twofold. First, these essays serve as a reminder that movements do not happen in a vacuum or without repercussions. Second-Wave Feminism spurred an anti-feminist response that fundamentally changed such longstanding institutions as the Southern Baptist Convention and the Republican Party, among others. Even though the pendulum swung back with great conservative force, it did not suffocate the movement as a whole. Second, though the major setbacks and the major victories of the movement are well-documented, this collection points to unexamined accomplishments, including the rise of female economists and a focus on women's economic status, the expansion of women's spirituality, and a growing politicization that underscores a powerful gender gap in voting. And the influence extends well into the twenty-first century. New ripples—the impact that Second-Wave activism had on Latina women and their eventual success as political candidates, or the way in which the movement worked in tandem with the Civil Rights Movement for future generations of African American female state leaders—require scholars to reconceive of the wave in much broader terms.

As these essays demonstrate, movements, simply put, move. And sometimes their impact is not felt until decades later. Rather than condemn all the mistakes—the focus on the individual and the failure to understand intersectionality—that were surely made by the movement itself, by the media who handpicked their spokeswomen, and by the scholars who were too quick to create a definitive timeline and too often told only one part of the story, the critical light directed by the Third Wave and the sheer passage of time should reveal a more nuanced, balanced, honest, and accurate assessment of the legacy of this generation of activists 50 years later. The constant motion of women's activism, no matter how it has been perceived or recorded, has indeed produced change in ways both expected and unexpected. Part reflection, part recovery, this collection only scratches the surface of a "wave" that is much wider and deeper than has been acknowledged.

Chapter Summaries

In "Generations Later, Retelling the Story," Sara M. Evans counters the narrow narrative that is popularly used to describe the Second-Wave movement. Rather, she advocates for a broader consideration of a movement that remains active and in progress. The formal association of specific waves with key leaders limits our understanding of the grassroots, widespread activity that occurred and remains ongoing. Such an omission often accompanies top-down narratives of American history that simplify class, racial, and ethnic diversity within a movement, as well as the major contributions made by groups outside of the historical spotlight. As one of the groundbreaking scholars in the field, Evans encourages a new generation to view the movement as having exactly that: real, sustained, continuous movement. One of the primary criticisms of Second-Wave Feminism was that it catered only to the needs of privileged white women—a perspective that Evans reconsiders. More than that, the leaders of the Second Wave, and the principles for which they stood, were demonized as radical and destructive to American society. Opposition groups used these arguments to oppose the ERA and to serve as catalysts for bringing otherwise politically inactive conservative women into the political arena.

Marjorie J. Spruill uncovers the source for much of that antagonism by extending our common understanding of the Republican Party's racially motivated Southern Strategy to their conservative stance on women's rights. Professor Spruill, in her chapter, "Feminism, Antifeminism, and the Rise of a New Southern Strategy in the 1970s," notes that the political activism of feminists living in the South served as a catalyst for conservative groups to organize in opposition. When overt racist appeals were becoming increasingly unacceptable, following the successes of the Civil Rights Movement, the emergence of a politically active group of anti-feminists in the South provided the GOP with a new group of southern whites to convert. An unexpected result of the Second Wave was, in fact, the activation of conservative women and thier "family values" into the partisan divide. In particular, Professor Spruill gives specific attention to the organization of, and opposition to, the feminist-inspired International Women's Year conferences in 1977, as a critical turning point.

In addition to the evolving Republican Southern Strategy in response to Second-Wave Feminism, another unintended consequence of Second-Wave political activism was the development and popularization of the now ubiquitous voting pattern called the "gender gap." One of the leading scholars of women in contemporary American politics, Susan Carroll, contends that a "gender gap" in electoral politics has been used as a political and rhetorical devise by both feminists and anti-feminists. In Carroll's chapter, "The Gender Gap as a Tool for Women's Political Empowerment: The Formative Years, 1980–1984," she highlights a consistent difference in voting patterns between men and women, with the tendency of women to vote for Democratic presidential candidates and men to vote for Republican candidates. Carroll considers when this pattern was first observed, how it was framed, and the variety of ways that this trend has been used as a political tool by both liberals and conservatives. Even though First-Wave feminists hoped that once women were given the right to vote, they would immediately use their votes to bring about policy-related changes, the persistent and widespread differences in the vote choices of women and men became apparent only after the successes of Second-Wave feminists. The "gender gap" in voting first caught public attention following the election of President Ronald Reagan in 1980. Since then, subsequent concern over the gender gap, and developing a campaign strategy in light of the general pattern, have become common campaign practices. Carroll discusses these aspects of the gender gap in the efforts to ratify the ERA and the efforts to have a woman added to the Democratic presidential ticket in 1984.

Not all of the efforts of Second-Wave feminists were focused on direct political and electoral action—at least not in the traditional view of political action such as protests, voting strategies, and legal challenges. Another dimension of the multifaceted Second-Wave feminist movement was the intellectual influences that feminists had in academia and in traditional fields of study. Given the emphasis of Second-Wave Feminism on equality in the workplace and fair labor standards, it is not surprising that

Second-Wave feminists developed theoretical challenges to traditional economic theories. Cecilia Conrad explains how feminists influenced and faced opposition in the field of economics, and how feminist economic theories continue to challenge mainstream economic thought. In her chapter, "Feminist Economics: Second Wave, Tidal Wave, or Barely a Ripple?," Conrad examines the influence of the movement on three policy issues: pay equity, national income accounting, and economic development policy. She describes the evolution of feminist economic thought, its relationship to Second-Wave Feminism, its influence on the broader discipline of economics, and its impact on American public policy more generally.

Laura Foxworth argues that scholars have neglected to fully understand the influences that Second-Wave feminists have had on contemporary theology and the involvement of women in religious institutions. In Foxworth's "'No More Silence!': Feminist Activism and Religion in the Second Wave," she examines the relationship between Second-Wave Feminism, religion, the ERA, and the continued struggle for equality within churches in America. Foxworth points out that during the Second Wave, there was a surge of feminists who worked to influence and change orthodox theology. The proponents of this new feminist theology hoped to establish leadership roles for women, eliminate sexism, and end "patriarchal religious hierarchies." According to Foxworth, other feminists decided that the patriarchy in the church wasn't going to change, so they sought religious expressions outside of the traditional church. The result was an expansion of "woman's spirituality" and an elevated understanding of the female divine in the absence of male presence. Some feminist "reformers," however, did remain inside the church advocating for equality within the traditional religious institutions and practices, and these "less radical" reformers sometimes reached a much wider audience, at least until the debate over the ERA polarized women—often along religious lines. Still, Foxworth shows that despite a great deal of political opposition from traditional religious institutions, not all denominations or religious individuals, particularly in the South, however, opposed the ERA. Foxworth convincingly argues that while Second-Wave feminists generally focused their strategies on creating equality within the workplace, and in the electoral process, they also pursued equality within religious institutions.

In the chapter coauthored by Christina E. Bejarano and Valerie Martinez-Ebers, "Latina Mobilization: A Strategy for Increasing the

Political Participation of Latino Families," they claim that there is evidence of the growing political influence of Latinas in contemporary American politics, as well as the growing distinctiveness of Latinas in their partisanship and participation rates. Overall, Latinas' increased community participation may provide them with stronger civic skills and stronger ties to their community/institutions. In addition, Latinas' community involvement may also be linked to their higher political participation levels and increasing success rates as political candidates. Bajarano and Martinez-Ebers reason that it is important to focus on Latinas as catalysts of political change since they are perceived to be the key to propelling Latino families and communities into the political process. In fact, some research suggests that Latinas may be the driving force behind familial decisions to enter or stay out of the political arena altogether. The authors use multiple data sources and methods to discuss the various roles of Latinas in mobilizing the Latino community and their growing influence in American politics.

In "Black Women Lawmakers and Second-Wave Feminism: An Intersectional Analysis on Generational Cohorts within Southern State Legislatures from 1990 to 2014," Nadia E. Brown and her coauthors show how Second-Wave feminists indirectly paved the way for African American women to become political leaders, particularly at the state level. They examine differences in class and generational cohorts among African American female state legislators from 1990 to 2014. Further, they focus primarily on the American South since that is where many African Americans live and where female African Americans have had the most electoral success. Brown claims that while the Second Wave opened doors for female political activism and for women to learn from strong female political leadership, the movement focused largely on the concerns of white women and generally ignored the concerns of African American women—who live in a double bind at the intersection of race and gender. Brown and colleagues state that one consequence of the Voting Rights Act (VRA) was the development of majority–minority districts, and these districts provided an opportunity for African Americans to seek representation in state legislatures. Since the passage of the VRA, Brown notes that there have been at least three generations of African American women who have been elected to southern state legislatures. Brown and colleagues find that there are fewer African American female state legislators in the most recent generations and present arguments why this might be a reason for substantial concerns. Finally, Brown and colleagues present "life-histories" of two African American female state legislators from Maryland, and from this in-depth case study, the authors are able to provide a more nuanced description of how these two legislators focus their efforts on policies designed to help the most marginalized people in their community. These life histories also demonstrate how complex African American feminism is and the varied ways in which black women live at the intersections of race, gender, class, and age.

Claire Bond Potter fills yet another hole in the scholarship on Second-Wave Feminism in her chapter, "Not in Conflict, But in Coalition: Imagining Lesbians at the Center of the Second Wave." Potter does just that, moves lesbian activists to center stage as opposed to playing supporting roles in the margins where scholars have too often cast them. Lesbian activists were, Potter asserts, extreme and, in some ways, pure feminists because they sought to define feminine sexuality completely independent of men, and they considered themselves the heartbeat of the movement. Moreover, lesbian communities offered examples of not only a sexual life, but a political and economic life unobstructed by institutionalized patriarchy. And because lesbian activists were not stuck in the dichotomous vision of men versus women, they were able to heighten awareness about the class and sexuality and racial differences between women in and of themselves. Despite NOW leader Betty Friedan's ridicule as the "lavender menace," lesbians played major roles in numerous Second-Wave organizations, argues Potter, roles that extended beyond the 1970s to a legacy of leadership particularly during the AIDS crisis of the 1990s. Yet they have failed to receive the scholarly attention they deserve—until now.

Finally, it is fitting that in her concluding chapter Lisa Corrigan confirms the initial claim made by Sara M. Evans: that the wave metaphor should be replaced by a broader, more inclusive history that accurately depicts the continuous and overlapping efforts of women activists. And our work is just beginning, notes Corrigan, who challenges feminist historians, political scientists, and economists, like those featured in this collection, to continue to place women's activism at the center of our political landscape. Now, with the gift of hindsight and the awareness of the mistakes and the limitations of the Second Wave, is the time to reflect on the feminist cause in America and to chart its path forward.

NOTES

1. Stephanie Gilmore, ed. 2008. *Feminist Coalitions: Historical Perspectives on Second-Wave Feminism in the United States* (Urbana: University of Illinois Press), p. 2.
2. Charlotte Krolokke and Anne Scott Sorenson. 2006. *Gender Communication Theories and Analyses: From Silence to Performance* (London: Sage Publications), pp. 12–13.
3. Becky Thompson. 2010. "Multiracial Feminisim" in. *No Permanent Waves: Recasting Histories of U.S. Feminism* edited by Nancy A. Hewitt (New Brunswick, NJ: Rutgers University Press), p. 39.
4. Robin Morgan. 1970. *Sisterhood is Powerful: An Anthology of Writings from the Women's Liberation Movement* (New York: Vintage).
5. Linda Nicholson, ed., 1997. *The Second Wave: A Reader in Feminist Theory* (New York: Routledge), p. 4.
6. Rory C. Dicker. 2008. *A History of U.S. Feminisms* (Berkeley, CA: Seal Press), p. 72.
7. Estelle B. Freedman. 2002. *No Turning Back: The History of Feminism and the Future of Women* (New York: Ballantine Books), p. 89.
8. Dicker, 2008. *A History of U.S. Feminisms*, p. 99.
9. See Benita Roth. 2004. *Separate Roads to Feminism: Black, Chicana, and White Feminist Movements in America's Second Wave* (New York: Cambridge University Press).
10. Anne M. Valk. 2008. *Radical Sisters: Second-Wave Feminism and Black Liberation in Washington, D.C.* (Urbana, IL: University of Illinois Press), p. 3.
11. Carol Giardina. 2010. *Freedom for Women: Forging the Women's Liberation Movement, 1953–1970* (Gainesville: University Press of Florida), p. 212.
12. Nancy MacLean, 2009. *The American Women's Movement, 1945–2000: A Brief History with Documents* (Boston, MA: Bedford/St. Martin's), p. 14.
13. See Judith Evans. 1995. *Feminist Theory Today: An Introduction to Second-Wave Feminism* (London: Sage Publications).
14. The Combahee River Collective. 1997 [1977]. "A Black Feminist Statement" in *The Second Wave: A Feminist Reader* edited by Linda Nicholson (New York: Routledge), pp. 63–70.
15. Thompson, 2010. "Multiracial Feminisim," p. 45.
16. Audre Lorde, quoted in Dicker, 2008. *A History of U.S. Feminisms*, p. 91.
17. Dorothy Sue Cobble, Linda Gordon, and Astrid Henry. 2014. *Feminism Unfinished: A Short, Surprising History of American Women's Movement* (New York: Liveright Publishing Corporation), p. 71.

18. Sherna Berger Gluck. 1998. "Whose Feminism, Whose History? Reflections on Excavating the History of (the) U.S. Women's Movement(s)," in *Community Activism and Feminist Politics: Organizing across Race, Class, and Gender*, edited by Nancy A. Naples (New York: Routledge), p. 32.
19. Martha Weinman Lears. 1968. "The Second Feminist Wave." *New York Times Magazine* (10 March), p. 24.
20. Simone De Beauvoir. 1953. *The Second Sex*, translated by HM Parshley (London: Jonathan Cape). The book was original published in 1949.
21. Thompson, 2010. "Multiracial Feminism," p. 41.
22. Cobble, Gordon, and Henry, 2014. *Feminism Unfinished*, pp. 122–124.
23. Gilmore, ed., 2008. *Feminist Coalitions*, p. 5.
24. Roth, 2004. *Separate Roads to Feminism*, p. 211.
25. Debra Baker Beck, "The 'F' Word: How the Media Frame Feminism," *National Women's Studies Association Journal* 10 (Spring 1998): 139–153.
26. Quoted in Krolokke and Sorenson, 2006. *Gender Communication Theories and Analyses*, p. 15 and Julia T. Wood, *Who Cares?: Women, Care, and Culture* (Carbondale: University of Southern IllinoisPress, 1994), p. 106.
27. Gloria Steinem, quoted in Dicker, 2008. *A History of U.S. Feminisms*, p. 17.
28. Roth, 2004. *Separate Roads to Feminism*, p. 2fn. See also: Chela Sandoval. 1990. "Feminism and Racism: A Report on the 1981 National Women's Studies Association Conference" in *Making Face, Making Soul/Hacienda Caras: Creative and Critical Perspectives on Women of Color* edited by Gloria Anzaldúa (San Francisco, CA: An Aunt Lute Foundation Book).
29. Dicker, 2008. *A History of U.S. Feminisms*, pp. 107–108.
30. Imelda Whelehan. 1995. *Modern Feminist Thought: From the Second Wave to "Post-Feminism"* (New York: New York University Press), p. 36.
31. Natalie Fuehrer Taylor. 2009. "The Personal is Political: Women's Magazines for the 'I'm-Not-a-Feminist-But' Generation" in *You've Come a Long Way, Baby: Women, Politics, and Popular Culture* edited by Lilly J. Goren (Lexington: University Press of Kentucky), p. 216.
32. MacLean, 2009. *The American Women's Movement*, p. 18.
33. Thompson, 2010. "Multiracial Feminism," pp. 50–51.
34. Leslie Heywood and Jennifer Drake, eds. 1997. *Third Wave Agenda: Being Feminist, Doing Feminism* (Minneapolis, MN: University of Minnesota Press), p. 1.
35. Cobble, Gordon, and Henry, 2014. *Feminism Unfinished*, p. 170.
36. Heywood and Drakes, eds., 1997. *Third Wave Agenda*, p. 14.
37. Phyllis Schlafly. 2009 [1972]. "What's Wrong with 'Equal Rights' for Women?" in *The American Women's Movement*, edited by MacLean, p. 117.

38. Jerry Falwell. 1997 [original date unknown]. "The Feminist Movement" in *Antifeminism in America: A Collection of Readings from the Literature of the Opponents to U.S. Feminism, 1848 to the Present* edited by Angela Howard and Sasha Ranaé Adams Tarrant (New York: Garland Publishing, Inc.), pp. 142–143.
39. Susan Faludi. 1991. *Backlash: The Undeclared War Against American Women* (New York: Crown Publishers), p. xviii.
40. Janet K. Boles. 1979. *The Politics of the Equal Rights Amendment: Conflict and the Decision Process.* (New York: Longman), p. 88.
41. Deborah Siegel. 2007. *Sisterhood, Interrupted: From Radical Women to Girls Gone Wild* (New York: Palgrave Macmillan), p. 12. See also: Taylor, 2009. "The Personal is Political," p. 215.
42. Kate Eichhorn. 2013. *The Archival Turn in Feminism: Outrage in Order* (Philadelphia: Temple University Press), p. viii.
43. Kathleen Hannah/Bikini Kill. 2007 [1992]. "Riot Grrrl Manifesto" in *The Essential Feminist Reader* edited by Estelle B. Freedman (New York: The Modern Library), p. 394.
44. Rebecca Walker 2007 [1992]. "Becoming the Third Wave" in *The Essential Feminist Reader* edited by Freedman, p. 400.
45. Ruth Rosen. 2000. *The World Split Open: How the Modern Women's Movement Changed America* (New York: Viking Penguin), p. 344.
46. See: Hewitt, ed., 2010. *No Permanent Waves.*

CHAPTER 2

Generations Later, Retelling the Story

Sara M. Evans

Abstract As the half-century anniversaries begin, study of the Second Wave is in vogue in both print and visual media as it has never been before. In this chapter, Sara M. Evans reflects on some of the ways the story is being told now, the power of iconic representations, and new questions arising from the experience of new generations. Addressing many of the myths and generalizations about the movement, Evans counters the oversimplification of the Second-Wave feminists as uniformly white, middle class, selfish, and anti-sex. This characterization, Evans argues, misses the role of minorities, the poor, and other feminist perspectives on sexuality that were a growing part of the Second-Wave feminist movement. Thus, as opposed to seeing themselves as a continuation of the Second Wave, many Third-Wave feminists saw themselves as a completely new "rupture with the past." Evans then reviews more recent historical work, some of which takes a broad international view, while others explore a narrower context and examine the history of feminists and feminism within a particular community. These studies clearly show the multiracial, international, multiclass, and selfless actions of many feminists and feminist groups. Rather than

---

The original version of the book was revised: Final corrections have been incorporated. The erratum to this chapter is available at https://doi.org/10.1007/978-3-319-62117-3_11

S.M. Evans (✉)
University of Minnesota, Minneapolis, USA

© The Author(s) 2018
A. Maxwell and T. Shields (eds.), *The Legacy of Second-Wave Feminism in American Politics*, https://doi.org/10.1007/978-3-319-62117-3_2

being a monolithic American movement of white middle-class women, led by only a few visible leaders, the women's movement continues to be a patchwork of groups, many not even aware of one another, and many who disagree with one another on various topics, but all working together for improving some aspect of women's lives. Ultimately, Evans insists that viewing the women's movement in "waves" that seem to begin and end at specific points in time obscures the fight that many Second-, Third-, and multiple-wave feminists continue to wage.

The year 2013 marked the fiftieth anniversary of the President's Commission on Women Report that spelled out in considerable detail the discrimination embedded in our laws and practices and the hardships this entailed. The commission described a world in which poor and working women lacked access to childcare; businesswomen could not obtain credit in their own names; working women received lower wages than men in the same jobs and were "disqualified" for higher-paying jobs; graduate and professional schools held female admissions to quotas of 5% or less, and many states barred women from jury duty.

In 1963 Congress also passed the Equal Pay Act to make it illegal to pay differentially on the basis of sex for the exact same job, and Betty Friedan published her blockbuster, *The Feminine Mystique*, that railed less against legal restrictions than the psychic toll of the social role of "housewife" as prescribed in the popular culture, Freudian psychology, and higher education.

We are at the beginning of what is going to be a very long series of anniversaries for the women's movement as well as the Civil Rights Movement, the anti-Vietnam War movement, and a host of other "rights-based" movements that grew from and were inspired by them. This means that we are at last going to have that story told, and retold. My interest here is to explore some of the myths that serve as blinders, blocking our ability to tell the full story, and to explore some of the complexities revealed in recent scholarship that make such a telling both critically important and extremely difficult.[1]

Stereotypes Take Over

For the first two decades during and after the initial feminist eruption in the 1960s and 1970s, historians paid little attention to its story, in part because it was so recent. Mainly, however, they were busy establishing women's history as a legitimate field of inquiry (a project that was itself part of the feminist upsurge) and looking for the deep roots of women's agency in the past: in daily life, labor struggles, the experience of slavery, the evolution of cultural definitions of masculinity and femininity, and so forth. The very range of subjects examined makes it clear that historians, deeply influenced by socialist feminism as well as the emerging social history fields of African American, working class, and family history, construed the new field of women's history as a project to understand the past lives of *all* women.[2]

There were a handful of books on late twentieth-century feminism, my own among them, but for the most part the "Second Wave" receded into a series of stereotypic assumptions, namely that feminists in the 1970s were "white, middle-class, and strident." It is ironic that in the 1980s, even as parts of the feminist movement were gaining in strength and sophistication, popular culture proclaimed a "postfeminist" age, and most young women wanted nothing to do with those they thought of as angry/ugly/strident/lesbian (or paradoxically, asexual) feminists. Indeed, I used to read the following quote from a 1927 article in *Harper's* entitled "Feminist—New Style" to my women's history classes: "Feminism has become a term of opprobrium to the modern young woman. For the word suggests either the old school of fighting feminists who wore flat heels and had very little feminine charm, or the current species who antagonize men with their constant clamor about maiden names, equal rights, women's place in the world, and many other causes."[3] My students agreed that it sounded awfully familiar.

Feminist scholars in the 1980s and 1990s, mostly interested in the literary and theoretical, and struggling with the theoretical conundrums of gender, race, and class, fixed the perception of Second-Wave feminists in the 1970s as white, middle class, self-interested, and antisex. They declared themselves a "third wave" under the rubric of "intersectionality," presuming an almost total rupture with earlier feminist theorizing.[4]

When Third-Wave feminists named the Second Wave, which was not a term used by activists at the time, they pointed to an intellectual genealogy that in effect took the part for the whole. One of the most powerful analyses in this vein is Jane Gerhard's *Desiring Revolution: Second Wave Feminism and the Rewriting of American Sexual Thought* published in 2001.[5] *Desiring Revolution* is an important and insightful book, but by tracing the lineage of a particular conversation about sexuality, and positioning that conversation as constitutive of Second-Wave thought, she reinforces the larger narrative from the point of view of the 1990s Third

Wave that has made it more difficult to see the complexity of the movement in the 1970s and 1980s.

Gerhard traces the evolution of a white feminist "subject" from early radical feminist assertions of sexual freedom such as Anne Koedt's "Myth of the Vaginal Orgasm" in 1968 through the 1975–1985 cultural feminist emphasis on female difference and victimization in the work of writers such as Adrienne Rich, Nancy Choderow, Mary Daly, Audre Lorde, Susan Brownmiller, Myra Dinerstein, Andrea Dworkin, and Catharine MacKinnon.[6] The latter provided the theoretical underpinning for a growing anti-pornography movement in the late 1970s. For Gerhardt, when "sexual freedom" advocates clashed publicly with anti-pornography activists at the 1982 Scholar and Feminist Conference at Barnard College, the ensuing "sex wars" served as a turning point in which the Second-Wave worldview unraveled. Gerhardt concludes: "Second-wave feminists … saw sexuality as the most salient component of women's identity. This assumption, above all, paradoxically gave Second-Wave Feminism much of its radicalism and set the terms for its undoing. The fictional white woman who unconsciously dominated Second-Wave feminist sex theory could no longer stand in unproblematically for the 'feminist,' no matter how much she desired revolution."[7]

While this intellectual genealogy is without question an important strand in the evolution of feminist theory, it obscures the debates that never stopped. As a result, in Gerhardt's telling, at the Barnard Conference defenders of sexual freedom and individualism along with feminists of color seem to spring out of nowhere to create a tumultuous debate. What is missing here is (a) that the debate had been there all along, (b) that strategic alliances between white feminists and feminists of color had never disappeared and were, in fact, on the increase, and (c) that limiting Second-Wave Feminism to the feminist subcultures that evolved in the academy and in events like music festivals renders the on-the-ground battles about issues such as employment equity, welfare rights, credit, and divorce invisible in one of the most compelling versions of feminist history.

As feminist intellectual history mainstreamed the Third-Wave paradigms of multiculturalism, identity politics, and intersectionality, the resulting conception of the Second Wave as white and middle class erased the early interventions of women of color in the 1970s by seeing newer ideas as a rupture with the past rather than a continuation of it. When a new generation of historians sought to reconstruct an on-the-ground understanding of feminism as a social movement, they were frustrated by the pervasive grip of the Second- versus Third-Wave account. In 2008, Stephanie Gilmore found "the standard narrative that the women's movement was composed predominantly of white and middle class women" to be an obstacle to understanding the diversity and complexity of that movement. She lamented that "in many ways, it seems that the movement and its actors are suspended in historical—or rather, ahistorical—amber, unable to move or be moved."[8]

In its less theoretical and more activist versions, the story of the women's movement was left to be retold from time to time in the popular culture where a more triumphalist narrative arc pulled its story and images from the mass media of the time. This different version, however, was similarly rooted in images that were predominately white and middle class.[9] Key elements of this account include the following:

- According to the media, there were a few great leaders, such as Betty Friedan and Gloria Steinem.[10]
- Victories can be traced in the legislative and court battles of the sixties and early seventies: The Equal Pay Act (1963), Title VII of the Civil Rights Act (1964), Congressional passage of the Equal Rights Amendment (ERA, 1972), the Women's Educational Equity Act (WEEA, 1972), Title IX (1972), *Roe v. Wade* (1973), the Equal Credit Opportunity Act (1974).
- In addition to the above, key events in this narrative include the 1970 "strike" when thousands of women demonstrated across the country, the massive Houston Conference in 1977, and the ultimately losing battle for the ERA in state legislatures.

MAKERS: Women Who Make America, one of the best, recent documentaries on the movement that aired on PBS in February 2013 was almost inevitably stamped with that media-driven (and often New York- and Washington-centered) narrative, though I think the producers made a serious effort to include African Americans and working-class women. The result, however, even in a three-hour documentary, is lots of absent narratives. There are very few Asian American or Latina feminists in *MAKERS*, leaving the very eloquent black women interviewees to stand in for all minorities. Religion is virtually absent, passing over the flourishing debates around feminist theology and the ordination of women, as well as the emerging "cultural feminist" search for ancient sources of female spiritual power and affirmation. The role of the arts also gets short shrift, though feminism found expression in every art form, and women challenged their exclusion throughout the art world. And, finally, one gets no sense that the movement, from the beginning, was international in scope. It should be no surprise, however, that most of the complexity as well as the rough edges of the story of feminism disappear when you only have 3 hours to tell it. After all, *Eyes on the Prize* was 14 hours long, and even then there were hundreds of local heroes, especially women, who remained offscreen and unnoticed.

The problem with that dominant narrative, despite the fact that one cannot tell the story without it, is that feminism in the 1970s was a decentered movement, whose parts were not necessarily in communication with one another. In fact, often they did not even know one another. Each of those parts, in its own location, was in complex relationships and interactions with other movements that were active at the same time. We should also add that the movement's legacies, while considerable and worthy of celebration, are also complex and limited. Future generations need to understand how the problems that remain were shaped by that story without, in the process, failing to draw inspiration from its triumphs.

Reclaiming the Story

For the last two decades, scholars have turned their attention to unearthing the more complex and rich story of the Second Wave in ways that can help us understand the legacies we live with. The first step, as Stephanie Gilmore argues, is to have a "capacious definition of feminism," which scholars are beginning to do in a variety of ways. The second is to explore the movement through a variety of lenses that can, together, enable a multifaceted narrative to emerge. Finally, it is critical that we unearth and analyze broader societal patterns that can tell us a great deal about the complicated legacies of that movement.

Community studies that cast a broad net, for example, illumine multiple threads of feminist activism based on neighborhood, class, race, and ethnicity, tracing out the points of intersection, conflict, and collaboration.[11] As soon as they do this, it becomes clear that stereotypes cannot hold. Stephanie Gilmore dismantles the "liberal/radical" divide in her study of the National Organization of Women (NOW) chapters in Memphis, Columbus, and San Francisco, finding members who saw themselves as deeply radical and militant as well as those who were more liberal and mainstream.[12] In some places NOW was the only visible feminist presence, and for a time it drew in activists of all stripes. Judith Ezekiel's study of Dayton, Ohio, by contrast, finds that where there was no NOW chapter, Women's Liberation, a direct offshoot of the New Left, grew in multiple directions, generating projects and institutions some of which were very radical, while others had a more liberal political bent.[13] In the late sixties, the radical and liberal branches of the movement had distinctive roots and different generational constituencies, but by the early 1970s the exponential growth of the movement blurred the boundaries rapidly.

Similarly, the "all-white" image of the movement cannot stand in the face of new scholarship. In every branch of the identity-based "rights revolution"—black, Chicano/Latino, Asian American, American Indian—as well as in mainstream institutions such as churches, unions, and mass media—there was a feminist upsurge.[14] And throughout the 1970s, feminists built coalitions that crossed classes, races, and regions, despite a historical context that made coalitions extremely difficult.[15]

Though the movement was unquestionably multiracial, specific organizations were only rarely interracial. Anne Valk's *Radical Sisters: Second-Wave Feminism and Black Liberation in Washington, D.C.*, for instance, explores a complex landscape in the 1960s and 1970s where multiple movements focused on women, black liberation, and economic justice existed in continual interaction.[16] Valk analyzes these separate strands of activism as they intersected and interacted over time. White radical feminists, struggling to build a movement based on gender solidarity, stumbled over and wrestled with the realities of differences among women. African American women engaged with welfare rights and black liberation honed new political skills while they also grew increasingly aware of gender oppression. These separate streams came together in the movement against sexual violence, generating, according to Valk, "distinct black and Third World feminist movements. Separate but interconnected, these branches of feminism provided a foundation for further women's movements that extended into the 1980s and beyond."[17] It is interesting to contemplate the coexistence of these grassroots movements in Washington, DC, where, in those same years, there was enormous feminist ferment in and around the federal government and policy think tanks and in the DC headquarters of numerous national women's organizations.[18]

The complexity of this feminist tapestry may go far toward explaining the movement's massive achievements in the early 1970s. Carrie Baker's analysis of grassroots activism in the 1960s that led to and framed landmark appellate court decisions on the issue of sexual harassment makes it clear that a close-up study of specific legal changes cannot escape the coexistence and intersections of these multiple strands. The brilliant lawyer and legal scholar Catharine MacKinnon is commonly credited with inventing the legal concept of sexual harassment.[19] Yet the term was created by a local organization in Ithaca, New York, led by feminist activists with roots in one of Washington, DC's most famous lesbian separatist groups, the Furies Collective, as well as other radical women's liberation groups such as New York Radical Women and the *Rat* Collective. Radicals, however, worked together with women in the ACLU Women's Rights Project under the direction of Ruth Bader Ginsberg as well as clerical workers, undergraduates, and a local NOW chapter. A second group that developed out of a rape crisis center in Washington, DC, abetted their organizing and educational work. These activist groups, in the mid-1970s, completely belie the notion that liberal, radical, lesbian, and socialist feminists existed in highly separated ideological and activist worlds. While there were indeed ideological battles and raging wars of words, some women moved with apparent ease from one to another. And on the ground, focused on a concrete issue, "women found common cause across difference to create feminist change."[20] Attention to the "stars" would miss the ferment, which in fact drove those changes.[21]

Another innovative study by Ann Enke steps away from the stories the movement told about itself to look for the movement in specific, contested public spaces: public civic spaces such as city parks and ball fields and newly invented public spaces created by the women's movement such as coffee houses in church basements, health clinics, women's centers, feminist bookstores, and credit unions. In *Finding the Movement* we are getting closer to the underground force of those shifting plates when we locate women in the 1960s who would never call themselves "feminists" but who stake firm claims to formerly forbidden spaces and find themselves emulated by the feminists. Detroit's "Soul Sisters" were a black women's softball team in the 1960s that had already claimed public space for serious, hard-playing, tough, black, lesbian, working-class athletes. When socialist feminists and lesbians in Chicago set out in the early to mid-1970s to create softball teams, they modeled themselves on women who would never have accepted the label "feminist."[22]

In her exploration of institutions like coffee houses, bookstores, and health clinics, Enke gives us a deeper understanding of the power of race and class to divide an emerging movement and its often unstable coalitions. In self-identified feminist institutions, coalitions between white, middle-class founders and working-class and minority women sometimes grew but too often foundered. Under pressure to survive, both financially and politically, some spaces of interaction collapsed or migrated to neighborhoods marked as white and middle class; others institutionalized and professionalized, losing their activist edge. It was not simply a failure of ideas—as later theorists of feminist intersectionality imagined—but a consequence of the class, race, and sexual inflections of spaces in which people lived and worked and the communities that their activist spaces enabled or discouraged, sometimes by intention but often by happenstance and inertia. The result frequently eroded the coalition building that these creative, fluid, and unruly spaces had seemed to promise, leading feminist groups, despite their self-conscious laments, to emerge from the 1980s still deeply divided by class and race.[23]

If we can remove the distorted lenses of stereotypes, perhaps we can understand better the changing dynamics of the women's movement over time. There is definitely something to understand about the apparently sudden upsurge of women's rights activism in the 1960s and its evolution through the 1970s. By the 1980s, the dynamics were clearly different, though parts of the movement, such as the programs against domestic violence and sexual harassment and the intellectual ferment in and around the academic enterprise of women's studies, continued to grow despite an increasingly hostile political context.

From the outset, the simultaneity of feminist insurgencies in numerous communities and social movements was not simply a North American phenomenon. As I have described elsewhere, the global student uprisings in 1968, sparked by opposition to the Vietnam War as well as generational demands for greater freedom, catalyzed feminist organizing and ideas on virtually every continent.[24] It is startling to realize how similar the dynamics were in very different political and cultural contexts: France, Germany, Italy, Mexico, Argentina, and Japan. But from the point of view of the USA where one can tell similar stories about women's experiences in the Civil Rights Movement, the New Left, Black Power, Chicano, American Indian, and Native American movements, one should not be surprised. In every case, women gained political skills and self-respect at the same time that they became increasingly aware of gender oppression. And they put those newly honed skills to the task of understanding and changing that reality.

In the case of 1968, specifically, late twentieth-century feminism arose around the globe, at least in part, because of an interestingly similar constellation of generation, class, and gender in radical student movements. The university-based parts of those movements were often seen as a revolt of sons against their fathers, a refusal to proceed lockstep into hierarchical structures of power (corporate, military, or political) that regulated their lives in oppressive ways and wrecked imperialist, racist, and class oppression both in their own countries and around the world. Children of the Cold War, entering a rising middle class in the 1960s but inspired by revolts of peasants, workers, and racial minorities around the world, imagined the possibility of a new kind of personal freedom. These sons eschewed some of those markers of manhood, not only traditional careers but also traditional sexual propriety leading to proper breadwinner jobs and marital obligations. Their long hair invited brutal police responses in places as different as Germany and Mexico.

Young women participated in student revolts throughout the world in equal numbers, often against severe parental pressure, though they were rarely visible in the top leadership. Their revolt against patriarchy, however, was fundamentally different from that of their male comrades, as it required a challenge to traditional female roles. To the extent that their brothers in the struggle invented new signs of manhood such as sexual access to young women in their class without the trappings of marriage and monopolized positions of leadership, women began to challenge the restrictions they experienced within the very movements that had liberated them and raised their expectations. The erotic intensity of street demonstrations, building occupations, and apocalyptic expectations could only be liberating for women when they redefined themselves as sexually autonomous, capable of defining their own desires. Their anger when this was not the case elicited furious manifestos in numerous countries once young women found their voice. "The international 1968" offers a fascinating intersection of generation, class, at a very specific moment in time. But similar things also occurred in very different contexts, suggesting that in the late twentieth-century women, especially younger women, found new ways to imagine a world in which being female was no longer a second-class status in whatever other contexts they found themselves. That imagining, and the multitude of resulting struggles to overturn laws, open opportunities, change power relationships within families, undermine heterosexual norms, establish reproductive rights, equalize women's access to the labor force, and revalue the work that they traditionally do, also generated a massive political and cultural backlash that framed the evolution of those struggles into the 1980s and beyond.

In the USA, the context of radical, utopian, even apocalyptic movements such as Black Power, antiwar movements, and campus insurrections in the late 1960s and early 1970s prompted many to imagine that radical change—even revolution—was just around the corner. It framed some of the more extreme feminist experiments (e.g, separatist communes like the Furies) as well as the countercultural strategy of starting institutions—bookstores, health clinics, rape crisis centers, shelters for battered women, daycare centers—that would model new possibilities to the world. Those institutions themselves, as Anne Enke has shown, created new forms of public space where the meanings of the movement were invented and enacted by diverse and changing communities.[25] Yet media images of young, white, and middle-class activists obscured the similar expectations of dramatic change welling up in settings ranging from labor unions to religious institutions and welfare rights organizations.

An Unfinished Revolution

As we begin to unravel the complexities of the movement, we are also beginning to understand the broader societal impact of feminist activism and some of the paths not taken. Changes wrought by the movement have left a swath of unresolved problems affecting the lives of large numbers of women, marked by class as well as race. Katherine Turk's study of Title VII explores some of the broader implications of the strategic shift in NOW and much of mainstream feminism toward individual opportunity as symbolized by the ERA and away from policies that acknowledge the different realities of women and men in the labor force and the family. In doing so, she also complicates the label "liberal feminist" by showing that, like self-defined radicals, liberals also wrestled with the deeper meanings of the changes they sought.

In an article in the *Journal of American History*, Turk focuses on the Chicago branch of NOW which had built a nationally influential campaign against Sears for its practices of refusing to hire women in higher ticket sales jobs, confining them to the lowest paid clerical and retail jobs. Internal battles for the leadership of NOW in the mid-1970s, however, sidelined the Chicago group led by Mary Jean Collins and Anne Ladke. As a result, NOW became a more streamlined and centralized organization focused on the ERA, leaving local campaigns like the SEARS campaign stranded. Turk then follows the trajectory of NOW under the leadership of Karen DeCrow and then Eleanor Smeal away from the concerns of working women in low-paid jobs and toward an agenda emphasizing individual rights and opportunity. This shift, Turk argues, was not just tactical; it was ideological, abandoning broader feminist ideas about economic justice, employees' rights, and citizenship.[26] In her broader study of Title VII, she argues that the SEARS campaign was part of a shift within liberal feminism away from emphasizing sex difference between women and men toward an emphasis on individual mobility, individual rights, and meritocracy. This had the effect of undermining "the possibility of shared female solidarity while contributing to the societal devaluation of the labors of workers in feminized positions."[27] Doors opened to professional opportunities, but the majority of working women remain confined to the lowest wage, female-dominated (and mostly unorganized) clerical and service jobs.[28]

Alison Lefkovitz's recent dissertation on marriage in the time of women's liberation bolsters Turk's conclusion that low-income and poor women have basically been left behind in the changes wrought by feminism.[29] Her study explores the dismantling of coverture, not so much by federal laws and courts but by state laws regulating marriage and divorce. Feminists made multiple arguments about marriage in the early 1970s. Some proposed simple, formal equality while more radical critiques demanded that the institution of marriage itself be dismantled, as it could not be reformed. What is interesting here is the behavior of thousands of men and women in response to shifting legal requirements that linked no-fault divorce and state-level equal rights amendments. In effect, and without clear intention, the new legal regime effectively dismantled the male breadwinner/female housewife model of marriage that had been fundamental to marriage law for centuries and was the foundation for legal coverture. Lefkovitz describes "how a host of lawmakers, judges, activists, and ordinary men and women ... struggled to redefine family and marriage without gender."[30] Men, for example, challenged the gendered premises of alimony, which soon became maintenance based on a percentage of contribution by either spouse to the household. Women achieved some legal recognition of the value of their household labor when that justified the division of household property rather than assuming that it belonged to the man.

The complex consequences of removing prescribed gender roles from the legal understanding of marriage were twofold. Anxiety about the failing family galvanized the right-wing opposition to feminism. Lefkovitz argues "the convergence of class, gender, sexual, and even race equality at woman's position in the family evoked fears that helped construct the new Republican Party by bringing in a broad swath of men and women who objected to changes to the traditional family structure."[31] The organized power of that reaction helps to explain the fierce resistance to gay marriage, which became in a legal sense totally logical once marriage and gender were disconnected. It also fed the refusal of policymakers to extend the recognition that women's labor in the home has monetary value to poor women on welfare. In 1972, Johnnie Tillmon had argued that simply "paying women a living wage for doing the work we are already doing, child raising and housekeeping" would end the welfare crisis "just like that."[32] But wages for housework never gained any traction, and poor women were left with a diminished capacity to argue effectively for their own needs.

WOMEN IN MOTION: LEGACIES OF A TURBULENT TIME

No metaphor can capture the power and complexity of what many call the "Second Wave," but we will always grope for images that move us in that direction. Women were in motion. Women seized the opportunity to sue their employers, fought for access to male-defined spaces from iron and coal mines to street repair crews, ordained ministries, art galleries, professions, athletics both amateur and professional, and the leadership of their own social movements, and struggled openly to revalue women's traditional labors in the home and in the labor force. The movement was never all white and middle class, but in fact consisted of multiple, simultaneous streams that erupted in almost all corners of American society. At the same time, the public, media-driven face of activism in the 1970s was more often white and middle class than not. Feminist movements struggled in different ways to define the nature of gender oppression and the most effective remedies. Some developed theories and actions that (in very different ways) prioritized sexuality and the body. Some turned to legislatures and courts, moving gradually toward a liberal, individualist definition of both problem and solution.

Some demanded access to civic public spaces or created their own new forms of public space, too often migrating spatially away from places where divergent communities intersected and toward locations increasingly stamped as white and middle class.

Among the hardest things to convey in narrative form are the intersecting possibilities of every moment and the fact that activists themselves had very different conceptions of what was going on. No one could know how it would turn out. And in a time of apocalyptic expectations—indeed, that may be the hardest thing of all to convey—the fierce debates had resonances we can hardly imagine from decades down the road. The movement was filled with conflict, both intellectual and personal. It was messy. How do we tell that? Many versions just smooth it over, making everything seem inevitable, while a few portray divisions as deeper and more absolute than they were.[33] When we pull back to take in a larger view it is clear that maelstrom deeply altered the world as we know it, creating changes that younger generations cannot fathom if we do not tell them.

Another part of the story, however, must be the unintended consequences as changed ways of living and speaking were appropriated, resisted, and reworked in the daily lives of millions of women and men as well as in a host of court decisions and laws. Change was always partial, and we need a clear assessment of both the gains and the failures. Specifically, feminists must analyze the consequences of an extremely incomplete challenge to the masculinist structure of the labor force that routinely devalues labor traditionally associated with women and allows employers to escape all responsibility for the difficulty of supporting families with low wages and no benefits. No health care, sick leave, vacation, or retirement are standard for the low-wage, part-time jobs that many poor women have as their only option. And at the other end of the scale, high-income professional women must live in a work culture that makes little or no allowance for the responsibilities of family life and children. What they can afford to do is to hire other women, at low wages, to do that work, but they cannot insist that their employers ease their workload so that they can be more involved in family life without severe penalties in terms of professional stature and advancement. Marriage may have no gender, but the labor force still does in very class-specific ways.

Finally, our retelling must also recognize that the evolution of feminism was shaped by the organized force of its opposition, the broader political currents in the country, and the changing nature of the political economy. Feminism was so deeply unsettling that reaction against it reshaped the political landscape, bringing into being a highly ideological right wing focused on the cultural issues of abortion and gay rights and fanatically opposed to the ERA and Affirmative Action. That, too, is part of its legacy.

Every generation has to define its own battles, but they do so in contexts created by what went before. Future generations need to know the full story of the feminist upsurge in the late twentieth century because they live with the consequences. It is an empowering and sobering story of great dreams, partial victories, and unresolved dilemmas. If it was a tidal wave, a storm, an earthquake, a set of pulses—pick your metaphor—it is not over. Not only have most former activists not packed up their bags and declared victory, but also each newer generation has generated new initiatives to address the issues that affect them the most. This continuity is the baton that we hand on along with stories of a time when imagining a better future and acting to bring it about went hand in hand.

Notes

1. It occurred to me to think about how the woman's rights story was being told 50 years after Seneca Falls. That would be 1898, when the vote had been granted in only a handful of states and municipalities and victory on the national level was not in sight. Only a few of the early activists were still alive then. Elizabeth Cady Stanton lived until 1902 and Susan B. Anthony to 1906, but most of their coworkers were long gone, though some of their daughters, for example, Alice Stone Blackwell and Harriot Stanton Blatch, were still active in the arena of women's rights. Interestingly, the narrative of their movement had already been framed in the first three volumes of *History of Woman Suffrage*, which appeared between 1881 and 1886, written and edited by Susan B. Anthony, Matilda Joselyn Gage, and Elizabeth Cady Stanton. Volume 4 in 1902 was the last to be edited by Anthony. Because there had been a deep split in the movement after the Civil War, Lucy Stone and others in the National American Woman Suffrage Association received relatively short shrift. Volumes 5 and 6 appeared in 1922, 2 years after passage of the Nineteenth Amendment. Their tone, by contrast to the first four, is far more triumphalist, and the story has a sense of inevitability that the earlier volumes could not achieve. For many generations, this monumental effort fixed the story of the "first wave" as the story of the long struggle

for woman suffrage with a relatively small cast of characters. It was finally complicated by Eleanor Flexner in 1959 whose book, *Century of Struggle: The Women's Rights Movement in the United States* (Cambridge, MA: Harvard University Press, 1959), broadened "women's rights" to include the struggles (most of them actually named in the original document of 1848) for access to legal rights, education, and labor rights, and to more fully acknowledge the separate struggles of black women in a time first of slavery and then of segregation. Today scholars are uncovering additional hidden histories of women of color whose stories add further layers of richness and complexity. So, even that first one was not a single "wave" but a complex constellation of movements and struggles addressing the multiple ways that gender intersects with the realities of race, class, religion, region, and ethnicity.

2. To get a sense of this early paradigm-shifting work, see for example: Linda Gordon, *Woman's Body, Woman's Right: A Social History of Birth Control in America* (New York: Grossman, 1976); Alice Kessler-Harris, *Out to Work: A History of Wage Earning Women in the United States* (New York: Oxford University Press, 1982); Gerda Lerner, *The Grimke Sisters of South Carolina: Pioneers for Abolition and Women's Rights* (Boston: Houghton Mifflin, 1967) and *Black Women in White America: A Documentary History* (New York: Pantheon, 1972); Nancy Cott, *Root of Bitterness: Documents of the Social History of American Women* (New York: Dutton, 1972) and *The Bonds of Womanhood* (New Haven, CT: Yale University Press, 1977); Mari Jo Buhle, *Women and American Socialism: 1870–1920* (Urbana: University of Illinois Press, 1981); Ellen DuBois, *Feminism and Suffrage: The Emergence of an Independent Women's Movement in America, 1848–1869* (Ithaca, NY: Cornell University Press, 1978); Mary P. Ryan, *Womanhood in America: From Colonial Times to the Present* (New York: New Viewpoints, 1975); Linda Kerber, *Women of the Republic: Intellect and Ideology in Revolutionary America* (Chapel Hill: University of North Carolina Press, 1980); Mary Beth Norton, *Liberty's Daughters: The Revolutionary Experience of American Women, 1750–1800* (Boston: Little Brown, 1980).

3. Dorothy Dunbar Bromley, "Feminist—New Style," *Harper's* 155 (October 1927): 552.

4. For an excellent analysis of this process, see Leela Fernandes, "Unsettling 'Third Wave Feminism': Feminist Waves, Intersectionality, and Identity Politics in Retrospect," in *No Permanent Waves: Recasting Histories of U.S. Feminism*, ed. Nancy A. Hewitt (New Brunswick, NJ: Rutgers University Press, 2010), 98–118.

5. Jane Gerhardt, *Desiring Revolution: Second Wave Feminism and the Rewriting of American Sexual Thought* (New York: Columbia University Press, 2001).

6. Anne Koedt, "The Myth of the Vaginal Orgasm," *Notes from the Second Year* (New York: New York Radical Feminists, 1970), 37–41. Koedt's article also appeared in *Radical Feminism*, ed. Anne Koedt, Ellen Levine, and Anita Rapone (New York: Quadrangle Books, 1973), 198–207, and a briefer version in *Notes from the First* Year (1968). Adrienne Rich, *Of Woman Born: Motherhood as Experience and Institution* (New York: Norton, 1976); Audre Lorde, *Zami: A New Spelling of My Name* (Watertown, MA: Persephone Press, 1982); Mary Daly, *Gyn-Ecology* (Boston: Beacon Press, 1978); Nancy Chodorow, *The Reproduction of Mothering: Psychoanalysis and the Sociology of Gender* (Berkeley: University of California Press, 1978); Myra Dinerstein, *The Mermaid and the Minotaur: Sexual Arrangements and Human Malaise* (New York: Harper & Row, 1976); Andrea Dworkin, *Pornography: Men Possessing Women* (New York: Putnam, 1981); Catharine A. Mackinnon, *Sexual Harassment of Working Women: A Case of Sex Discrimination* (New Haven, CT: Yale University Press, 1979).
7. Gerhardt, *Desiring Revolution*, 195.
8. Stephanie Gilmore, "Thinking about Feminist Coalitions," in *Feminist Coalitions: Historical Perspectives on Second-Wave Feminism in the United States*, ed. Stephanie Gilmore (Urbana: University of Illinois Press, 2008), 2. The few historical studies available in the 1980s, such as Alice Echols's *Daring to Be Bad*, traced a story of declension from (white) radical feminism in the late 1960s and early 1970s to (white) cultural feminism in the late 1970s. My own work in *Personal Politics* rooted the women's liberation movement in the experience of the Civil Rights Movement, community organizing experiences in poor urban communities, and the student antiwar movement. On the multiple roots of feminism, see Benita Roth, *Separate Roads to Feminism: Black, Chicana, and White Feminist Movements in America's Second Wave* (New York: Cambridge University Press, 2004).
9. See, for example, Susan Douglas, *Where the Girls Are: Growing Up Female with the Mass Media* (New York: Times Books, 1994). For an analysis of the intersection between feminism and popular television shows, see Bonnie J. Dow, *Prime-Time Feminism: Television, Media Culture, and the Women's Movement Since 1970* (Philadelphia: University of Pennsylvania Press, 1996).
10. I am sure that Steinem did not want to be our Susan B. Anthony and though Friedan probably *did* want to be our Elizabeth Cady Stanton, there were many other contenders (I think of Shulamith Firestone, Kate Millett, Susan Brownmiller, and bell hooks for starters).
11. For a quick introduction to some of what is out there in this area, see Gilmore's collection, *Feminist Coalitions*, and Part 2 of Nancy Hewitt's, *No Permanent Waves*.

12. Stephanie Gilmore, *Groundswell: Grassroots Feminist Activism in Postwar America* (New York: Routledge, 2012).
13. Judith Ezekiel, *Feminism in the Heartland* (Columbus: Ohio State University Press, 2002).
14. On the multiracial roots of contemporary feminism, see Becky Thompson, "Multiracial Feminism: Recasting the Chronology of Second Wave Feminism," originally in *Feminist Studies* 28, no. 2 (Summer 2002), reprinted in Hewitt, ed., *No Permanent Waves*, 39–60, and Benita Roth, *Separate Roads to Feminism: Black, Chicana, and White Feminist Movements in America's Second Wave* (New York: Cambridge University Press, 2004). See also Maylei Blackwell, *Chicana Power! Contested Histories of Feminism in the Chicano Movement* (Austin: University of Texas Press, 2011); Sonia Shah, *Dragon Ladies: Asian American Feminists Breathe Fire* (Boston: South End Press, 1997); Kimberly Springer, *Living for the Revolution: Black Feminist Organizations, 1968–1980* (Durham, NC: Duke University Press, 2005); Devon Abbott Mihesuah, *Indigenous American Women: Decolonization, Empowerment, Activism*. Lincoln, NE: University of Nebraska Press, 2003); Paula Gunn Allen, *The Sacred Hoop: Recovering the Feminine in American Indian Traditions* (Boston: Beacon Press, 1986); Johnetta B. Cole and Beverly Guy-Sheftall, *Gender Talk: The Struggle for Women's Equality in African American Communities* (New York: Ballantine Books, 2003); Cherrie Moraga and Gloria Anzaldua, eds., *This Bridge Called My Back: Writings by Radical Women of Color* (New York: Persephone Press, 1981); Barbara Smith, ed., *Home Girls: A Black Feminist Anthology* (New York: Kitchen Table Women of Color Press, 1983); Alice Walker, *In Search of Our Mother's Gardens: Womanist Prose* (San Diego: Harcourt Brace Jovanovich, 1983).
15. See Stephanie Gilmore, ed., *Feminist Coalitions: Historical Perspectives on Second-Wave Feminism in the United States* (Urbana: University of Illinois Press, 2008).
16. Anne M. Valk, *Radical Sisters: Second-Wave Feminism and Black Liberation in Washington, D.C.* (Urbana: University of Illinois Press, 2010).
17. Valk, *Radical Sisters*, 186.
18. For firsthand accounts of the latter, see Irene Tinker, ed., *Women in Washington: Advocates for Public Policy* (Beverly Hills: Sage Publications, 1983).
19. Catharine Mackinnon, *Sexual Harassment of Working Women* (New Haven, CT: Yale University Press, 1979).
20. Carrie N. Baker, *The Women's Movement against Sexual Harassment* (New York: Cambridge University Press, 2007), quote on p. 4.

21. A growing group of 1970s feminists have written memoirs, among them Susan Brownmiller, Sheila Tobias, Betty Friedan, Arvonne Fraser, Gloria Steinem, Gloria Anzeldua, Alice Walker, Alix Dobkin, Andrea Dworkin, bell hooks, Audre Lorde, Robin Morgan, and Katha Pollitt. For the most part, of course, it is the famous ones whose accounts are seriously considered by major publishers. Some states like Iowa and Minnesota have published books of brief memoirs by activist women from those states, and the State Historical Society of Wisconsin houses an impressive oral history program designed to elicit the stories of midwestern feminists. There is also Rachel Blau DuPlessis and Ann Barr Snitow, eds., *The Feminist Memoir Project: Voices from Women's Liberation* (New York: Three Rivers Press, 1998), and Rosalyn Fraad Baxandall and Linda Gordon, eds., *Dear Sisters: Dispatches from the Women's Liberation Movement* (New York: Basic Books, 2000). One of the largest resources for memoir is MAKERS.com with more than one hundred first-person interviews in addition to the documentary. The great value of all of these stories is that readers and viewers get to witness the movement through the lens of a specific life.
22. Anne Enke, *Finding the Movement: Sexuality, Contested Space, and Feminist Activism* (Durham, NC: Duke University Press, 2007).
23. Ibid.
24. Sara M. Evans, "Sons, Daughters, and Patriarchy: Gender and the 1968 Generation," *American Historical Review* 114 (April 2009): 331–47.
25. Enke, *Finding the Movement*.
26. See Katherine Turk, "Out of the Revolution, Into the Mainstream: Employment Activism in the NOW Sears Campaign and the Growing Pains of Liberal Feminism," *Journal of American History* (September 2010): 399–423, and Katherine Lee Turk, "Equality on Trial: Women and Work in the Age of Title VII" (PhD diss., University of Chicago, 2011). The Chicago NOW chapter was also influenced by the Midwest Academy, a Chicago organizer training center founded by Heather Booth. Booth was one of the early members of the first women's liberation group in Chicago and a founder of the socialist feminist Chicago Women's Liberation Union.
27. Turk, "Equality on Trial," 416.
28. In the 1980s, with colleague Barbara Nelson, I undertook a study of comparable worth in Minnesota. This policy, initially from the era of WWII, was revived in a series of labor union initiated lawsuits. Bolstered by a National Academy of Sciences study chaired by economist Heidi Hartman (a socialist feminist and former editor of *Feminist Studies*), it briefly appeared that state and perhaps national legislation could mandate the reevaluation of female-dominated jobs to bring their pay in line

with similarly skilled male-dominated jobs. While Minnesota did, in fact enact such laws for state and local employees, the lack of broad grassroots support and the active hostility of the EEOC, then headed by Clarence Thomas, made the promise of comparable worth short lived indeed. See Sara M. Evans and Barbara J. Nelson, *Wage Justice: Comparable Worth and the Paradox of Technocratic Reform* (Chicago: University of Chicago Press, 1989).
29. Alison Lefkovitz, "Marriage in the Era of Women's Liberation" (PhD diss., University of Chicago, 2010).
30. Ibid., 9.
31. Ibid., 8.
32. Johnnie Tillmon, "Welfare Is a Women's Issue," Liberation News Service (1972), quoted in Lefkovitz, 2.
33. For analyses that vividly describe conflict, especially in the radical wing of the movement, see Alice Echols, *Daring to Be Bad*, and Susan Brownmiller, *In Our Time: Memoir of a Revolution* (New York: Dial Press, 1999).

CHAPTER 3

Feminism, Anti-Feminism, and The Rise of a New Southern Strategy in the 1970s

Marjorie J. Spruill

Abstract In this chapter, Marjorie J. Spruill argues that Second-Wave Feminism cannot be fully understood without examining the countermovements that also gained strength in the 1970s. While the Second-Wave feminists achieved substantial success in changing cultural expectations, laws, and policies in favor of equality for women, their success was also the reason why many conservative women mobilized in opposition. These conservative opposition groups rarely called themselves anti-feminists. Instead, they often called themselves "pro-family" and saw traditional family values under attack by feminists. They advocated for political leaders to restore "values" rather than promote "liberty" or "equality." Conservative women became angered at the bipartisan support they saw the women's movement receiving and began developing political strategies to oppose "women's libbers," eventually condemning feminist efforts as both anti-God and anti-American. Specifically, Spruill examines

---

The original version of the book was revised: Final corrections have been incorporated. The erratum to this chapter is available at
https://doi.org/10.1007/978-3-319-62117-3_11

M.J. Spruill (✉)
University of South Carolina, Columbia, USA

© The Author(s) 2018
A. Maxwell and T. Shields (eds.), *The Legacy of Second-Wave Feminism in American Politics*, https://doi.org/10.1007/978-3-319-62117-3_3

carefully the battles leading up to the International Women's Year (IWY) conferences. She notes that the state-level conferences preceding the national meeting allowed anti-feminist groups the opportunity to learn how to mobilize, become politically active, and to see clearly how working across denominational boundaries allowed conservative groups—Baptists, Mormons, evangelical Protestants, Catholics, and Pentecostals—an opportunity to defeat feminist objectives. Spruill argues that the beginning of the religious right was the formation of these interdenominational coalitions designed to oppose the efforts of feminists leading up to the IWY. Moreover, while the new GOP support was nationwide, there was a particular concentration of new support in the South, where religious and social conservatives were opposed to many of the issues espoused by feminists including abortion, homosexuality, minority rights, and government-supported programs such as health care. Thus, Spruill contends, as it became increasingly unacceptable to use overtly racist appeals to gain southern conservative Democratic votes, opposition to the women's movement, and portraying the women's movement as an extension of the Civil Rights Movement, became for Republicans a new "southern strategy."

In the 1970s, there were two women's movements whose ideas and actions had a major impact on American politics. The first was the resurgence of the American women's rights movement often called the "Second Wave" that enjoyed tremendous success early in the decade. There was also a movement of conservative women who rose up in opposition that grew increasingly powerful as the decade progressed.[1] Women's rights advocates proudly embraced the term *feminist*. Their opponents rarely described themselves as *anti-feminist* and, in the late 1970s, chose the label *pro-family* as their efforts to block or reverse feminist-sponsored reforms turned into an enduring political movement. Nevertheless, their activities continued to be reactive, aimed largely at countering and discrediting the "women's lib" movement that they blamed for undermining traditional gender roles and family structure. Any consideration of the legacy of 1970s feminism requires an understanding of the mutual influence and antagonism between these two movements that had major consequences for American society and politics.

As feminists lobbied for policies they saw as fitting "today's realities" including the massive movement of wives and mothers into the labor force, women committed to traditional gender roles opposed them in an effort to preserve a way of life they saw as under attack and endangered.

With increasing strength and unity, they demanded that politicians focus on "family values" rather than women's rights—two concepts they saw as in opposition. Both groups claimed to represent majority opinion and tried to convince political leaders that they were the women most important to please.[2]

The competition for influence led more women to become politically active and pushed women's issues to the forefront of national political debates. It contributed to the nation's "right turn" and the emergence of the "culture wars" that have continued since. It also had profound consequences for American party politics.[3]

For most of the decade, the women's rights movement had strong bipartisan support. As conservative women demonstrated their strength and numbers and the power of women's and gender issues to mobilize voters, however, the Republican Party changed sides, and by 1980 cast its lot with the pro-family movement.[4] This strategy was particularly beneficial to the GOP in the American South where the adoption of a new and profoundly anti-feminist southern strategy helped the party fulfill long-held goals of converting disgruntled Democrats.[5] Thus, the feminist movement that in the 1970s profoundly altered cultural assumptions, laws, and policies regarding gender roles also touched off a backlash led by conservative women that profoundly altered American politics, leading ultimately to a major political realignment in the 1980s.

Reform and Reaction

As the decade of the 1970s began, the modern women's rights movement that emerged in the 1960s was having a powerful effect on American society with the aid of both major national political parties. Public opinion favored equal rights for women, and even politicians conservative on social issues felt obliged to support feminist reforms. At the national level, all branches of the federal government—legislative, judicial, and executive—revised laws and policies in keeping with this new wave of egalitarianism. Feminists were increasingly influential in both major political parties and worked together in bipartisan coalitions, most notably the National Women's Political Caucus (NWPC) founded in 1971. During the 92nd Congress, 1971–1972, more women's rights bills were passed than in all previous legislative sessions combined.[6]

In 1972, the Equal Rights Amendment (ERA) that would have made discrimination on the basis of sex unconstitutional was approved by overwhelming majorities, signifying how powerful the women's movement had become. Liberal Democrats such as Teddy Kennedy and Bella Abzug backed it but so did staunchly conservative Republicans including South Carolina's Strom Thurmond. Senator Sam Erwin of North Carolina had scant success recruiting even other southern conservatives as he tried to defeat the ERA or modify it to include traditional protections for women. State legislatures rushed to ratify the proposed amendment, some with little or no debate. Within months, the Supreme Court handed feminists another victory in the 1973 *Roe v. Wade* decision, which legalized abortion.[7]

Conservative women were furious at this massive "capitulation" to feminists. In their eyes, the movement for women's rights had gone much too far, demanding radical change in women's roles and the family that they found offensive and threatening. They were appalled that feminists were on the verge of securing ratification of a constitutional amendment that would prevent lawmakers from drawing distinctions between the sexes. They were particularly disturbed that ERA sponsors had rejected modifications intended to protect women's right to support from their husbands and to exclude them from the draft.[8]

Most of the women disturbed by feminist gains were devoutly religious and believed in innate, indeed divinely created differences between women and men that mandated traditional gender roles, patriarchal families, and differential treatment of the sexes under the law. Feminism appeared to them as a dire threat not only to the security and happiness of American women, but to the survival of the nation—which drew its strength from the strength of the American family. Anti-feminist rhetoric often overlapped with the anti-communist rhetoric with which many of them long been familiar including depiction of their feminist foes as "ungodly." Whereas some viewed feminists as simply misguided, many viewed feminism as just the latest manifestation of efforts by saboteurs within the USA, a plot by secular humanists or communists or both, unwittingly or deliberately undermining America by turning it away from God and teaching women to shun their God-given responsibilities.[9]

By 1973, the resentment of conservative women had erupted in bitter protests against feminists and the politicians who supported them. They founded numerous ad hoc organizations to arouse public opinion against the ERA and convey their concerns about the amendment's potential impact. Many ERA opponents including Phyllis Schlafly, founder of STOP ERA, a veteran of the Republican Party's right wing and a devout

Catholic, also supported the "pro-life movement" and insisted that the ERA would make it impossible to overturn *Roe* or to limit its effects. By mid-decade, ERA opponents had made major progress in slowing down the ERA bandwagon, and two states had voted to rescind ratification.[10]

As the federal government continued to show strong support for women's rights, however, what began as opposition to specific legislation became a full-blown social movement determined to roll back feminist gains. In 1975, Phyllis Schlafly established a new organization, the Eagle Forum, promoted as "the alternative to women's lib."[11] In the South, a group called Women Who Want to be Women (WWWW), founded by Church of Christ leader Lottie Beth Hobbs in 1974, grew out of an effort to rescind ratification of the ERA in Texas and quickly spread throughout the region. The two organizations cooperated with each other with Hobbs becoming a vice president of the Eagle Forum and helping Schlafly build support among southern Protestants.[12]

These were two of the largest and more prominent of the many organizations conservative women formed to oppose feminism. By the late 1970s, the revolt of conservative women had coalesced into an influential political movement primarily devoted to preserving the traditional family and restoring the nation's moral compass. It inspired and facilitated the development of a "religious right" as conservative women and men opposed to various aspects of the feminist agenda cooperated with one another to leverage their political power and end what they saw as an unholy alliance between feminists and the federal government. These developments—which continue to affect national politics today—were a part of the legacy of 1970s feminism that to feminists and their liberal and moderate supporters was as unanticipated as it was undesirable—though a strong backlash was a clear testament to their success.

The competition between feminist and anti-feminist women reached a fevered pitch in 1977 during a series of congressionally funded conferences held to solicit women's input on future policy. Women were invited to attend open meetings in their states and territories where they would vote on recommendations and delegates to send to a "National Women's Conference" held in Houston, Texas, at the end of the year. There a "National Plan of Action" would be adopted which was to guide future federal policy.[13] These conferences inadvertently polarized and further politicized American women as participants vied for the right to speak for American women. Though over 150,000 people took part in them, the press and pundits gave them a tremendous amount of attention, and both feminist and conservative leaders considered them to be watershed events; they played a far more important role in the transformation of American political culture than has been recognized.[14]

Intended to advance the status of women, these assemblies were called International Women's Year (IWY) conferences because of their original connection to a United Nations' effort on behalf of women worldwide. Proclaiming 1975 as "International Women's Year," the UN sponsored a major conference in Mexico City, which produced a "World Plan of Action." President Gerald Ford appointed a National Commission on the Observance of International Women's Year to coordinate US participation in the UN program. It was also charged with recommending internal reforms that would make the USA a "more perfect nation" in regard to women's equality. In late 1975, at the urging of feminists in Congress, most notably Congresswoman Bella Abzug (D-NY), a champion of feminist reforms and a participant in the Mexico City conference, Congress extended the life of the National Commission to organize the state and national IWY conferences and appropriated $5 million to fund them.[15]

The conferences eventually took place in 1977, delayed until after the 1976 bicentennial celebrations and the presidential election. Following fifty-six state and territorial meetings, the culminating National Women's Conference was a feminist extravaganza, a celebration of the movement's accomplishments that put feminists and feminist goals on display like few other events in its history. Including the delegates, thousands of observers including one hundred women from other nations and 1500 representatives of the press, 20,000 people descended upon Houston for the conference held the weekend of November 18–21. In the glare of national publicity, the delegates adopted a "National Plan of Action" to be presented to the president and Congress.[16]

The National Women's Conference, according to historian Sara Evans, was the "high tide" of the Second Wave of American feminism. Delegates included well-known leaders of national women's organizations from the venerable League of Women Voters (LWV) to the relatively new feminist organization, the National Organization for Women (NOW), but as organizers had hoped, many of them were newcomers to the women's movement. They were an extraordinarily diverse group: IWY leaders had gone to great lengths to include women from every race and ethnicity as well as economic background. Civil Rights Movement veterans, most notably Coretta Scott King, were highly visible.[17]

That the conference attracted stars in every field including academics, actors, and athletes demonstrated that the IWY was something with which the nation's most famous and accomplished women wished to be identified. For women active in politics, it was an event not to be missed. That the Houston conference featured the most prominent women in both political parties, including former first ladies Lady Bird Johnson and Betty Ford and then current first lady Rosalynn Carter, was a testimony to the high level of bipartisan support the movement enjoyed.[18]

Amid pageantry, stirring oratory, and impassioned floor demonstrations, the delegates adopted twenty-six recommendations for federal action. These included government-supported child care, ratification of the ERA, and protection of reproductive rights. There was a strong minority rights plank: few would forget its concluding section read by Coretta Scott King stating that from Houston there should go forth "a new force, a new understanding, a new sisterhood against all injustice that has been born here. We will not be divided and defeated again."[19] The delegates also adopted a "sexual preference" plank. Putting aside previous divisions, in Houston feminists called for eliminating all discrimination against homosexuals, adding to the women's rights agenda an issue new to American politics and extremely controversial.[20] The Houston conference became a celebration of newfound solidarity among feminists, but of course that was not the same as solidarity among American women.

From the beginning, conservative women opposed the IWY program. They were dismayed that President Gerald Ford appointed only feminists to the National Commission and were angry when one of its first acts was to declare that ratification of the ERA as early as possible was a primary goal. They demanded that Congress repeal the act mandating the IWY conferences, predicting that feminists would use the conferences for their own ends.[21] They were appalled when Jimmy Carter also appointed an all-feminist commission including women regarded by conservatives as "some of the most radical women's libbers in the country."[22] Adding insult to injury, he named Abzug, a woman they regarded as an archenemy, as the IWY's "presiding officer."[23] As the National Commission made plans for the 1977 state IWY meetings and the culminating national conference in Houston, women opposed to the feminist movement protested that they and their views were not represented. "Every women's lib leader in the country has been involved in State and National IWY Planning Committees," they stated, "while prominent women who oppose IWY goals have been pointedly excluded, with the exception of a few 'tokens.'"[24]

Conservative women were indignant that IWY leaders, who went to great lengths to involve women of many racial, ethnic, and economic backgrounds as conference organizers and participants, showed no such concern when it came to ideological diversity and differing views regarding women's rights. In appointing state IWY organizing committees, the National Commission followed guidelines stated in the enabling act adopted by Congress (drafted largely by Abzug) calling for involvement of representatives of "groups which work to advance the rights of women" as well as "members of the general public with special emphasis on the representation of low-income women, members of diverse racial, ethnic, and religious groups, and women of all ages."[25] Though they included some feminists who personally opposed abortion, IWY organizers viewed women working to defeat the ERA as working against women's interests and felt no obligation to include them.

IWY leaders were happy to have conservative women and any women not yet supporting feminism attend the conferences as participants, however, assuming that they would find exposure to feminists and feminist views to be persuasive. They expected that the IWY would increase grassroots support for the feminist movement as well as unite feminists and it did. Yet, as conservative women mobilized to challenge feminists for control of the preliminary IWY meetings in the states, they were clearly there to oppose, not consider, feminism. Ironically, the conservative challenge inspired greater solidarity among feminists. It attracted the participation of radicals who tended to scorn state and federal commissions on women and their work; that, however, inspired greater conservative turnout and solidarity. The IWY conferences had the effect of expanding the constituencies, clarifying the goals, and galvanizing the supporters of both movements.[26]

Conservatives Mobilize

The nation's most prominent anti-feminist, Phyllis Schlafly, claimed that "Houston" was a major feminist blunder that played directly into her hands.[27] The need to oppose feminists at taxpayer-funded conferences where a "blueprint" for federal action would be adopted offered her and other leaders an ideal way to mobilize and unify conservative women. Insisting that the establishment of the feminist-dominated IWY program was further proof that the federal government was taking one side of a national debate, they established the "IWY Citizens Review Committee" (CRC) to monitor IWY, which they denounced as a "Federally Funded Festival for Frustrated Feminists" and "Abzugate." The CRC also coordinated conservatives' efforts to influence if not control the state IWY meetings and the recommendations and delegates selected.[28]

The IWY not only presented conservative women with a challenge they could not ignore, as feminists developed an expansive National Plan of Action during IWY, they also created a broad target for anti-feminist foes. Though for years feminist strategists had sought to disassociate the ERA from controversial issues including abortion and gay rights, during IWY they took a different course, embracing these and other issues anathema to social and religious conservatives.[29]

As the feminist agenda became manifest during the state IWY meetings in late spring and summer of 1977, conservative opposition grew. At most meetings and all of the earliest ones, feminists were numerically dominant and approved feminist recommendations and delegates. What feminists called the "anti-change forces" made strong showings in many states, however, and as the IWY meetings continued, they managed to gain control of several of them.[30]

The first major victory for conservatives came in mid-June in Oklahoma. State Eagle Forum and CRC leader Diane Edmondson reported they "relied heavily on the fundamentalist church groups here to tell their members to attend and vote against the feminist slate. They helped us because about 1000 of the 1200 attending were anti-feminists."[31] This triumph was followed shortly by another in Utah where heavy Mormon participation ensured that feminist proposals went down in defeat.[32] Conservatives turned out in great numbers in southern states including Florida and Alabama and achieved a complete "takeover" in Mississippi.[33] In the last few weeks of state meetings, feminists prevailed only in New York and West Virginia. In the end, conservatives managed to elect only 20% of the delegates to Houston but, considering the feminist advantage, they considered it to be a victory. As Schlafly had said from the beginning, if they could not succeed in "taking over" the IWY conferences they would try to "make the libbers sorry they ever had the state conferences."[34]

The efforts of conservatives to challenge feminists at the IWY meetings drew strength from defenders of traditional gender roles and opponents of big government, which were often overlapping categories.

IWY Citizens Review Committee literature proclaimed that the state meetings were "designed and controlled as an elaborate charade—at taxpayers' expense—to rubber-stamp the pet projects of women's lib leaders like Bella Abzug ... including ERA, federally-funded abortions-on-demand, and militant demands from lesbian groups, [that] have been rejected by voters and lawmakers time and again."[35] They appealed with dramatic success to conservative Catholics, Mormons, and fundamentalist and evangelic Protestants—groups long hostile to one another, each seeing itself as the one true religion and denying the others' legitimacy. As they mobilized to oppose feminist proposals and candidates—and at times succeeded in getting their own recommendations and candidates approved—they learned that by working together they could win—a key factor in the development of the "religious right."

Conservatives found it particularly galling that feminists were proposing large-scale spending for social programs they found objectionable, including government-sponsored childcare, re-education of "displaced homemakers," and shelters for "battered women" (seen as weakening the traditional family), as well as increased aid for welfare recipients and a national system of health care. As one South Carolina IWY critic, state representative Norma Russell, charged, the resolutions "railroaded through gave no thought to costs to implement them. The leadership of this conference is endorsing making government a 'sugar daddy' from the cradle to the grave!!"[36] Furthermore, that the IWY program had UN origins and promoted international cooperation alarmed isolationists; the IWY, they claimed, was part of a plot to undermine national sovereignty and establish "one-world government."[37]

In addition, the anti-IWY drive drew support from racial conservatives, especially in the South. Many of the IWY Citizens Review leaders were leaders of Women for Constitutional Government, an organization established in the 1960s to oppose integration and to defend "racial integrity" and Christian values.[38] Ku Klux Klan leaders in some states boasted of their success in mobilizing women to attend the rallies and of "controlling" the Mississippi IWY conference, which sent an all-white delegation and anti-ERA, anti-abortion, anti-homosexuality, anti-daycare, anti-Social Security, and anti-UN (and pro-South Africa) resolutions to Houston.[39]

The anti-IWY effort also drew support from pro-life organizations. Nellie Gray, president and founder of March for Life, the group that sponsors annual protests on the anniversary of *Roe v. Wade*, was one of the key CRC leaders. National Right to Life newsletters reported with outrage the fact that feminists at the IWY meetings were promoting women's right to abortion.[40] Many women opposed to abortion but previously uncommitted or even supporting the ERA decided during IWY to align themselves with the anti-feminist coalition. Pro-life organizations played a key role in mobilizing conservative participation. Many were Catholic organizations, but a growing number of conservative Protestants were becoming involved in the movement against abortion including in the South where pro-life leaders were making a strong effort to recruit them.[41] Pro-life leaders, recognizing that they had to have southern support in order to win a human life amendment to the Constitution, had begun a major campaign to gain the support of conservative Protestants in the region that may have boosted conservative turnout at IWY meetings in southern states.[42]

The nascent movements for and against gay rights became a major factor in the IWY struggle somewhat unexpectedly. Before 1977, feminists had been at odds with one another over whether or not to include protection of the rights of lesbians on the feminist agenda, though NOW formally endorsed it in 1971.[43] National and state commissions on the status of women had avoided the issue, and it was not addressed by the Ford-appointed IWY commission. However, two developments early in 1977—the sudden rise of an anti-gay movement in Florida led by Anita Bryant and the appointment by President Jimmy Carter of gay rights leader Jean O'Leary to the National Commission on IWY—ensured that this new and extraordinarily volatile issue would be among those over which feminists and conservatives fought at the IWY state meetings and in Houston. The viciousness of Bryant's homophobic campaign that portrayed gays as child molesters and perverts inspired feminists to rally behind the gay rights effort and to include an anti-discrimination plank in the National Plan of Action despite the fears of many that it would become an "albatross" around their necks.[44]

As the state IWY meetings came to an end, the IWY Citizens Review Committee tried to stop the Houston conference from happening. Senator Jesse Helms (R-NC), who had become one of Schlafly's leading allies in the fight against ERA, joined the fight against IWY; in September 1977, he sponsored congressional hearings where women from the CRC testified about discrimination, "railroading," and "lesbian aggressiveness" at the state IWY meetings and demanded that the IWY be brought to an end before more taxpayers' money was wasted.

When it was clear the Houston conference would still go on, however, they tried to turn it to their advantage.⁴⁵

Aware that it would draw huge attention from the press, CRC leaders planned a protest rally to make it clear the National Women's Conference did not speak for them. Lottie Beth Hobbs, the WWWW leader, a Texan, boldly reserved Houston's Astro Arena and launched plans for a massive protest. Schlafly was fearful, worried that with so little time to prepare, an anti-IWY rally would draw a small crowd and be an embarrassment, but as she happily acknowledged later, she was completely wrong: The Pro-Family Rally, she said afterward, "was one of the most amazing events that ever happened," one that proved "that Pro-Family Americans have the dedication and the determination to win."⁴⁶ Outraged by what they had seen at the state IWY meetings, protesters poured in, many from Texas and nearby states but also from all over the nation. Triumphant conservative leaders were exultant, attributing their success to God "with a little help from Christian women."⁴⁷

As the National Women's Conference proceeded, throngs of women, some accompanied by men and children, filled Houston's Astro Arena to overflowing. Estimates about crowd size varied (10,000–20,000), but it rivaled the IWY rally in size and intensity. The tone and nature of the crowd was quite different, however. Many waved flags and carried Bibles and, according to the press, nearly all of them were white. They cheered as an all-star lineup of conservative leaders denounced the IWY and the entire feminist agenda as a combined assault on the American family. Leaders of the anti-ERA movement were joined by prominent pro-life leaders, reflecting the new level of cooperation between anti-abortion forces and the movement to stop the ERA. The leader of the new movement against homosexuality, Anita Bryant, sent a videotaped message.⁴⁸

In her address, Hobbs denounced not just the plan but the philosophy behind it, insisting that the "barriers" the feminists sought to destroy were not "barriers" at all but "safeguards" carefully built into the system by "wise men and women" and that their removal would plunge the nation "into social and moral destruction."⁴⁹ Schlafly stated the feminist movement was out to "drive the homemaker out of the home," "forbid you to identify with the traditional roles as wives and mothers," and substitute "two sex-neutral parents" for fathers and mothers. The crowd roared in response as she declared, "American women do not want ERA, abortion, lesbian rights, and they do not want child care in the hands of government."

Schlafly proclaimed that God was on their side and that they could "turn back this tide" if they continued to work together.[50]

Rally organizers seized the occasion to announce the birth of a "pro-family movement" determined to reverse feminist gains and take control of the nation from feminists and their allies who threatened to destroy American families and thus the nation. Afterward, many in the crowd told reporters this was their "political baptism" and that the millions Congress had spent on the IWY might have been worth it if it awakened Christian women to the dangers facing the nation and the need to become active in politics.[51]

The carefully orchestrated performances in Houston at the National Women's Conference and the Pro-Family Rally focused attention on the two competing women's movements as nothing had before—a consciousness-raising experience for the entire nation. Considering that national polls showed that only 20% of American women identified with the Schlafly agenda—approximately the same percentage of conservative delegates elected to Houston—feminists were appalled at the success of conservative women in attracting the attention of the press and in convincing politicians that they were the women most important to please.[52]

After Houston

After Houston, both feminists and conservatives were fired up, ready to fight for their goals. Over the next 2 years, feminists clashed with President Carter over implementation of the National Plan of Action. Recognizing that the IWY had become a polarizing issue, he tried to distance himself from it and eventually fired Abzug when she criticized him publicly for his lack of action on "the Plan." That made her a martyr in the eyes of many feminists and led feminists to divide among themselves about supporting Carter's reelection. Abzug herself supported Ted Kennedy's challenge to Carter for the Democratic Party's nomination. She led Kennedy forces at the 1980 party convention and helped saddle Carter with a platform far more liberal than he wanted and difficult to run on.[53]

Meanwhile, the new pro-family movement, united by opposition to feminism and inspired by its own display of strength, worked with the "New Right" to boost the power of the most conservative factions within the Republican Party and elect their hero, Ronald Reagan.[54] New Right strategists could not help but notice their success in mobilizing social conservatives and religious groups—including Catholics, evangelical Protestants, and Mormons who had in the past despised one another—in a campaign against feminism and feminist control of IWY. The uprising of conservative women not only boosted the confidence of a dispirited right but put them on the path to success.[55]

As even party leaders previously considered to be moderate or progressive such as George Herbert Walker Bush, Reagan's primary competitor for the 1980 Republican nomination, began to cater to what was becoming known as "the religious right," the GOP ended its decades-long support for the ERA, came out squarely against abortion, and marginalized feminists in the party who, looking back, regarded this period as the beginning of the "Republican War against Women." Republican leaders who had long sought methods to break apart the New Deal coalition embraced anti-feminism as a wedge issue with which to appeal to social conservatives across the nation.[56] Joining resentment against government regulation of business and high taxes with resentment of government-sponsored social change, they recognized, was a likely formula for success.

This effort was certainly not limited to the South, but the region presented special opportunities and tremendous potential rewards. If the Republicans could gain the support of large numbers of disaffected southern white conservatives, they could realize their dream of becoming a majority party. In the South, there were many social conservatives with profoundly conservative views about women and the family, and many were from evangelical or fundamentalist groups that discouraged participation in politics as worldly and corrupting. That meant there were large numbers of people likely to respond to the pro-family, anti-feminist message who would be new voters—an untapped resource for politicians including Jesse Helms who knew how to appeal to them.[57] Then, there were large numbers of registered Democrats unhappy with the national Democratic Party's support of civil rights that had tended to vote Republican in presidential politics but had not changed parties. They were inconsistent in their support for the GOP, and the fact that many born-again Christians in the region had voted for Carter had been an important factor in his election.[58] If the party could employ an anti-feminist strategy that appealed to Christian conservatives, one that also tapped the massive reservoir of southern white resentment about having been "overcome" by the Civil Rights Movement backed by the federal government, the results could be striking. In addition, if they could direct anti-feminist, racist, and anti-federal sentiments against the Democratic Party, they might even strike gold.

The IWY helped the GOP do just that. It mobilized and politicized social conservatives and prepared them for their work ahead. The opportunities to enhance skills in networking, coalition building, convention planning, and media relations were particularly important for the thousands of women not previously active in politics who had been mobilized during the 1977 anti-IWY challenge. Afterward, these women not only saw themselves as part of God's army, they were able to work with greater effectiveness. IWY leader Rosemary Thomson (who likened the rise of Christian women during in 1977 to the Great Awakening) insisted proudly that IWY had been their "boot camp," preparing them "for the offensive in the battle for our families and our faith."[59]

The IWY also linked radical and "un-Christian" feminism, racial liberalism, and federal activism to one another and to the Democratic Party. It alienated thousands of conservatives from the Democratic Party and gave them ammunition they could use to mobilize others. Anti-feminism was at the heart of a new southern strategy that over the next few years helped the GOP achieve longstanding goals in the region. IWY became a new and effective rallying cry through which to harness the newly demonstrated power of anti-feminism.

Between the November 1977 showdown in Houston and the November 1980 presidential election, the pro-family forces continued their fight against feminism and for the traditional family. Southern women returning from the conservatives' rally in Houston were fired up and ready to work. Within days, two Mississippi women sent out a letter to like-minded "friends" reporting on the spectacular showing of Christian conservatives and calling for action. "We have just returned from a meeting which drew more women than Bella Abzug's International Women's Year conference. At the same hour that Bella's IWY Conference was opening … more than 15,000 women were arriving for a PRO-FAMILY, PRO-LIFE Meeting, in opposition to the Equal Rights Amendment, Abortion and Civil rights for Homosexuality." They predicted that politics would never be the same. "Leaving Houston's Astro Arena, we felt we had witnessed a great breakthrough, a turning point for our country."[60]

Women of the new pro-family movement hastened to spread the word about what they had seen and how the IWY had revealed the "true intentions" of feminists and the urgent need to stop them.

Conservative women insisted that all they had to do was show people the National Plan of Action to move like-minded women to action. One Houston veteran stated that it was "the best recruiting tool I've ever had .... I just spend twenty minutes reading it to them. That's all I have to do."[61]

In the South as across the nation, one of the conservatives' main targets was the state commissions on the status of women that since the early 1960s were the primary workhorses behind the women's movement. After John F. Kennedy appointed a presidential commission on the status of women, governors and legislatures across the nation created similar commissions and generally appointed women progressives to these bodies that surveyed state laws and policies for gender discrimination and recommended reforms.[62] Conservative women saw the commissions as state-level counterparts of the IWY, similarly outrageous for using taxpayers' dollars to fund feminism. Efforts to do away with the commissions had begun in South Carolina back in 1973, but after IWY, conservative women went after the commissions with renewed purpose and vigor and managed to get many of them abolished or defunded. South Carolina state legislator Norma Russell, who had been elected to the National Women's Conference and was a leader among the conservative delegates, introduced legislation to try to kill the state's commission on women using "sunset laws."[63]

When unable to abolish commissions, they insisted (understandably) on the addition of conservative appointees, which usually resulted in gridlock and rendered the commissions useless to feminists. Arkansas feminists, including Diane Blair, who had been a leader of her state's commission on women and active in the National Association of State Commissions on the Status of Women, reluctantly concluded that in the changed political climate, these would no longer be a viable mechanism for achieving feminist goals.[64]

As for the ERA, after IWY there was little chance of success. Most of the unratified states were in the South and several including Florida, Virginia, and North Carolina became "battleground states" where feminists believed they stood a chance of winning and focused their efforts. But southern ERA advocates became increasingly frustrated and dispirited as they continued to "fly the colors" for what was for the time a lost cause.[65] One South Carolina NOW leader recalls how she resented the subtle or unsubtle suggestions that northern women "blamed southern women" for the ERA's defeat.[66] Meanwhile, after Houston their conservative opponents were not only better organized but more determined than ever and buoyed by a sense of impending victory.[67]

The 3-year extension of the deadline prolonged the battle but produced no new victories. Many southern politicians who had come out early for ERA or had come around on Carter's urging were increasingly resentful at being saddled with the amendment, particularly those in states heavily dependent on tourism and hurt by the ERA boycott. Many congressmen who had earlier supported the ERA and still claimed to be supporters voted against extension.

Rescission movements gained strength, benefiting from the coalescence and coordination of conservative energy through the pro-family movement. Studies have shown that for the rest of the ERA battle, the opponents were much more knowledgeable than proponents about where their political representatives stood on the amendment, more passionate about the issue, and more likely to take political action. One study indicated that, despite the national polls, within the nonratifying states there was a precipitous decline in support for the ERA that dropped below 40%.[68]

Schlafly and many other conservative women attributed the change to the IWY. She wrote: "At the IWY event in Houston, the ERAers, the abortionists, and the lesbians made the decision to March in unison for their common goals. The conference enthusiastically passed what the media called the 'hot button' issues: ERA, abortion and abortion funding, and lesbian and gay rights. The IWY Conference doomed ERA because it showed the television audience that ERA and the feminist movement were outside the mainstream of America. ERA never passed anywhere in the post-IWY period."[69]

IWY AS RALLYING CRY

As the 1980 election approached, women of the pro-family movement and their GOP allies found that invoking IWY was highly effective in mobilizing voters including those alienated by feminist positions on racial and religious issues. In their view it was the perfect tool with which to appeal to those who wanted to take back their country from the moderates and liberals who had been using the power and resources of an inflated federal government to force unwanted change upon the nation.

The association between the IWY and the Civil Rights Movement was as clear and obvious as it was deliberate, and conservatives actively exploited it. IWY leaders seeking to diversify and strengthen their movement in the South had actively encouraged participation of African American women in an effort to bring white and black feminists together.

In appointing state organizers, they sought out African American women who were veterans of the Civil Rights Movement. The Mississippi IWY Coordinating Committee, for instance, included women who were members of the Mississippi Advisory Committee to the US Civil Rights Commission and of the NAACP; two of them including Mayor Unita Blackwell (later a McArthur "genius award" winner) were officeholders whose elections had been made possible by the Voting Rights Act of 1965.[70]

IWY state meetings honored Civil Rights Movement leaders such as Modjeska Simkins of South Carolina, an icon of the movement who was elected as a delegate to Houston. There she was part of a group calling themselves "Women for Racial and Economic Equality" that, in the name of Fannie Lou Hamer, protested the seating of the all-white Mississippi delegation.[71] At the national IWY conference, First Lady of the Civil Rights Movement Coretta Scott King—one of Carter's appointees to the National Commission—was afforded almost as much honor and attention as Lady Bird Johnson, Betty Ford, or Rosalynn Carter.

Efforts to encourage sisterhood between black and white feminists worked. In their final report to the National Commission, the biracial state IWY coordinating committee vanquished in the Mississippi takeover stated: "The State Meeting made clear to us that sexism and racism are the same. Those who are against equal rights for women are also opposed to equal rights for blacks. Therefore both black and white women have to fight both sexism and racism or whichever one they may choose, it really means the same thing."[72] Similar comments came from South Carolina. Dr. Marianna Davis, IWY chair in South Carolina, said she came to believe for the first time that the women's movement was her movement too—that the two causes were inseparable.[73] A highlight of the Houston conference was the adoption of the minority rights plank signifying a convergence of the women's and minority rights movements, upon which delegates spontaneously joined hands and sang "We Shall Overcome."[74]

However, white supremacists were equally fired up by the idea that the women's movement was an extension of the Civil Rights Movement, and they mobilized in part as an opportunity to strike back. As noted above, conservatives associated with strong opposition to racial integration and the Civil Rights Movement were much in evidence during the IWY challenge: Women for Constitutional Government members were members of the IWY Citizens Review Committee, and some testified at the Helms hearings it organized. John Birch Society members including many men were part of the conservative coalitions. Members of the American Party, the party that nominated George Wallace in 1968, took part, as did members of more extremist and violent groups including the White Nationalist Movement and the Ku Klux Klan.[75]

Modjeska Simkins said she recognized old foes at the South Carolina state meeting including JBS and KKK members. When she was nominated for a slot on the state delegation to Houston, they put out what she called "a communist smear sheet" on her, a page from the records of the McCarthy-era House Un-American Activities Committee (HUAC)—though she still received the second highest number of votes in the election.[76]

As noted, the IWY in Mississippi sent an all-white delegation to Houston that included several men (the only men elected as delegates) and the wife of the state KKK leader. She insisted that she was not a Klan member, but attended meetings "as a concerned citizen." When interviewed by the press, she observed that communists had tried to take over the country through the blacks and were now hoping to control the nation through a majority composed of blacks and women. Her husband added, "Women's rights and civil rights go hand in hand."[77]

The conservative coalition that called itself "Mississippians for God, Country, and Family" also included Richard Barrett, the founder and leader of the Nationalist Movement, a white supremacist organization. Mississippi IWY Coordinating Committee member and Civil Rights Movement veteran Unita Blackwell was quoted as saying, "Even if they say they are for God, country, and family," they were "the same group of people that have always oppressed black people" in the state all along.[78]

In Houston, some members of the Mississippi delegation made racist statements to the press, such as that most of the black women participating in IWY were brought in by the feminists and that they were offering the "poor and underprivileged" a "gravy train."[79] Andrea Dworkin, covering the IWY conference for *Ms.* magazine, described hearing racist comments as well as anti-Semitic comments, including the denunciation of feminism as a "Jew" conspiracy.[80]

Ku Klux Klan imperial wizard Robert Shelton, the infamous Alabama Klan leader, boasted that the Klan had controlled state IWY meetings in several states. He announced that Klansmen would be going to Houston "to protect our women from all the militant lesbians who will be there."[81] He protested as injustice the use of taxpayers' money to organize the IWY state meetings, saying that if Congress should do that "then it should give $5 million to the Klan to fight for segregation." He acknowledged that in 1977, "we got into this too late to be effective, but we'll keep working. While we are an independent organization, we work with any group with a Christian base; and, yes, we are working with some Christian groups—it's time they have come out and taken a stand against the women's movement and the IWY meetings in particular."[82]

At the time and later, Schlafly denied knowledge of any KKK involvement in IWY or anti-ERA activities or ever having met a member of the Klan and said such boasting was their trying to "mooch in" and "take credit for what we were doing." She described herself, however, as "very tolerant" and said she had welcomed the support of groups with similar determination to oppose feminism. Schlafly also insisted that the pro-family movement was proud to claim African Americans as part of their coalition.[83] Organizers of the Houston protest invited two African Americans as speakers at the rally, Dr. Mildred Jefferson, president of Right to Life, and state legislator Clay Smothers, clearly hoping to counter the idea that racism was a part of their agenda.[84]

However, Smothers, a recent convert to the Republican Party who had attended the 1972 Democratic National Convention as a Wallace delegate and instead nominated himself, undermined that notion.[85] His speech to the Houston pro-family rally played heavily to white supremacist as well as homophobic sentiments. According to the *New York Times*, the nearly all-white crowd went wild, whistling and cheering, as he said he already had enough civil rights to "choke a hungry goat" and "proclaimed his desire to "segregate" himself from the "misfits and perverts" coming to the IWY in Houston.[86]

To some analysts of southern politics, it seemed that the IWY revived the fighting spirit of white conservatives who had been "overcome" by the Civil Rights Movement but saw in IWY a new opportunity to strike out against federal "intervention." After the Mississippi takeover, Bill Minor, a leading analyst of Mississippi politics, observed in his column that the state had just gotten "a look-see" at "a new form of militant conservatism" that had "emerged to replace the old-time anti-black militancy of the White Citizens Councils and the Ku Klux Klan." The new militant conservatism, he wrote, was "ostensibly not racist," but "comes out of a strong reactionary backlash led by religious fundamentalism, self-acclaimed patriotic organizations and some old-time staunchly conservative political groups." Minor stated, "Their overall enemy now is not the black man but 'liberalism' in any form, as they see it," and that, in place of opposition to civil rights and voting rights bills, they were focused on "such issues as ERA, gay rights, and abortion."[87]

Invoking IWY gave the GOP a means of appealing to angry white conservatives on these issues while also channeling their anger about the new state of affairs since the Civil Rights Act of 1964 and 1965 barely 10 years earlier. In his 1982 autobiography, white nationalist leader Richard Barrett spelled that out, stating that IWY, "a government-backed, stacked deck, pro-lesbian menagerie," had "afforded the common people the first opportunity since the anti-integration protests to make known, in large turnouts, that they were neither colonial lackeys nor unthinking slaves of Washington," adding that after IWY, "the moral, womanly woman became increasingly prominent in my speeches."[88] At a time when it was more important than ever to appeal to disaffected white Democrats without overt racism, denunciation of IWY was a prime example of the use of "coded language." The IWY allowed Republicans to direct the accumulated outrage of southern white conservatives against Jimmy Carter and the Democrats and they did.

No one seemed to remember and certainly did not mention that IWY began under a Republican president who appointed Republican feminists to lead it—never mind that the Republican Party had supported the ERA much longer and more consistently than had the Democrats. That the IWY actually took place under Carter's watch was highly beneficial to GOP strategists, and they took full advantage of it.[89] Carter had given it over to women they perceived as "godless." And, as one speaker at the Pro-Family Rally proclaimed, Carter's wife was at "the wrong rally"— an act so resented among Christian conservatives that one religious right newspaper called for the clothes that she and the other first ladies had worn at the National Woman's Conference to be publicly burned.[90]

Republican strategists used IWY as a rallying cry and with great effectiveness. In Richard Viguerie's *The New Right: We're Ready to Lead*, published in the fall of 1980 just in time for the presidential election, he boasted that the New Right was registering millions of new voters in preparation for the most important election of the twentieth century and attributed much of that success to the IWY. The new voters, he said, included many who "had turned out for the pro-family rally in Houston to counter Bella Abzug's 'women's lib conference.'" Quoting Heritage Foundation founder Paul Weyrich, he warned that "as pro-family groups become better educated in the political process," a lot of politicians "who today thumb their noses at the whole notion of a pro-family coalition are going to be humbled."[91]

That Carter had been elected in 1976 in part because of born-again Christians accounted for the viciousness of their attacks on him during the 1980 election. They were like lovers scorned. As Viguerie put it, given that they were "much more important" in Carter's election even than the blacks, conservatives found it "difficult to understand why for almost four years Carter had given the born-again Christian the back of his hand," instead surrounding himself with "many people who routinely reject Biblical principles regarding sexual behavior, family responsibility, abortion, and other key moral issues." He gloated about the rift that had emerged between Carter and more liberal Democrats and that groups Carter thought were his base instead backed Teddy Kennedy.[92]

Rev. Jerry Falwell, leader of the Moral Majority, a Christian right activist group founded with the encouragement of New Right leaders in 1979, proclaimed that the newly mobilized "great Christian army" was on the move. It was about to show "the godless minority of treacherous individuals who have been permitted to formulate national policy ... [that] they do not represent the majority" and that they will no longer "permit the destruction of their country by godless, liberal philosophies."[93]

Thus, that Carter inherited the IWY, declined invitations to attend, implemented but little of the National Plan of Action, and fired Abzug in a humiliating fashion did not matter. Republican strategists recognized the value of IWY to their cause and hung the IWY—like an albatross—around his neck. Southern conservatives, many pundits later claimed, provided Reagan with the margin of victory.[94] Ronald Reagan, who forcefully embraced the pro-life, pro-family, and anti-feminist rhetoric of which angry white southerners had become so fond, won the election and the hearts and minds of many who would soon become Republicans.

A New Southern Strategy

Between 1970 and 1980, there was a profound change in American political culture. As the decade began, the vociferousness of the women's rights movement and the quiescence of women conservatives encouraged politicians to support feminist goals. However, the organization of conservative women in opposition to feminism made it very clear that

American women were divided on these issues. During IWY, those divisions became more visible and even more politically consequential as women leaning toward feminist or anti-feminist positions coalesced into warring factions determined to enhance their political clout. The uprising of conservative women gave politicians permission and motive to oppose feminism: it gave politicians incentive to support "family values" instead of women's rights—and encouraged them and the nation to see the two as contradictory.

By 1980, the two parties had chosen sides in the great debate over women's and gender issues. Anti-feminism would continue to be a central part of Republican policy for many years—as would the claim that the GOP was the party most supportive to American families, the defender of the traditional family against redefinition. Especially in that it gave Republicans a new and highly effective "southern strategy," the IWY played a role in one of the most important episodes of political realignment in American history. The IWY helped turn the South red.

Notes

1. The author wishes to thank the National Endowment for the Humanities, the Radcliffe Institute for Advanced Study, the Woodrow Wilson International Center for Scholars, the Gerald R. Ford Foundation, and the University of South Carolina for grants that supported this research.
2. NCOIWY, *The Spirit of Houston: The First National Women's Conference: An Official Report to the President, the Congress and the People of the United States* (Washington, DC: GPO, 1978); Phyllis Schlafly, *The Power of the Positive Woman* (New Rochelle, NY: Arlington House, 1977); Rosemary Thomson, *The Price of LIBerty* (Carol Stream, IL: Creation House, 1978).
3. Marjorie J. Spruill, "Gender and America's Right Turn," in *Rightward Bound: Making America Conservative in the 1970s*, ed. Bruce J. Schulman and Julian E. Zelizer (Cambridge, MA: Harvard University Press, 2008), 71–89.
4. Tanya Melich, *The Republican War against Women: An Insider's Report from Behind the Lines* (New York: Bantam Books, 1998); Catherine E. Rymph, *Republican Women: Feminism and Conservatism from Suffrage through the Rise of the New Right* (Chapel Hill: University of North Carolina Press, 2006); Donald T. Critchlow, *Phyllis Schlafly and Grassroots Conservatism: A Woman's Crusade* (Princeton, NJ: Princeton University Press, 2005).

5. There is an impressive and expanding body of literature on the growth of Republican support in the South though more focused on race, religion, and "the social issues" generally than on women's activism. For a few examples, see Earl Black and Merle Black, *The Rise of Southern Republicans* (Cambridge, MA: Harvard University Press, 2002); Glenn Feldman, ed., *Painting Dixie Red: When, Where, Why, and How the South Became Republican* (Gainesville: University Press of Florida, 2011); Daniel K Williams, *God's Own Party: The Making of the Christian Right* (Oxford: Oxford University Press, 2012).
6. Susan M. Hartmann, *From Margin to Mainstream: American Women and Politics since 1960* (New York: Knopf, 1989), 71–129; Sara M. Evans, *Tidal Wave: How Women Changed America at Century's End* (New York: Free Press, 2003), 61–97; Flora Davis, *Moving the Mountain: The Women's Movement in America Since 1960* (Urbana: University of Illinois Press, 1999), 147–195.
7. Hartmann, *From Margin to Mainstream*, 103–106; Evans, *Tidal Wave*, 65–67; Donald G. Mathews and Jane Sherron De Hart, *Sex, Gender, and the Politics of ERA: A State and the Nation* (New York: Oxford University Press, 1990), 35–53; Carol Felsenthal, *The Sweetheart of the Silent Majority: The Biography of Phyllis Schlafly* (Garden City, NY: Doubleday and Company, 1981), 233–239.
8. Thomson, *Price of LIBerty*, 51; Schlafly, *Power of the Positive Woman*; Felsenthal, *Sweetheart of the Silent Majority*, 235–241; Mathews and De Hart, *Sex, Gender, and the Politics of ERA*, 50–51.
9. For an example of the blend of anti-feminist and anti-communist rhetoric, see Thomson, *Price of LIBerty*; Schlafly, *Power of the Positive Woman*.
10. Felsenthal, *Sweetheart of the Silent Majority*; Critchlow, *Phyllis Schlafly*; Ruth Murray Brown, *For a "Christian America": A History of the Religious Right* (Amherst, NY: Prometheus Books, 2002); Felsenthal, *Sweetheart of the Silent Majority*.
11. "Eagle Forum: The Alternative to Women's Lib" (Brochure, 1975), Nancy Moore Papers, South Carolina Political Collections, University of South Carolina Libraries, Columbia, S.C. (hereafter SCPC); Felsenthal, *Sweetheart of the Silent Majority*; Critchlow, *Phyllis Schlafly*.
12. William Martin, *With God on Our Side: The Rise of the Religious Right in America* (New York: Broadway Books, 1996); Brown, *For a "Christian America,"* 65–66; Janet K. Boles, *The Politics of the Equal Rights Amendment: Conflict and the Decision Process* (New York: Longman, 1979); Brown, *For a "Christian America"*; Nancy Elizabeth Baker, "Too Much to Lose, Too Little to Gain: The Role of Rescission Movements in the Equal Rights Amendment Battle, 1972–1982" (3106609,

Harvard University, 2003), ProQuest Dissertations & Theses (PQDT) (305332209).
13. National Commission on the Observance of International Women's Year, *The Spirit of Houston: The First National Women's Conference: An Official Report to the President, the Congress and the People of the United States* (Washington, DC: US GPO, 1978); Caroline Bird and National Commission on the Observance of International Women's Year, *What Women Want: From the Official Report to the President, the Congress, and the People of the United States* (New York: Simon and Schuster, 1979); Kathryn Kish Sklar and Thomas Dublin, *Women and Social Movements in the United States 1600–2000* (Alexandria, VA; Binghamton, NY: Alexander Street Press; Center for the Historical Study of Women and Gender at the State University of New York, Binghamton, 2007), http://asp6new.alexanderstreet.com/was2.
14. Spruill, "Gender and America's Right Turn"; Gloria Steinem, *Outrageous Acts and Everyday Rebellions* (New York: H. Holt, 1995); Thomson, *Price of LIBerty*.
15. *Spirit of Houston*, 9–12. Other primary sponsors of the act were Democrat Patsy Mink of Hawaii and Republican Margaret Heckler of Massachusetts.
16. NCOIWY, SNCOIWY, *Spirit of Houston*, 119–70; "What Next for U.S. Women: Houston Produces New Alliances and a Drive for Grass-roots Power," *Time*, December 5, 1977, 19–22, 25–26; Anna Quindlen, "Women End Parley With Plan for Rights: Women End Meeting in Houston with a 25-Point Agenda for Rights," *New York Times*, November 22, 1977. http://search.proquest.com.pallas2.tcl.sc.edu/hnpnewyorktimes/docview/123146340/abstract/21E73E78B4DF4E07PQ/4?accountid=13965; Sally Quinn, "The Pedestal Has Crashed: Pride and Paranoia in Houston," *Washington Post*, B1, November 23, 1977.
17. *Spirit of Houston*, 119–126.
18. Ibid., 119–126, 138–140.
19. Bird and NCOIWY, *What Women Want*; *Spirit of Houston*, 147–157, quotation p. 157.
20. NCOIWY, *Spirit of Houston*, 165–166.
21. *Phyllis Schlafly Report*, June 1976.
22. Carter reappointed several members of the Ford Commission and added several Democrats including representatives of key Democratic constituencies plus Betty Ford. The appointees who conservatives considered radical were Eleanor Smeal of NOW; Gloria Steinem, editor of *Ms.* magazine; and Jean O'Leary, co-chair of the National Gay and

Lesbian Task Force. "President Announces IWY Commission Members," *Women Today*, April 14, 1975.
23. James J. Kilpatrick, "Carter Hands $5 Million Kitty Over to Bella," *Human Events*, April 16, 1977.
24. *Spirit of Houston*, 99–102; Thomson, *Price of LIBerty*, 92, 93; quotation from "IWY CITIZEN'S REVIEW MEMO#1," October 28, 1977, p. 2, Box 3, Marion Gressette Papers, SCPC; *Phyllis Schlafly Report*, January 1976; *Eagle Forum Newsletter*, May 1977, March 1977; Phyllis Schlafly to "Dear Friend," September 1977, Box 3, Folder 2, Dunaway Papers, Emory University; Hartmann, *From Margin to Mainstream*, 137–141, 147; Felsenthal, *Sweetheart of the Silent Majority*, 253.
25. "Public Law 94-167" in Appendix, *Spirit of Houston*, 251–252.
26. Irene Wolt, "'California Feminists Beat Back Right Wing,' by Irene Wolt, Independent Socialist Paper (*In These Times*), July 6–12, 1977, California Report to IWY National Commission, National Commission Papers, SL," *In These Times*, July 6, 1977, California Report to IWY National Commission, NCOIWY Papers, SL.
27. Phyllis Schlafly, "What Really Happened in Houston," *Phyllis Schlafly Report*, December 1977.
28. Citizens' Review Committee for I.W.Y. NEWS MEMO#1, October 28, 1977, International Women's Year, 1977, Topical, Box 8, Folder 1, L. Marion Gressette Papers, SCPC.
29. See the National Plan of Action, *Spirit of Houston*, pp. 13–98.
30. Bird and NCOIWY, *What Women Want*, 99–117.
31. Edmondson quotation in Carolyn Kortge (Wichita, Kansas) *Eagle & Beacon*, August 3, 1977 (clipping in Briefing Book, NCOIWY Papers); "Final Report of the Oklahoma IWY Coordinating Committee, July 18, 1977, Carton 3, NCOIWY, SL; James J. Kilpatrick, "A Conservative View," "Bella's Troops Routed in Oklahoma," clipping n.d., Box TY07196#2, NCOIWY, SL.
32. On the Mormon role in the IWY and ERA battles generally, see Martha Sonntag Bradley, *Pedestals and Podiums: Utah Women, Religious Authority and Equal Rights* (Salt Lake City: Signature Books, 2005); Neil Young, "'The ERA Is a Moral Issue: The Mormon Church, LDS Women and the Defeat of the Equal Rights Amendment," *American Quarterly* 59, no. 3 (2007): 623–644; See also the Utah IWY Coordinating Committee's official report, "State Report from Utah to National Commission for Observance of IWY," Box 3. Utah (1) folder, NCOIWY Papers, SL.
33. "Women's Rights Backlash Troubles Carter Aide," July 10, 1977, *Gadsden (AL) Times*, NCOIWY Papers, SL; "Conservative Move Among Women Grows: Two Groups Oppose ERA," July 18, 1977, *Alabama*

Journal, Montgomery, AL; Marjorie Julian Spruill, "The Mississippi 'Takeover': Feminists, Antifeminists, and the International Women's Year Conference of 1977," in *Mississippi Women: Their Histories, Their Lives*, Vol. 2, ed. Martha H. Swain, Elizabeth Anne Payne, and Marjorie Julian Spruill (Athens: University of Georgia Press, 2003).
34. "Women's Meets End as Battles," clipping, AP story, no paper or date, ca. July 11, 1977, NCOIWY Papers, SL; Schlafly, *Phyllis Schafly Report*, June 1976.
35. Citizens' Review Committee for I.W.Y., "NEWS MEMO#1—INFORMATION BACKGROUNDER—Houston INTERNATIONAL WOMEN'S YEAR CONFERENCE—NOV. 18–21, 1977," Box 3, Marion Gressette Papers, SCPC; Elaine Donnelly Papers, Bentley Library, University of Michigan, Ann Arbor.
36. "Press Release—June 17, 1977—by Norma C. Russell," p. 2, Box 3, "L. Marion Gressette Papers," n.d., SCPC.
37. On opposition to UN ties and "the international flavor" of the IWY program and fears that the Plan of Action would represent the desires of "a few fringe radical feminists, revolutionaries and internationalists," see "IWY Tax Dollars for Revolution," *The Mindszenty Report*, July 1977, Gressette Papers, SCPC; The concern about "one-world government" is discussed at length in Erin M. Kempker, "Battling 'Big Sister' Government: Hoosier Women and the Politics of International Women's Year," *Journal of Women's History* 24, no. 2 (Summer 2012): 144–170.
38. Elizabeth Gillespie McRae, "White Womanhood, White Supremacy, and the Rise of Massive Resistance," in *Massive Resistance: Southern Opposition to the Second Reconstruction*, ed. Clive Webb (New York: Oxford University Press, 2005).
39. Bob Schwartzman, "Klan Cardholder Wanted to Help," *Wall Street Journal*, September 2, 1977; Carolyn Kortge, "Schlafly Says Women's Movement Is Dying in an Anti-Feminist Surge," *Wichita (KS) Eagle & Beacon*, August 3, 1977; Vera Glaser, "Women's Year: Peril on the Right," *Pennsylvania Inquirer*, August 23, 1977.
40. Jennifer Donnally, "The Politics of Abortion and the Rise of the New Right" (PhD diss., University of North Carolina at Chapel Hill, 2013); "IWY Folds Tent—300,000 Protest Signatures Flown to White House," *National Right to Life News*, January 1978.
41. Donnally, "Politics of Abortion"; Neil J. Young, "We Gather Together: Catholics, Mormons, Southern Baptists and the Question of Interfaith Politics, 1972–1984" (PhD diss., Columbia University, 2008).
42. Patricia Parish Williams, "Right to Life: The Southern Strategy," *Southern Exposure* 4, no. 4, *Generations of Women in the South* (Winter 1977): 82–85.

43. Davis, *Moving the Mountain*, 262–268.
44. *Spirit of Houston*, 166; Laura Kalman, *Right Star Rising: A New Politics, 1974–1980* (New York: Norton, 2010), 256–59.; *Spirit of Houston*, 155–156; Marci Shatzman, "Gay Women's Victory No Guarantee of Acceptance," *On Women*, November 25, 1977, *Evening Bulletin*, Philadelphia, PA, Clippings, September–November 1977, Folder: Nov 1977 GAY/LESBIAN RIGHTS, Carton 120, NOW Records MC 496, Schlesinger Library.
45. Thomson, *Price of LIBerty*, 99–101; Elizabeth Moore, "Witnesses Say Feminist Faction Suppressed Others," *NRTL News*, October 1977; "Boost for Pro-Life Seen in Responses to IWY Meetings: Helms Plans Special Hearings," *NRTL News*, September 1977.
46. Schlafly, "What Really Happened in Houston"; Thomson, *Price of LIBerty*, 138.
47. Thomson, *Price of LIBerty*, 138–150, quotation 144.
48. Pat Reed, "Pro-Family Groups Ink Proposals," *Daily Breakthrough*, November 20, 1977, WASM, http://asp6new.alexanderstreet.com.pallas2.tcl.sc.edu/was2/was2.object.details.aspx?dorpid=1001257239&fulltext=pat.%20reed; Judy Klemesrud, "10,000 Foes of Equal Rights Plan in 'Pro-Family Rally' in Houston," *New York Times*, November 20, 1977; Phyllis Schlafly, "Pro-Family Rally Attracts 20,000," *Phyllis Schlafly Report*, December 1977; Thomson, *Price of LIBerty*, 138–150.
49. Reed, "Pro-Family Groups Ink Proposals."
50. Sally Quinn, "The Pedestal Has Crashed: Pride and Paranoia in Houston," *Washington Post*, November 23, 1977; Thomson, *Price of LIBerty*, 146.
51. Thomson, *Price of LIBerty*, 138–150; Rosemary Thomson, *Withstanding Humanism's Challenge for Families: Anatomy of a White House Conference* (Morton: Braun Press, 1981), 22.
52. NCOIWY, *Spirit of Houston*, 130.
53. Hartmann, *From Margin to Mainstream*; Susan M. Hartmann, "Feminism, Public Policy, and the Carter Administration," in *The Carter Presidency: Policy Choices in the Post–New Deal Era*, ed. Gary M. Fink and Hugh Davis Graham (Lawrence: University Press of Kansas, 1998); Emily Cook, "Women White House Advisors in the Carter Administration Dissertation 1995" (PhD diss., Vanderbilt University, 1995); Donald T. Critchlow, "Mobilizing Women: The 'Social Issues,'" in *The Reagan Presidency: Pragmatic Conservatism and Its Legacies*, ed. W. Elliott Brownlee and Hugh Davis Graham (Lawrence: University Press of Kansas, 2004), 300, 321; Suzanne Braun Levine and Mary Thom, *Bella Abzug: How One Tough Broad from the Bronx Fought Jim Crow and Joe McCarthy, Pissed Off Jimmy Carter, Battled for the Rights*

of Women and Workers, Rallied Against War and for the Planet, and Shook up Politics Along the Way: An Oral History (New York: Farrar, Straus and Giroux, 2007), 227.
54. Elaine Donnelly, "What Women Wanted—Reagan Appealed to and Developed a Generation of Female Conservatives," *National Review Online*, June 7, 2004, http://www.freerepublic.com/focus/news/1151429/posts.
55. Critchlow, "Mobilizing Women."
56. Melich, *Republican War Against Women*; Rymph, *Republican Women*, 188–238.
57. William A. Link, *Righteous Warrior: Jesse Helms and the Rise of Modern Conservatism* (New York: St. Martin's Press, 2008); Paul Boyer, "The Evangelical Resurgence in 1970s American Protestantism," in *Rightward Bound: Making America Conservative in the 1970s* (Cambridge, MA: Harvard University Press, 2008), 43–49.
58. Young, "We Gather Together"; Earl Black and Merle Black, *The Rise of Southern Republicans* (Cambridge, MA: Harvard University Press, 2002); Kalman, *Right Star Rising*.
59. Thomson, *Price of LIBerty*, 7; Thomson, *Withstanding Humanism's Challenge*, 22.
60. Mrs. Paul Hogue and Mrs. Houston Howie, Dear Friends, November 23, 1977, Gressette Papers, SCPC.
61. Brown, *For a "Christian America,"* 117.
62. Cynthia Harrison, *On Account of Sex: The Politics of Women's Issues, 1945–1968* (Berkeley: University of California Press, 1988); Kathleen A. Laughlin, "How Did State Commissions on the Status of Women Overcome Historic Antagonisms between Equal Rights and Labor Feminists to Create a New Feminist Mainstream, 1963–1973?," *Women and Social Movements in the United States*, http://asp6new.alexanderstreet.com.pallas2.tcl.sc.edu/was2/was2.object.details.aspx?dorpid=1000681891. (Accessed February 6, 2015).
63. Marjorie Spruill, "The Conservative Challenge to Feminist Influence on State Commissions on the Status of Women," *Women and Social Movements in the United States*, http://asp6new.alexanderstreet.com.pallas2.tcl.sc.edu/was2/was2.object.details.aspx?dorpid=1002104578&fulltext=spruill#en1. (Accessed May 9, 2015); South Carolina Commission on Women Papers, South Carolina Department of Archives and History, Columbia.
64. Anita Miller, "The Uncertain Future of Women's Commissions," *Graduate Woman* 74 (June 1980): 10–15; Janine A. Parry, "'What Women Wanted': Arkansas Women's Commissions and the ERA," *Arkansas Historical Quarterly* 59, no. 3 (2000): 265–298, http://www.jstor.org/stable/40027988.

65. Kimberly Voss, "The Florida Fight for Equality: The Equal Rights Amendment, Senator Lori Wilson and Mediated Catfights in the 1970s," *Florida Historical Quarterly* 88, no. 2 (Fall 2009): 36; Mathews and De Hart, *Sex, Gender, and the Politics of ERA*; Megan Shockley, Cynthia Kierner, and Jennifer Loux, *Changing History: Four Hundred Years of Virginia Women* (Richmond: Library of Virginia, 2013); Mathews and De Hart, *Sex, Gender, and the Politics of ERA*.
66. Eunice ("Tootsie") Holland Class Visit to Marjorie Spruill Senior Seminar, Spring 2007, South Carolina Women's Rights Collection (SCWRC), SCPC.
67. Donald T. Critchlow and Cynthia L. Stachecki, "The Equal Rights Amendment Reconsidered: Politics, Policy, and Social Mobilization in a Democracy," *Journal of Policy History* 20, no. 1 (2008): 163–165.
68. Critchlow and Stachecki, "The Equal Rights Amendment Reconsidered," 163.
69. Phyllis Schlafly, "A Short History of E.R.A.," *Eagle Forum*, September 1986, http://www.eagleforum.org/psr/1986/sept86/psrsep86.html.
70. Spruill, "Mississippi Takeover."
71. South Carolina International Women's Year Committee et al., eds., *Final Report of the State Meeting: "The South Carolina Woman: Heritage to Horizons"* (Columbia: South Carolina International Women's Year, 1977); "Women for Racial and Economic Equality" (Flyer, National Women's Conference, Houston, Texas, 1977), Copy in possession of the author.
72. Final Report, Mississippi IWY Coordinating Commission, NCOIWY Papers, SL.
73. Marianna Davis Interview, November 20, 1977, IWY Interviews, "Constance Ashton Myers Oral History Collection," n.d., South Caroliniana Library, University of South Carolina, Columbia.
74. Bird and NCOIWY, *What Women Want*, 35.
75. Brown, *For a "Christian America"*; Caitlin Mans, "'Heritage to Horizons': The History of the 1977 International Women's Year Conference in South Carolina" (University of South Carolina, 2013); Nancy Weaver, "Delegates Brace for IWY Storm: State Again Fuels U.S. Controversy. Delegates-Elect: 20 Whites, 6 Men, All Conservative," *Clarion-Ledger*, November 17, 1977; Spruill, "Mississippi Takeover."
76. Modjeska Simkins, Interview, June 11, 1977, "Myers IWY Interviews, SCL."
77. Nancy Weaver, "Klansman's Wife Equate Women's Rights With Communism," *Clarion-Ledger*, November 17, 1977.
78. Spruill, "Mississippi Takeover."

79. "Meet the Delegates: Mississippi Style," *Daily Breakthrough*, November 19, 1977.
80. Andrea Dworkin, *Right-Wing Women* (New York: Perigee Books, 1983), 33, 112–117.
81. Peggy Simpson, "Feminists, Conservatives Face Houston Standoff," *Commercial Appeal*, September 11, 1977.
82. Betty J. Blair, "Klan's 'Spies' Plan to Disrupt Feminist Parley," *Detroit News*, September 1, 1977. Reprinted in National Women's Conference Official Briefing Book: Houston, Texas, November 18 to 21, 1977 (Washington, DC: National Commission on the Observance of International Women's Year, 1977), 227. Included in *How Did the National Women's Conference in Houston in 1977 Shape a Feminist Agenda for the Future?*
83. Interview with Phyllis Schlafly, Marjorie J. Spruill, February 22, 2005, in possession of the author.
84. Thomson, *Price of LIBerty*, 145–146. Thomson rejoiced that "people of all races" were at the rally but the press reported that there were very few.
85. Jonathan Levin, "42 Delegations Assist Frances In Balloting for V.P. Choice," Washington Bureau Amarillo *Globe-Times*, July 14, 1972, 7, http://www.newspapers.com/newspage/29954998/. (Accessed June 5 2014); Jann S. Wenner, ed., *Hunter S. Thompson, Fear and Loathing at Rolling Stone: The Essential Writing of Hunter S. Thompson* (New York: Simon & Schuster, 2011), 232.
86. Klemesrud, "10,000 Foes."
87. "Militant Conservatives Form New Coalition," July 14, 1977, DDT.
88. Richard Barrett, *The Commission* (Jackson, MS: Barrett, 1982), 149.
89. Article from *Conservative Digest*, May/June 1980, Container 124 folder "Pro-Family Movement," ERAmerica, LC.
90. Thomson, *Price of LIBerty*, 147; Clipping, NOW Papers, SL.
91. Richard A. Viguerie, *The New Right: We're Ready to Lead* (Falls Church, VA: The Viguerie Company, 1980), 165, 197.
92. Ibid., 156–158.
93. Ibid., Introduction.
94. Young, "We Gather Together."

CHAPTER 4

"No More Silence!": Feminist Activism and Religion in the Second Wave

Laura Foxworth

Abstract Similar to the political goals of Second-Wave feminists, proponents of feminist theology, which also surged in the early 1970s, sought to establish leadership roles for women in the church and end "patriarchal religious hierarchies." In this chapter, Laura Foxworth examines the complex relationship between Second-Wave Feminism and the ongoing struggle for equality within American religious institutions. Although the National Organization of Women (NOW) created a task force to explore the relationship between feminism and organized religion, Foxworth notes that it was rarely utilized and its influence was limited. Frustrated with their lack of progress, many women, contends Foxworth, sought religious expression outside of the church. The result was an expansion of "woman's spirituality" and an elevated understanding of the female divine in the absence of male presence. Other moderate feminist reformers who remained inside the church, advocating for equality within traditional religious practices, faced specific opposition to the Equal Rights

---

The original version of the book was revised: Final corrections have been incorporated. The erratum to this chapter is available at
https://doi.org/10.1007/978-3-319-62117-3_11

L. Foxworth (✉)
University of South Carolina, Clemson, USA

© The Author(s) 2018
A. Maxwell and T. Shields (eds.), *The Legacy of Second-Wave Feminism in American Politics*, https://doi.org/10.1007/978-3-319-62117-3_4

Amendment (ERA). Foxworth explores how religious leaders, both male and female, often argued that people of faith should oppose the ERA, particularly in the South where opposition to both feminism and the ERA was often the strongest. Phyllis Schlafly and other popular leaders of the emerging "Religious Right," for example, quoted various Bible verses to support their opposition to the ERA. Foxworth concludes that while Second-Wave feminists primarily fought to create secular equality, they inspired a powerful movement within religious institutions as well. Though the lasting influence of Second-Wave Feminism remains the growing numbers of women who are ordained in many denominations, as well as the increased leadership opportunities for women of faith, the level of inequality in the contemporary church remains incredibly high.

Alice Hageman, a lecturer on women and ministry at Harvard Divinity School in the early 1970s, regularly heard pastors use biblical texts to perpetuate sexism in churches. She cringed at the prospect of another sermon on the New Testament book of I Timothy, which contained the directive: "Let a woman learn in silence, with all submissiveness. I permit no woman to teach or to have authority over men; she is to keep silent." Hageman was hired at Harvard Divinity at the behest of the school's new Women's Caucus which was established in 1971 to investigate the legacy of women's subordination within Judeo-Christian traditions. By forming academic and social networks with other religious feminists, the Caucus asserted that women's voices would not be silenced. Its members sought deeper spiritual fulfillment, Hageman stated, "within the Church if possible, outside the Church if necessary."[1]

By the mid-1970s, a strong contingent of feminist theologians, philosophers, and political thinkers posed formidable challenges to the tenets of Christianity, Judaism, and other patriarchal religious institutions. Mary Daly, Rosemary Reuther, and Elsie Thomas Culver were among the activists who decried modern religion's continued subjugation of women despite political recognition of women's civil rights earlier in the 1960s. With initial concerns that mirrored the secular objectives of the Second-Wave feminist movement, they advocated the elimination of prejudice against women in religious organizations, guaranteed opportunities for female leadership and advancement in denominational employment, and completed eradication of patriarchal religious hierarchies and dogma. Daly's own spiritual journey outside of the Catholic Church in the early 1970s inspired many women to further investigate female-centered spiritual expression and life "beyond God the father." As Hageman predicted, longstanding frustration prompted many feminists to leave churches behind. "Reformers," however, remained members of traditional religious institutions throughout the Second Wave and worked from within to promote gender equity. Though radicals feminists and reformers remained at odds for many decades, on separate paths they furthered the cultural reach of the movement in contemporary religion.

The consciousness-raising publications of feminist scholars of religion during the Second-Wave feminist movement have been well documented by modern practitioners of religion and women's studies. Outside of these disciplines, however, scholars have generally focused on antifeminists' faith-based activism during this time period. The Religious Right crafted powerful arguments about the mutual exclusivity of feminism and religious piety in the mid-1970s and 1980s, but this perspective should not monopolize the contemporary historical narrative. This generalization further marginalizes the history of women whose religious and feminist beliefs intertwined to form the ideological underpinning of their activism.

When the Religious Right began to thwart feminists' efforts to support ratification of the Equal Rights Amendment (ERA) in the mid-1970s, feminist reformers extended their activism from local churches and synagogues into the public square. As they spoke at civic gatherings, they explained to crowds that they favored the ERA precisely because it was consistent with their religious beliefs. Though supporters were not able to achieve ratification by the extended congressional deadline in 1982, religious feminist campaigns for the ERA provided activists with established networks and political experience that aided their battles for gender equality within religious organizations. Though many of these communities still provide support for religious feminists to this day, most operate on the periphery of political consciousness. In the aftermath of the ERA's failure, the narrative of religious feminist activists has been obfuscated, perhaps even subjugated, by the political legacy of religious antifeminism. On behalf of these women, we should demand "No more silence!"

"The Silence has been Broken"

In the 1960s, religious feminists began to evaluate secular feminist political goals within a religious context in a search of a more holistic feminist ideology. Not surprisingly, many of these processes took place in seminaries and universities as scholars re-evaluated their fields during the women's liberation movement. In response to the Second Vatican Council of the Roman Catholic Church in 1965, there was initially a great deal of hope among feminists for its potential to change its social policies in relation to the modern world.[2]

The Catholic hierarchy never delivered on the promises of social changes to gender roles. Mary Daly felt hope after witnessing the same Catholic event and wrote much of *The Church and the Second Sex* directly afterward. This 1968 publication extended Simone de Beauvoir's analysis of the subjugation of women to more fully explore the role that the Catholic Church played in this social construct. At the core of her findings was her observation of a fundamental dichotomy in scriptural depictions of women: that of the ideal godly woman and the inferior subservient woman; this "contradiction" resulted in difficulty in practical application of the Bible in women's lives, and the Catholic Church did little during the papacies of Pius XI and Pius XII to help rectify this tension. The Church, focusing on Mary's virginal purity, continually emphasized women's "special status" and did little in the late nineteenth and early twentieth centuries to help women's early quest for equal rights. In contrast to the writings of Simone de Beauvoir, an atheist, Daly claimed that hers was a "theology of hope," meant not to undermine the meaning of religion in women's lives, but, "with God's help," to improve women's experiences within the Church. Daly viewed her publication as a call for a "radical transformation" of the Church and offered her critiques from the perspective of a "Christian who is truly sensitive to the problem of women and the Church."[3]

Responding to initial optimism surrounding the Second Vatican Council and word of a newly formed National Organization for Women (NOW), Elizabeth Farians, professor of theology at Sacred Heart College, contacted Betty Friedan to investigate the possibility of integrating religious concerns into its agenda. NOW was particularly well suited for this alliance; its founding members included Catholic nuns Sister Joel Read and Austin Doherty, Presbyterian minister Rev. Dean Lewis, a representative of the National Council of Churches, and Pauli Murray, an African American Episcopalian who was ordained as the denomination's first black female priest.[4] With the rationale that "discrimination based on sex is destructive of religious values," NOW's board of directors approved Farians's proposal to create a Task Force on Women and Religion and it was up and running by the end of 1967. Its primary goal was "to develop a meaningful theological approach to the understanding of personhood, sex, man, and woman" and it sought to accomplish this task by collecting ecumenical data on gender inequality and informing members of religious leadership opportunities and job openings.[5] The task force strongly advocated equal participation of women in church functions, equal pay in religious employment, equal educational opportunities in seminaries, and the development of women's studies curriculum in seminaries.

By the late 1960s, NOW began establishing chapters at the local level, and Elizabeth Farians wanted the task force's ideas implemented into a comprehensive grassroots strategy. Soon she realized that religious feminist goals were not communicated fully to new chapters; too often the organization's national structure inadvertently prevented information from trickling down to the grassroots.[6] Farians worried that potential ignorance on religious matters could, if "spread through the mass media ... damage the image and effectiveness of N.O.W., or alienate large groups of members or potential members."[7] The task force, comprised of theologians and professors of religion, was well equipped to address these audiences knowledgeably, but its consultation was rare. Despite this underutilization, the task force continued developing goals for action. They wanted to establish a "working relationship" with American Roman Catholic bishops to promote open dialogue on women's issues, and they also supported an "ongoing effort to cooperate (or if you prefer, infiltrate) as many religious orientated organizations as possible."[8]

In 1969, NOW's Task Force on Women and Religion planned one such "infiltration" to protest a local Catholic Church's rule mandating head coverings for women, which it found indicative of a subjugated status. The inspiration for this protest, which Farians referred to as the "National Unveiling," occurred at Milwaukee's St. John de Nepomuc Church when Father James J. Wamser reprimanded a woman for attending church without a covered head. He based this position on a 50-year-old Code of Canon Law that regulated modest dress for women.[9] At the following service, an Easter Sunday mass, fifteen members of Milwaukee's NOW chapter attended St. John de Nepomuc—some wore hats and some attended without. When they approached the Communion rail, those wearing hats removed them in coordinated protest when Father Wamser again criticized the "bareheaded women" for their violation of Canon Law.[10] As they left the altar, the protestors passed out pamphlets to the congregation which read: "Hats off now, women! Let us not be humiliated. Let us not be treated as second class Christians. Let us not be intimidated. Let us be men and women, equal in Christ!"[11]

Indeed, this was more than a simple matter of Easter bonnets. NOW members drew an explicit connection between mandatory head coverings and the religious subjugation of women: a bare head symbolized the eradication of double standards in the Church. When denominational papers upheld the 1917 Canon, it confirmed for Farians the Church's commitment to the gendered status quo. For a woman once so inspired by the Vatican's potential for change, this response ultimately fell flat. Elizabeth Farians later explained:

> We freely grant that the hat issue is not perfect, but it is the best we have been able to come up (or off) with after much discussion and brain-storming by dozens of people over a period of two years. We feel something must be done to keep women acting on the problem of prejudice in the church. We hope this act will dramatize the problem without offending. Incidentally, I'm not sure it's as "old hat" as you say.[12]

Farians was encouraged by the decision of some denominations that set up committees to study women, including Presbyterians USA, National Council of Catholic Women, and Disciples of Christ. Women were ordained in the United Methodist Church, United Presbyterian Church, Lutheran Church of America, American Baptist, and even Southern Baptist churches in the early 1970s. In 1971, the American Academy of Religion formed a women's caucus dedicated to studying women's issues in the profession.[13] The following year Sally Priesand was ordained as a rabbi (Reform Jewish Seminary), and in 1973, a Jewish women's movement formally organized and resulted in the Conservatives' United Synagogues of America's resolution to allow women as rabbinical students at the Jewish Theological Seminary of America.[14]

It seemed that women in ministry were winning some important battles at the national level. Despite these gains, NOW's Task Force for Women and Religion remained continuously underutilized at the grassroots level. Though the size of NOW expanded to 700 chapters and 40,000 members by 1974, the influence of the Task Force for Women and Religion was limited at best.[15] Another problem was the willingness of chapter members to address the subject of women and religion. Explained Ann Sayre, Cincinnati NOW's Task Force coordinator:

"Chapter members tend to be either indifferent to religion or radicals, as we are, not reformists." She suspected that if local NOW members still attended traditional church services, they kept it to themselves.[16]

"THE GREAT DIVIDE"[17]

Indeed, some radical feminists came to the conclusion that there was no hope for change in organized religion. In 1968, Robin Morgan, author of *Going Too Far*, opined that the oppressive past was too deeply entrenched for any meaningful transformation to occur in mainstream religious communities. As she considered closing out her religious past, she, and other radicals:

> justly condemn[ed] the gray, co-optative mask of modern Protestantism (clamped over the self-righteous expressions of Luther and Knox); the virulent woman-hatred in fundamentalist Christianity; the woman-fear and woman-loathing rampant in Judaism to this day (as if the scars of that religion's matriarchal origin and its overthrow were still not eradicated from the Jewish collective unconscious); the female-as-temptress or the female-as-nonentity in, respectively, the exoteric and esoteric sophistries of Buddhist, Zen, or Western existential thought; the vitriol spewed on women for centuries in Moslem cultures ... So we left their churches, and are still leaving. And the birth of what has been called female spirituality is a new phenomenon in the women's movement. This has given me much personal joy.[18]

Daly's 1973 publication, *Beyond God the Father: Toward a Philosophy of Women's Liberation*, similarly revealed her shift away from the church's boundaries and new focus on spiritual expression outside of patriarchal jurisdiction. Many others followed Morgan's and Daly's "exodus movement." Looking for feminist-friendly spirituality, they looked outside the bounds of Christianity, Judaism, and even Eastern religions for a doctrine that epitomized their egalitarian ideals.

These women felt empowered by spiritual expression that bore no resemblance to the confining institutions that subjugated their experiences, and they produced a litany of feminist writings, rituals, dances, and other art expressions. Focusing on woman's innate connection to nature, many forms of "woman's spirituality" revisited ancient symbols and mythology to find new feminist meaning. Participants turned their attention to God the Mother, Mother Nature, and Goddess deities as embodiments of the female divine. These expressions of feminism elevated female figures, while simultaneously eradicating a male dominance of spiritual practices.

In assessing these new traditions, Mary Daly predicted: "The women's movement will present a growing threat to patriarchal religion less by attacking it than by simply leaving it behind. Few of the leaders in the movement evince an interest in institutional religion, having recognized it as an instrument of their betrayal."[19] To a certain extent, Daly's prediction—that women would follow her "exodus" out of churches—was accurate. Several key studies published in the 1970s found a strong negative correlation between feminist activism and strong religious affiliation. J. A. Dempewolff's 1974 study found that 57% of feminists had "none or mild religious interest", whereas 75% of nonfeminists demonstrated "moderate or strong interest."[20]

In other ways, Daly's prediction missed the mark. The strongest effects of feminists' departures from church congregations were not experienced by advocates of traditional gender hierarchy. Instead, their absences made things more difficult for the reformists, or feminists who remained in churches to advocate for gender equality. In order to do so, reformists had to "play ball" with patriarchal biblical interpretations and male-led church committees, but they had help from the writings of theologians Rosemary Reuther and Phyllis Trible and feminist hermeneutics to support their endeavors. Trible's analysis of Genesis demonstrated that one could return to Hebrew texts to "depatriarchalize" the interpretation of scriptural passages, especially those used to justify gender discrimination in churches.

Evangelical churches were especially resistant to feminist ideas because of literal biblical interpretations that seemingly prescribed hierarchical gender roles. For the women in these churches, Nancy Hardesty and Letha Scanzoni's *All We're Meant to Be* was a helpful resource for facilitating denominational dialogue. Written for a lay Protestant audience, with a study guide in the back for Sunday School groups, Hardesty and Scanzoni's text presented a decidedly mild articulation of women's liberation that spoke the vocabulary of this particular audience. They wrote that women's liberation was not just a political movement, but rather, "a *state of mind* in which a woman comes to view herself as Jesus Christ sees her—as a woman created in God's image whom he wants to make free to be whole, to grow, to learn, to utilize fully the talents and gifts God has given her as a unique individual." They advocated a form of gender equality that appealed to women's spiritual devotion and translated feminist ideas using religious language. *All We're Meant to Be* took the women's movement—albeit in a less radical form—to a much wider audience. Yet the call for feminist activism was still clear: "We cannot hide behind the skirts of our alleged inferiority or under our domestic bushels. We must speak out for ourselves, not wait for men to do it for us. We must join with other women who are crusading for an end to discrimination and for freedom for all people."[21]

Regardless of consciousness-raising within religious circles, progress was slow in some resistant organizations. Episcopalians fought a battle over women's ordination rights when eleven women were ordained by retired officiates in an attempt to force the denomination's hand. When bishops refused to accept the ordinations, the denomination faced internal strife. NOW's Task Force on Women and Religion indicted the bishops for their unwillingness to dismantle the status quo, and in Minneapolis, they staged a nailing of "95 theses" to the Episcopal General Convention meeting; they called the "Unfinished Reformation" a "NOW Witness," boldly appropriating the spiritual precept of speaking one's personal truth as religious testimony. Members encouraged churches to "complete the reformation by purging themselves of sexism, racism, [and] homophobia" and held prayer vigils to underscore their protest. The idea was that they could effectively support women's ordination and gain publicity by "preaching" to the Episcopalians about the issues of sex, race, and class discrimination. The task force correctly assumed that the denomination was "undergoing the kind of internal stress that will make it most susceptible" to feminist critique.[22] Finally, in 1976 its General Assembly ruled that the ordinations were valid and they could rise to the priesthood.[23]

In the midst of other important battles, NOW's Task Force on Women and Religion was often less of a priority than its leaders would have liked. Joyce Slayton Mitchell, director at that time, acknowledged that "as much as I feel like it's a job that should have priority—religion still scares most feminists." She felt pressure from NOW members all over the country who wrote asking for help on issues in their local congregations.[24] Another member of the task force, Georgia Fuller, wrote: "We are not considered a vital task force by the leadership and grassroots of NOW—but we're TRYING!"[25]

A Call to Action for Religious Feminists: The ERA

According to movement historian Sara Evans, by the mid-1970s, the Second–Wave feminist movement experienced a "crest"—it was powerful and experiencing forward motion that could not be stopped. In 1972, after extensive lobbying on Capitol Hill, Congress passed the Equal Rights Amendment and sent to the states this capstone feminist legislation that would ensure full legal and civil equality for women. Though there was an initial wave of ratification in many states, this momentum fell short of tallying the required thirty-eight states. In just a few short years, Evans noted, the amendment became "a critical mobilizing symbol" for those who supported feminism and for those who opposed the amendment.[26]

Just as political scientists demonstrated strong correlations between general preferences for feminism and nonreligion, they found even stronger evidence linking religious affiliation to a definitive stance on the ERA. Kent Tedin's study of 154 women who attended ERA hearings in Texas showed that 50% of polled ERA supporters were not associated with any religious denomination. He deemed religion a "very strong predictor of pro-anti-ERA activism," even more significant a factor than social class. In another study that used the same sample of 154 women, Tedin and Brady found that 98% of polled opponents to the ERA were church members. Religious beliefs were "very important" (the highest possible choice) to 92% of these same individuals. Tedin and Brady argued, therefore, that social scientists could consider political beliefs for these women "as extensions of their religious beliefs."[27]

In 1972, Phyllis Schlafly wrote that biological sex roles were "not the fault of selfish and domineering men, or of the establishment, or of any clique of conspirators who want to oppress women. It's simply the way God made us." She argued that women's ability to experience pregnancy and childbirth evidenced inalienable distinctions between men and women; she quipped, "If you don't like this fundamental difference, you will have to take up your complaint with God because He created us this way." Schlafly strongly opposed the ERA, and her newsletter, the *Phyllis Schlafly Report*, attracted support from other conservatives who disfavored ratification. Her most successful argument to oppose the amendment was the claim that it would harm American families by destroying the divinely ordained gender hierarchy. Schlafly's ideas resonated with evangelical women, many of whom were stay-at-home mothers, by highlighting radical portrayals of feminists who wanted to support gender equality through the ratification of the ERA. Citing materials from "The BITCH Manifesto" and W.I.T.C.H. (Women's International Terrorist Conspiracy From Hell), she claimed: "These women's libbers do, indeed, intend to 'break the barriers' of the Ten Commandments and the sanctity of the family."[28]

A devout Catholic, Schlafly's position closely mirrored that of the Catholic Church. By the mid-1970s, the National Council of Catholic Laity not only formally opposed the ERA but also supported states' rescission campaigns. Schlafly used biblical references to gender in order to support her political views and, in doing so, her implication was clear: Christians should not support the ERA. As she pointed out the radical aspects of women's liberation and claimed biblical truisms as a political truth, Phyllis Schlafly effectively disassociated religion from the women's movement. Schlafly quickly gained support from fundamentalist Protestants, Catholics, Orthodox Jews, and Mormons, and they provided the grassroots support she needed to establish STOP ERA headquarters in unratified states.[29]

The Catholic Church's position on the ERA generated a bifurcate response: It prompted a great deal of Catholic support for Schlafly's STOP ERA campaign, but it also inspired Catholic feminists to mobilize and challenge the Church's stance. Founders of Cincinnati's NOW chapter formed a religious organization for just that purpose. "Catholic Women for the ERA," by its very existence, negated the assumption that prominent voices in the Church spoke for all Catholics. The group proved more than a mere symbol, however, as it spread to other cities and spearheaded grassroots efforts to protest the Church's unwillingness to consider its stance on feminism.

When national feminist leaders commemorated the fifty-fourth anniversary of the Nineteenth Amendment's ratification by celebrating Women's Equality Day, Catholic Women for the ERA put its grassroots activism on display. On August 26, 1974, Cincinnati members approached Saint Peter in Chains Cathedral and posted on its doors a pro-ERA manifesto called "The Woman's Proclamation," which called upon Catholic leaders to reverse their positions on the amendment. In a continuation of its Women's Equality Day celebrations, Catholics for the ERA held a "medieval pageant" to celebrate the legacy of Christian women including Deborah, Mary, and Mary Magdelene of biblical texts, Joan of Arc, and Saints Catherine of Siena and Teresa of Avila. Women in local chapters of Catholic Women for the ERA were encouraged to send copies of "The Woman's Proclamation" to local Catholic leaders and host "pray-ins" for ratification in their private residences. The New York branch followed suit and posted the document on the doors of the city's iconic Saint Patrick Cathedral.[30]

Some Protestant denominations passed resolutions of support for the ERA, but perhaps even more significant was the activism of Church Women United. This ecumenical organization formed in 1941 and though originally incorporated into the National Council of Churches, the women's group became autonomous in 1971. Church Women United maintained a relationship with the National Council of Churches, however, and served as its liaison for women's issues. Upon the counsel of Church Women United, which endorsed the ERA before it passed in Congress, the National Council of Churches formally voiced its support in 1975 and remained a strong ally for ratification, even upholding NOW's boycott on unratified states in 1977.[31]

Church Women United also advocated for the establishment of the Religious Committee for ERA (RCERA), an activist organization designed to promote ratification in unratified states. Operating with national leadership from both Church Women United and the National Council of Churches, RCERA garnered support from over thirty Judeo-Christian organizations. Focusing on five unratified states (Missouri, Illinois, Indiana, North Carolina, and Florida), RCERA set up bases in the states but utilized preexisting religious networks to mobilize political support. According to Sister Mary Luke Tobin, one of RCERA's nine founding members, churches were slow to get on board but "the majority of them have redefined their belief about women's rights in the last 4 years and now we're ready to translate that into organizing in order to help get the ERA passed." To help this initiative, the organization provided churches in unratified states with community vigil kits and worship service liturgy that highlighted gender equality.[32]

In North Carolina, RCERA provided materials to the Resource Center for Women and Ministry in the South (RCWMS), a Judeo-Christian nonprofit organization closely connected to the North Carolina Council of Churches, which operated "*for* women, in favor of women." RCWMS's newsletter, *South of the Garden*, connected readers to RCERA's resources and those of groups that were already mobilized in the area, including the ACLU, NOW Task Force on Women and Religion, and the League of Women Voters. RCWMS director Jeanette

Stokes urged readers to educate themselves about the ERA and, considering the South's centrality to its ratification, encouraged them to contact legislators and become involved politically. Stokes knew that the amendment would help women in ministry achieve their employment goals so ratification was indeed quite relevant to the mission of the center.[33]

Meanwhile, following Phyllis Schlafly's direction, members of the burgeoning Religious Right led an assault against the ERA for its supposed detriment to families. It was on this platform that independent Baptists like Jerry Falwell and Tim and Beverly LaHaye found a national audience. Jerry Falwell claimed: "A definite violation of holy Scripture, ERA defies the mandate that 'the husband is the head of the church' (Ep. 5: 23). In 1 Peter 3: 7 we read that husbands are to give their wives honor as unto the weaker vessel."[34] As Falwell and others rejected all but literal biblical interpretation, they effectively deflected the conversation from the ERA to religious beliefs, a topic that caused many feminists to flinch. Even those who maintained Judeo-Christian affiliations tended to welcome feminist hermeneutics, which opened them up to fundamentalist critique that their embrace of biblical translation conveyed a less sincere faith.

The 1977 International Women's Year Conference in Houston, Texas, brought feminism to the center of American consciousness. Leaders thought it had great potential to win public support for many key political issues, including the ERA. The conference, inclusive to many interpretations of womanhood and personhood, had an interfaith Kumbaya room that provided space for meditation and quiet reflection in the midst of the energy-charged atmosphere. In many ways, this room represented the blended interests of the two split religious feminist ideologies. Its inclusive nature allowed for the expression of feminist spirituality and non-Western worship, but it also held Judeo-Christian church services for those inclined to attend. Helen Havers, a 42-year-old Protestant minister, served as officiant for these services and found them empowering. She explained to an interviewer at the conference: "I've just come from yet a third church service today in which many women told me afterwards they had received communion from a woman for the first time and it was tremendously meaningful for them, and so I know that I am a part of the women's movement by working in my specific area of religion." Like many other women, she realized that her religious faith and practice were intimately connected to her participation in the Second-Wave feminist movement.[35]

Outside the conference at the Pro-Life Pro-Family Conference, however, the Religious Right loudly protested the women's gathering as anti-God and anti-family. For them, the ERA's outcome would be either a religious victory or a spiritual defeat. In his North Carolina case study, Donald Mathews noted that this language differed from that of proponents who were religious; because "gender was not sacred for them," he argued, they viewed ratification as primarily a civic issue.[36] The platform passed by IWY delegates had multiple platforms, only one of which concerned the ERA, so the opposition linked the amendment with other, more controversial issues like gay rights and abortion. This connection, which Phyllis Schlafly observed long before the conference, appealed to conservatives' fears of widespread societal change and proved successful as a tactic for grassroots support. By the time the conference concluded, conservatives mobilized in full force against the ERA, utilizing the language of religion and family values to undercut feminist initiatives.[37]

In the aftermath of the IWY, feminists inspired by the conference pushed forward with renewed support for the ERA. Sara Evans claimed that even radical feminists who had previously found the ERA "too moderate a reform," started paying close attention when they considered "the real possibility of defeat."[38] Most problematic, however, was the prospect that feminists needed ratification from a southern state to achieve a two-thirds majority. This task was challenging because southern states were politically conservative and many local legislators were fundamentalists. Feminists did, however, turn their full attention to the southern states, in what Janet Boles has called "Phase III" of the ratification movement. Proponents used "almost all conceivable tactics" to support the ERA during its final years. One activist claimed, "The mainline denominations must declare again and again that the right-wing fundamentalists do not own the Judeo-Christian tradition nor 'the Christian vote'—and feminists must make clear that *the patriarchy does not own spirituality and morality.*"[39]

Southern coalitions fought for the ERA since Congress sent it to the states for ratification in 1972. The League of Women Voters worked together with newer NOW chapters and professional organizations in these areas to drum up grassroots support for ratification. Southern supporters struggled to establish credibility with legislators who were wary of the feminist agenda so they worked to disassociate from the stereotype of a "Yankee women's libber". Women who emphasized religious faith and denominational affiliation seemed less threatening to conservative lawmakers who opposed any attempt to transform traditional southern values and culture.

Rev. Diane Moseley implemented this tactic through organizing People of Faith for the ERA in South Carolina, an activist group dedicated to promoting ratification in the state. She recalled that religious feminists' voices were not being heard in the ERA debates due to prominent fundamentalist opposition. She explained:

> no one [in the state's ERA coalition] had brought up the issue of what to do [with] theological issues people were bringing up. A lot of folks in the opposition [were] talking about what God thought and how women should behave and their place in the universe. That's not right. I just simply disagree and I can back it up theologically. So I raised the question about forming a group that might speak to those issues ... I called up a couple of friends of mine that were Methodist and a couple of friends who were Catholic and I said, Let's do this! ... We began to gather people from denominations and Jewish women who were supportive.

People of Faith for the ERA demonstrated interfaith cooperation to show the legislature that support of the ERA was a valid perspective for religious persons. To accomplish this task, they held ecumenical rallies and prayer vigils similar to those organized by RCERA. Additionally, People of Faith for the ERA had a representative at the state house every time the ERA was on the legislative agenda. Moseley recalled: "We decided we would not scream or holler, we would not interrupt what they're doing, but we're going to be a ministry of presence."[40] They hoped to give traction to the state's ERA campaign by challenging the notion that only NOW members or other "libbers" supported ratification.

There was also a People of Faith for the ERA state lobby in Georgia, led by Margaret M. Curtis. A prolific author, Curtis wrote many letters to the editor of the *Atlanta Journal-Constitution* in support of the ERA. One of the perspectives that bothered her the most about Georgians' opposition to the ERA was the prevalence of religious intolerance. She explained:

> Because the media focused on Jewish feminist leaders like Gloria Steinem and Betty Friedan, there was a suspicion in some quarters that the ERA was a Jewish conspiracy. One legislator even said aloud that it was a shame the ERA's sponsor in the House was a Jewish woman. Although

Representative Cathey Steinberg was not the only sponsor of the ERA in Georgia (there were Christian sponsors as well), she received anti-Semitic letters and phone calls.[41]

Curtis refused to allow unanswered any published comments insinuating that feminists were "anti-God." In one letter to the editor of the *Atlanta Journal-Constitution*, Curtis explained: "Equality, justice and impartiality in laws are Biblical ideals, and unlike those who insist the Bible teaches the subjugation of women, I believe it teaches us to love, not dominate, each other. Even so, if a woman wants to bow down and pray to her husband three times a day, the ERA won't stop her."[42] Indeed, she faced a wary crowd in Georgia, but People of Faith for the ERA helped her dispel these kinds of myths concerning religion and re-educate the state's citizens about what the amendment would accomplish for women.

In Virginia, Sonia Johnson organized Mormons for ERA, an action which ultimately led to her excommunication from the Mormon Church in 1979. She was inspired to action after attending a church meeting that outlined its official position against the amendment. Johnson recalled: "[W]hen he read those words in that hostile room that night, they took hold of my heart like a great warm fist and have not let go for one single second, waking or sleeping since … Perhaps it was like being born again."[43] Johnson attempted to form pockets of feminist support within Mormon communities, but they were not able to reduce the millions of dollars that funneled to anti-ERA campaigns. She successfully exposed covert lobbying efforts, however, which forced Mormons anti-ERA activists to register as formal lobbyists.

Johnson's activism spread further than the borders of Virginia. Said Margaret Curtis: "Because of Sonia, Mormon women began to join our organization. This was invaluable, because they made us aware of the activities of our opposition. One member told us that the members of her ward were organized to write letters against the ERA to be sent to Georgia legislators. Even children as young as 11 were required to write."[44] Her insight helped southern supporters anticipate religious challenges and better understand anti-ERA networks. Johnson's bravery to stand up to her denomination also inspired feminists who challenged other conservative constituencies in support of the ERA. Johnson's story resonated with Jeanette Stokes, director of North Carolina's Resource Center for Women and Ministry in the South. Stokes, who considered Johnson a modern-day Anne Hutchinson, listened to her story at a NOW ERA fundraiser in Fayetteville; she observed that Johnson's excommunication had more to do with her willingness to buck the entrenched leadership's agenda than her position on the ERA. Regardless of their personal beliefs, Johnson lamented, Mormons lobbied against the ERA in order to demonstrate their faithfulness to the church "because the prophet says to." As she continued to raise awareness about the denomination's lobbying techniques, her public visibility increased and she was able to inspire new networks among religious ERA supporters at a crucial time.[45]

In 1981, one year before the extended deadline for ratification, the Religious Committee for ERA coordinated a national campaign to demonstrate the diverse basis for support for ratification among religious communities. Its leaders organized a National Prayer Vigil on the White House grounds, a candlelight service intended to evoke the Pillars of Fire, a symbol of liberation from Exodus.[46] In solidarity, People of Faith for the ERA in South Carolina hosted its own prayer vigil outside of the state house. To encourage legislators to attend, the organization sponsored a wine and cheese event prior to the vigil. Attracting "a gratifying cross-section of women and men, blacks and white, children and state leadership," the prayer vigil scheduled clergy and laymen from Methodist, Catholic, and AME denominations who presented diverse views but unified support for the ERA. Though the event attracted positive media attention, it did not produce the final push for ratification in South Carolina or other unratified states.[47]

The ERA did not become part of the Constitution despite supporters' efforts to raise awareness, re-educate, challenge stereotypes, and pray in earnest for ratification. This was a devastating blow for the women who invested a full decade in its pursuit. After the dust settled, however, it was clear that there were some long-term gains from the ERA ratification efforts. When a woman stood up to a religious group to express support for the amendment, she forced conversations on the feminist movement that otherwise may not have occurred. Most importantly, the ratification movement prompted coalition building among religious feminists in the South. Not only did members of individual denominations come together to affirm or protest their organizations' stances, but there was a great deal of interdenominational cooperation at the local level. As religious feminists attempted to refute the claims of ERA opponents, they learned that they had the power to reject the Religious Right's definitions of their political and religious beliefs.

The Legacy of Feminist Activism in Religion

At the end of the Second Wave, Gloria Steinem offered this reflection:

> Certainly the right wing has instructed us on the political uses of religion. We thank them for the lesson, as painful as it has been to learn. Some people who have remained inside those religions are rewriting the ceremonies to be more inclusive and democratic. But the origins of our current religions are still patriarchal ... Now, many women and men are looking more deeply at the patriarchal and the racist symbolism of organized religion and trying to universalize the sense of human possibilities and spirituality that lie in each of us.[48]

From the start of the Second Wave, feminists focused on the ways in which religion shaped women's lives, and just as they fought for equal rights and opportunities in businesses and government, so too did they protest injustice in religious institutions. As a result of the wide variety of spiritual writings and consciousness-raising sessions that came out of women's liberation, feminists had more opportunities to come to different conclusions about whether they wanted to remain participants in traditional religious organizations or leave "in exodus." Though this split between reformists and radicals remained a source of tension for many years in the women's movement, both groups continued to flourish at the end of the twentieth century. Support for women in ministry has also continued to flourish as networks grew after the Second Wave. If anything, they have become more globally inclusive; in the past few decades, feminist scholars also broadened their inquiries about sexism to non-Western religions in order to gain a comprehensive understanding of current prejudice against women in the world.[49]

Despite these efforts, the religio-political legacy of feminists has been overshadowed by the Religious Right's continued political eminence in the late twentieth and early twenty-first century. As a result, the idea of a religious feminist has evaded public consciousness. On June 20, 2011, a panel of commentators for the *Washington Post* evaluated Michele Bachmann's potential for a 2012 presidential run. Noting her popularity among evangelicals and espousal of traditional gender values, the columnist claimed that Bachmann's "blend of populism, Christian motherhood and political ambition is crafting a new form of evangelical feminism, one that may actually succeed with Republican voters." One week later, CNN's religious editor questioned, "Michele Bachmann, evangelical feminist?" Bachmann, a Lutheran, never claimed to be a feminist, but pundits gave her this label because of her belief that she was following God's will for her life and because she did not see conflicts between her beliefs about divinely ordained gender hierarchy and her potential bid for the highest office in the nation.[50]

As journalists continued to debate to what extent Bachmann was actually an "evangelical feminist" (which seemed even more pertinent after former vice-presidential candidate Sarah Palin took on the "feminist" moniker), very few referenced the longer legacy of the term. Sure, Bachmann was no women's libber, but was she an evangelical feminist? "Horsefeathers," said Cathleen Falsani, a former assistant editor for *Daughters of Sarah*, a religious feminist publication born in the 1970s. Reflecting on its roots, Falsani pointed out that what made "evangelical feminism" feminist was its insistence on gender equality in the church—women should face no limitations or subservient status due to sex. She noted that Bachmann had not actually claimed the label, but argued that if she did, "it would be as ridiculous as pinning a PETA button on a fox stole." Bachmann later revealed her admiration for Phyllis Schlafly, whom she deemed "the most accomplished woman in American politics" and lauded her conservative victories in the twentieth century.[51]

Despite a lack of widespread awareness, religious feminists have continued to call attention to the legacy of women in spiritual traditions. Muslim women, Jewish women, and other religious women from the Middle East recognized International Women's Day 2015 in Baqa al Garbiyya, Israel, by discussing some of the most basic human rights challenges they faced on a daily basis because of gender. Also recently, Supreme Court Justice Ruth Bader Ginsburg coauthored a feminist commentary about Passover that celebrates the women who chose to preserve baby Moses's life despite strict local regulations. Ginsburg closes the commentary: "Retelling the heroic stories of Yocheved, Shifra, Puah, Miriam and Batya reminds our daughters that with vision and the courage to act, they can carry forward the tradition those intrepid women launched … The Passover story recalls to all of us—women and men—that with vision and action we can join hands with others of like mind, kindling lights along paths leading out of the terrifying darkness." Similarly, the participants of International Women's Day recognized an opportunity for celebrating women's roles in faith communities and the potential for change and peace.[52]

These women's efforts represent the decades-long heritage of Second-Wave visionaries who wanted to increase the visibility and status of women in their own religious communities. In hindsight, there is a temptation to focus on the movement's failure to fully transform mainline religious doctrine to reflect gender equality. Similarly, one might criticize its inability to stop the Religious Right from preventing feminist success. Each time a female rabbi reads the Haggadah, each time a woman administers communion, each time a liturgy has gender-neutral language, and each time a religious marriage ceremony is performed for a homosexual couple, however, the legacy of religious activism in Second-Wave Feminism is renewed. As women continue their efforts to eliminate sexism in religion, they channel voices from sisters past and demand: "No more silence!"

Notes

1. Alice L. Hageman, ed., *Sexist Religion and Women in the Church* (New York: Association Press, 1974). The title of this chapter comes from the subtitle of Hageman's book: "No More Silence!" For a thorough account of the history of the Women's Caucus at Harvard Divinity School, see Ann Braude's 2005 Convocation address, available online at https://hds.harvard.edu/news/2005/09/19/short-half-century-fifty years-women-harvard-divinity-school#.
2. For more information about the Second Vatican Council, see Mary J. Henold, *Catholic and Feminist: The Surprising History of the American Catholic Feminist Movement* (Chapel Hill: University of North Carolina Press, 2008).
3. Mary Daly, *The Church and the Second Sex* (Boston: Beacon Press, 1968), 72, 221, 223.
4. Farians to Friedan, November 24, 1966, Box 1, Folder 5, Elizabeth Farians papers, Schlesinger Library, Radcliffe Institute, Harvard University; Ann Braude, "Religions and Modern Feminism," in *Encyclopedia of Women and Religion in North America* (Bloomington: Indiana University Press, 2006), 11–22; see also Ann Braude, "A Religious Feminist—Who Can Find Her? Historiographical Challenges from the National Organization for Women," *Journal of Religion* 84, no. 4 (October 2004): 555–572.
5. National Organization for Women Task Force Statement on Women and Religion, Box 1 Folder 5, Elizabeth Farians papers, Schlesinger Library, Radcliffe Institute, Harvard University; handwritten note on document: "Approved, Nov 20, 1967."

6. Farians to Katherine Clarenbach, August 7, 1968, Box 1, Folder 6, Elizabeth Farians papers, Schlesinger Library, Radcliffe Institute, Harvard University. For more information about the internal tension that plagued NOW's effectiveness in the late 1960s and early 1970s, see Jo Freeman, "The National Organization for Women," in *The Politics of Women's Liberation: A Case Study of the Emerging Social Movement and Its Relation to the Policy Process* (New York: McKay, 1975), 71–102.
7. Memo, Task Force on Women and Religion Meeting to National Board of Directors of N.O.W., May 26, 1968, Re: Consultation, Box 1, Folder 7, Elizabeth Farians papers, Schlesinger Library, Radcliffe Institute, Harvard University.
8. Report, Ecumenical Task Force on Women and Religion, June 1969, Box 1, Folder 9, Elizabeth Farians papers, Schlesinger Library, Radcliffe Institute, Harvard University.
9. "Hats in Air: Headgear Rule for Women Hard to Find," *Milwaukee Journal*, May 10, 1969, n.p., Box 1, Folder 9, Elizabeth Farians papers, Schlesinger Library, Radcliffe Institute, Harvard University. It was misprinted in some publications that it was part of a missal directive, but this was not true—it was in Church's Code of Canon Law—this discrepancy was noted in "The Mad Hatter…," n.p., n.d., Box 1, Folder 9, Elizabeth Farians papers, Schlesinger Library, Radcliffe Institute, Harvard University.
10. "Protesting Catholic Women Remove Hats at Communion Rail," Religious News Service, April 10, 1969, Box 1, Folder 9, Elizabeth Farians papers, Schlesinger Library, Radcliffe Institute, Harvard University.
11. "Hats Off Now Women!" pamphlet, National Organization for Women in Milwaukee, n.d., Box 1, Folder 9, Elizabeth Farians papers, Schlesinger Library, Radcliffe Institute, Harvard University.
12. Farians to Mrs. Richard Yeo, January 15, 1969, Box 1, Folder 9, Elizabeth Farians papers, Schlesinger Library, Radcliffe Institute, Harvard University.
13. Ronald Flowers, *Religion in Strange Times: The 1960s and 1970s* (Macon, GA: Mercer University Press, 1984), 225. Rita M. Gross, *Feminism and Religion* (Boston: Beacon Press, 1996), 46–47.
14. See Dale Nadine Weiss, "Jewish Feminist Women of Milwaukee, Wisconsin: Perspectives on Working for Social Justice" (EdD diss., Cardinal Stritch University, 2001): "The challenge for Jewish feminists became to create an identity-based politics that engaged women Jewishly [*sic*] as much as the Women's Movement engaged them politically. The feminist Jewish movement sought to include women who relate to their Jewishness primarily in a religious sense, and those who, as secular Jews,

understand Jewish identity through the lens of history and politics" (p. 37).
15. See Jo Freeman, "The National Organization for Women," 87. Freeman explains that there were many problems with task forces partly because there were so many, but also because of disorganization at the national level, which led frequently to miscommunications between local chapters and the national headquarters. Though this problem affected more than one task force, leaders of this particular task force often took the slights personally, feeling that NOW's leaders chose to place their issues on the periphery.
16. E. Ann Sayre to Joyce Slayton Mitchell, March 13, 1974, Box 1, Folder 1, Georgia Fuller papers, Schlesinger Library, Radcliffe Institute, Harvard University.
17. From Rita M. Gross, *Feminism and Religion* (Boston: Beacon Press, 1996), 52.
18. Robin Morgan, "Metaphysical Feminism," 386–92, in *The Politics of Women's Spirituality: Essays on the Rise of Spiritual Power within the Feminist Movement*, ed. Charlene Spretnak (Garden City, NY: Anchor Books, 1982); reprinted from *Going Too Far: The Personal Chronicle of a Feminist* (New York: Random House, 1968).
19. Mary Daly, "After the Death of God the Father: Women's Liberation and the Transformation of Christian Consciousness," in *Womanspirit Rising: A Feminist Reader in Religion*, ed. Carol P. Christ and Judith Plaskow (New York: Harper & Row, 1979), 57. Originally printed in *Commonweal* on March 12, 1971.
20. Carolyn Stoloff, "Who Joins Women's Liberation?" *Psychiatry* 36 (August 1973): 325–340; L. J. Ellis and P. M. Bentler, "Traditional Sex-Determined Role Standards and Sex Stereotypes," *Journal of Personality and Social Psychology* 25, no. 1 (January 1973): 28–34; J. A. Dempewolff, "Some Correlates of Feminism," *Psychological Reports* 34 (1974): 671–76; Edwin McClain, "Religious Orientation the Key to Psychodynamic Differences Between Feminists and Nonfeminists," *Journal for the Scientific Study of Religion* 18, no. 1 (1979): 40–45. Stoloff's 1973 study of college students found that supporters of women's liberation were "less religious" and Ellis and Bentler's study of the same year found they were "more ... nonreligious" than women who did not participate in women's liberation.
21. Nancy Hardesty and Letha Scanzoni, *All We're Meant to Be: A Biblical Approach to Women's Liberation* (Waco, TX: Word Books, 1974), 11–14, 208.
22. Georgia Fuller to Enid Griffin, August 29, 1976, Box 1, Folder 5, Georgia Fuller papers, Schlesinger Library, Radcliffe Institute, Harvard

University; Untitled document describing planned activities for September 26, 1976, likely authored by Mary-Louise McIntyre; Box 1, Folder 5, Georgia Fuller papers, Schlesinger Library, Radcliffe Institute, Harvard University; Memo, Georgia Fuller and Mary Louise McIntyre to NOW Treasurer, July 19, 1976, Re: Budget; Box 1, Folder 6, Georgia Fuller papers, Schlesinger Library, Radcliffe Institute, Harvard University.
23. Flowers, *Religion in Strange Times*, 219–220. See also Press Release, NOW Task Force on Religion, May 11, 1976, Box 1, Folder 4, Georgia Fuller papers, Schlesinger Library, Radcliffe Institute, Harvard University.
24. Joyce Slayton Mitchell to Ruth Hoppin, September 23, 1974, Box 1, Folder 1, Georgia Fuller papers, Schlesinger Library, Radcliffe Institute, Harvard University.
25. Georgia Fuller to Karen [no last name], July 3, 1976, Box 1, Folder 6, Georgia Fuller papers, Schlesinger Library, Radcliffe Institute, Harvard University.
26. See Sara M. Evans, *Tidal Wave: How Women Changed America at Century's End* (New York: Free Press, 2003), 128, 171.
27. See Kent L. Tedin, "Religious Preference and Pro/Anti Activism on the Equal Rights Amendment Issue," *Pacific Sociological Review* 21, no. 1 (January 1978): 55–66; David W. Brady and Kent L. Tedin, "Ladies in Pink: Religion and Political Ideology in the Anti-ERA Movement," *Social Science Quarterly* 56, no. 4 (March 1976): 564–575.
28. Phyllis Schlafly, "What's Wrong with 'Equal Rights' for Women?," *Phyllis Schlafly Report* 5, no. 7 (February 1972), Box 11, Kathryn Dunaway Papers, Manuscript, Archives, and Rare Book Library, Emory University.
29. Donald T. Critchlow, *Phyllis Schlafly and Grassroots Conservatism: A Woman's Crusade* (Princeton, NJ: Princeton University Press, 2005), 220–221.
30. "... Cincinnati: New Theses on the Cathedral Door," *Cincinnati Post-Times*, August 23, 1974, Box 1, Folder 12, Georgia Fuller papers, Schlesinger Library, Radcliffe Institute, Harvard University; News Release, Catholic Women for the ERA, August 26, 1974, Box 1, Folder 12, Georgia Fuller papers, Schlesinger Library, Radcliffe Institute, Harvard University; Ben L. Kaufman, "Local Catholic Women for Rights Amendment," *Cincinnati Enquirer*, August 25, 1974, Box 1, Folder 12, Georgia Fuller papers, Schlesinger Library, Radcliffe Institute, Harvard University.
31. Susan Hartmann, "Expanding Feminism's Field and Focus: Activism in the National Council of Churches in the 1960s and 1970s," in *Women and Twentieth-Century Protestantism*, ed. Margaret Lamberts Bendroth and Virginia Lieson Brereton (Urbana: University of Illinois Press, 2002), 49–69; Susan Hartmann, "Establishing Feminism Moral Authority: The

National Council of Churches," in *The Other Feminists: Activists in the Liberal Establishment* (New Haven, CT: Yale University Press, 1998), 92–131. For more information about Church Women United and its feminist awakening after participating in President Kennedy's Presidential Commission on the Status of Women, see Caryn E. Neumann, "Enabled by the Holy Spirit: Church Women United and the Development of Ecumenical Christian Feminism," in *Feminist Coalitions: Historical Perspectives on Second-Wave Feminism in the United States*, ed. Stephanie Gilmore (Urbana: University of Illinois Press, 2008), 113–134.

32. "Religious Committee Plans Push for Passage of ERA," *Washington Post*, September 24, 1976, B16.
33. *South of the Garden* 1, no. 1 (October 1978), Box 8, Folder: South of the Garden, Resource Center for Women and Ministry in the South Collection, David M. Rubenstein Rare Book & Manuscript Library, Duke University.
34. Jerry Falwell, *Listen, America!* (Garden City, NY: Doubleday, 1980), 151; cited in Charlene Spretnak, "The Christian Right's 'Holy War' Against Feminism," in *The Politics of Women's Spirituality: Essays on the rise of Spiritual Power within the Feminist Movement* edited by Charlene Spretnak (Garden City, NY: Anchor Books, 1982), 470–495.
35. Helen M. Havers, interviewer not identified, November 20, 1977. International Women's Year Archive, Oral History Collections, South Caroliniana Library, University of South Carolina.
36. Donald G. Mathews, "'Spiritual Warfare': Cultural Fundamentalism and the Equal Rights Amendment," *Religion and American Culture* 3, no. 2 (Summer 1993): 133.
37. For more information on the Religious Right after International Women's Year, see Critchlow, *Phyllis Schlafly and Grassroots Conservatism*; J. Brooks Flippen, *Jimmy Carter, the Politics of Family, and the Rise of the Religious Right* (Athens: University of Georgia Press, 2011); Daniel K. Williams, *God's Own Party: The Making of the Christian Right* (New York: Oxford University Press, 2010); and Neil J. Young, *We Gather Together: The Religious Right and the Problem of Interfaith Politics* (New York: Oxford University Press, 2015).
38. Evans, *Tidal Wave*, 172.
39. Janet K. Boles, "Building Support for the ERA: A Case of 'Too Much, Too Late,'" *PS* 15, no. 4 (Autumn 1982): 572–577; Spretnak, "The Christian Right's 'Holy War' Against Feminism," 470–495.
40. Diane Moseley interview, class visit March 22, 2010, translation by Shannon Brannon, University of South Carolina.

41. Margaret M. Curtis, *Life as a Feminist in Georgia: A Personal Recollection* (Atlanta: Georgia State University Library, 2010).
42. Margaret Miller Curtis, "Supports ERA," Letter to the Editor, *Atlanta Journal-Constitution*, August 6, 1980; W005_3A_02 (electronic version), Margaret Miller Curtis papers, W005, Donna Novak Coles Georgia Women's Movement Archives. Special Collections and Archives, Georgia State University, Atlanta.
43. Quoted in Evans, *Tidal Wave*, 173.
44. Curtis, "Supports ERA," 54.
45. *South of the Garden* 2, no. 6 (June 1980), Box 8, Folder: South of the Garden, Resource Center for Women and Ministry in the South Collection, David M. Rubenstein Rare Book & Manuscript Library, Duke University.
46. "Prayer Vigil Slated," Religious Committee for ERA, n.d., Box 5, Folder: ERA: Correspondence LL: 1978–1979, League of Women Voters of Columbia/Richland County Collection, South Carolina Political Collections, University of South Carolina.
47. Julie Lumpkin, "The ERA or The 345 Days Left to Ratify Committee," 1981, Box 24, Folder: ERA 1981, League of Women Voters of South Carolina Collection, South Carolina Political Collections, University of South Carolina.
48. Gloria Steinem, "Humanism and the Second Wave of Feminism," *Humanist* (May/June 1987): 15, 45.
49. For more information about the direction of recent scholarship, see Margaret Miles, "Mapping Feminist Histories of Religious Traditions," *Journal of Feminist Studies in Religion* 22, no. 1 (Spring 2006): 45–52, and published responses by Virginia Burrus, Tazim R. Kassan, and Rita M. Gross.
50. D. Michael Lindsay, "Michele Bachmann Leads a New Form of Evangelical Feminism," *Washington Post*, June 20, 2011, available online at http://www.washingtonpost.com/business/on-leadership/michele-bachmann-leads-a-new-form-of-evangelical-feminism/2011/06/20/AGztUGdH_story.html; Dan Gilgoff, "Michele Bachmann, evangelical feminist?" CNN.com, June 27, 2011, available online at http://religion.blogs.cnn.com/2011/06/27/michele-bachmann-as-evangelical-feminist/; Marie Griffith, "The New Evangelical Feminism of Bachmann and Palin," *Huffington Post*, September 5, 2011, available online at http://www.huffingtonpost.com/marie-griffith/evangelical-feminism_b_891579.html?ncid=edlinkusaolp00000008. Some media contributors did question that, if she was elected, would she be making the calls as commander in chief, or would she submit to her husband and serve as his proxy, or "Wife in Chief"? See Katha Pollitt, "Michele

Bachmann, Wife in Chief?" *The Nation*, September 12, 2011, 10; Joseph Farah, "The 'Submission' Question," WorldNetDaily, August 17, 2011; available online via NewsBank database.

51. Cathleen Falsani, "Is Michele Bachmann a Christian Feminist?" *Huffington Post*, July 14, 2011, available online at http://www.huffingtonpost.com/cathleen-falsani/michele_bachmann-feminist_b_899082.html; Bachmann quoted in Leo Hohmann, "Conservative Icon Still Going Strong at 90—Power Broker Politicians 'Would Tremble' When Phyllis Schlafly Walked in the Room," WorldNetDaily, WND Exclusive, August 15, 2014, accessed online via NewsBank database.

52. Katherine Marshall, "Religion and Women's Rights: International Women's Day in Israel," *Huffington Post*, March 15, 2015, available online at http://www.huffingtonpost.com/katherine-marshall/religion-and-womens-right_b_6873986.html?utm_hp_ref=religion; Justice Ruth Bader Ginsburg and Rabbi Lauren Holtzblatt, "The Heroic and Visionary Women of Passover," American Jewish World Service, Chag v'Chesed series, Pesach 5775, available online at http://ajws.org/what_we_do/education/publications/chag_vchesed/5775/cc_pesach_5775.pdf.

CHAPTER 5

Feminist Economics: Second Wave, Tidal Wave, or Barely a Ripple?

Cecilia Conrad

Abstract In this chapter, Cecilia Conrad discusses the influence of Second-Wave Feminism in the area of labor economics and on the discipline of economics itself. Conrad argues that Second-Wave feminists and the awareness they brought to gender-based pay differentials served as a catalyst for additional research on women's participation in the labor force and increasing numbers of women becoming economists. Moreover, not only did more women become economists, but also the field developed feminist challenges to dominant economic paradigms. While proponents of the leading economic theories often attribute pay differentials to differences between men and women in their education levels, their experiences, and their overall productivity, proponents of feminist economic theory argue that these explanations are incomplete and that at least some of the pay gap between men and women is the result of sexism, patriarchy, and discrimination.

The original version of the book was revised: Final corrections have been incorporated. The erratum to this chapter is available at https://doi.org/10.1007/978-3-319-62117-3_11

C. Conrad (✉)
Pomona College, Claremont, USA

In 1985, I began teaching the course "Sex, Discrimination and the Division of Labor" at Barnard College. First offered in the 1970s, the course likely would not have existed were it not for Second-Wave Feminism. Before the activism of the 1960s and 1970s, economists had demonstrated very little interest in the gender gap in pay, but the fact that women earned roughly 60 cents for every dollar earned by men became a rallying cry for Second-Wave Feminism. Women's activism stimulated political interest in this pay differential and the political interest stimulated demand for economic research. In addition, Second-Wave Feminism prompted scrutiny of the lack of gender diversity within the economics profession, leading to increases in the number of women economists. Not surprisingly, women economists had a slightly higher propensity to conduct research on women, and a subset of this group began to question the ability of the dominant neoclassical paradigm to explain gender differences in economic status. By the 1990s, these criticisms of neoclassical economics evolved into an alternative approach to economic analysis—a feminist economics. Feminist economics has yet to threaten the dominance of the neoclassical model, but it has steadily and stealthily changed the discourse around gender.

This chapter traces the emergence of feminist economics from Second-Wave Feminism's spotlight on the wage gap between men and women to the formation of the International Association for Feminist Economics (IAFFE) in 1991. It begins by providing a brief overview of the economic status of women in the 1960s and the growth in economic research on that status. The section "Competing Perspectives on the Male-Female Pay Gap" describes two competing perspectives about the male–female gap in earnings: a "perfect market" neoclassical perspective that attributed the gap to gender differences in education, work experience, and other productivity-related characteristics and a "discrimination" perspective that attributed at least some of the gap to sexism, workplace discrimination, and patriarchy. The section "Dueling Economists" uses testimony presented at congressional hearings on the status of women between 1970 and 2000 to illustrate how these two perspectives competed for policy influence. The section "The Emergence of Feminist Economics" describes the development of feminist economics as some adherents of the discrimination perspective became increasingly disenchanted with mainstream economic thought. The chapter identifies two legacies of Second-Wave Feminism for economics—the development of the new subfield, feminist economics, and a body of research on women's economic status around the globe.

In this chapter, I use the term *feminist* to label individuals committed to advancing equality of men and women, but I will make a distinction between economists who are feminist and feminist economists. I reserve the term feminist economist for economists who subscribe to a general set of principles, defined herein, that challenge the neoclassical paradigm in economics. Both an economist who is feminist and a feminist economist are advocates for the economic and social advancement of women and for their political rights. However, a feminist economist approaches the practice of economics with a critical lens. Feminist economics did not emerge as a separate field of economics until the 1990s, but its genesis, in part, was dissatisfaction of some economists, primarily women, with the explanations offered by mainstream economics for the economic inequality between men and women.

In this chapter, I build upon previous work on the history of economic thought on the status of women. Madden's 1972 survey of the "woman problem" in economics begins with the work of early feminists Mary Wollstonecraft and John Stuart Mill and ends with the development of economic models of discrimination in the 1960s (Madden 1972). Her account, like that of Robert Dimand (2005), stops short of the development of feminist economics. Claudia Goldin's Richard T. Ely lecture (Goldin 2006) links the evolution of women's economic roles and the work of economists to understand it, but she makes no mention of the feminist critique of mainstream economic theory. Several recent works offer a more thorough description of feminist economic thought than offered here. For example, Ann Mari May (2002) provides a readable summary of the basic principles of feminist economics. Janet Seiz (1995), Julie Nelson (1995), and Diana Strassman (1994) provide a feminist perspective on the models and methodology of economics. Three edited volumes provide a broad overview of the field: *The Elgar Companion to Feminist Economics* (Peterson and Lewis 1999), *Beyond Economic Man* (Ferber and Nelson 1993) and *Feminist Economics Today* (Ferber and Nelson 2003), and *Out of the Margins* (Feiner et al. 2013). This chapter focuses specifically on feminist perspectives on public policy to address gender inequality in the USA.[1]

WOMEN IN THE US LABOR MARKET 1960s, 1970s, AND 1980s

The 1963 report of John F. Kennedy's Commission on the Status of Women recognized changes in the economic roles of women and reported that women working full time earned 60 cents for every dollar earned by men (United States Government, Executive Office of the President, Council of Economic Advisors 1972, 20). This pay gap became a potent symbol for Second-Wave Feminism's push for women's social, political, and economic equality with men.

Fig. 5.1 Button Worn in 1980 Equal Rights Amendment March in Chicago, IL. *Source* Courtesy of Chris Savage http://www.eclectablog.com/2013/01/paycheck-fairness-act-introduced-again-will-the-gop-win-this-battle-in-the-war-on-women-too.html

Twenty years later, despite the passage of the Equal Pay Act of 1963 and the Civil Rights Act of 1964, the earnings of full-time, year-round working women continued to average roughly 60% of the earnings of full-time, year-round men, a fact immortalized in a popular women's movement button, circa 1980, shown in Fig. 5.1. The Book of Leviticus suggests the average woman earned 60% of the earnings of the average man even in biblical times;[2] however, we can only document that the ratio stayed relative constant between 1957, the year that the US Census Bureau began reporting this data, and 1980.

Figure 5.2 depicts the time series of the ratio of the median earnings of women to the median earnings of men for year-round, full-time workers from 1957 to 2012. After 1980, the ratio began to increase and today the median earnings ratio is 0.77 or, in other words, the average female workers earn roughly 77 cents for every dollar earned by the average male worker.

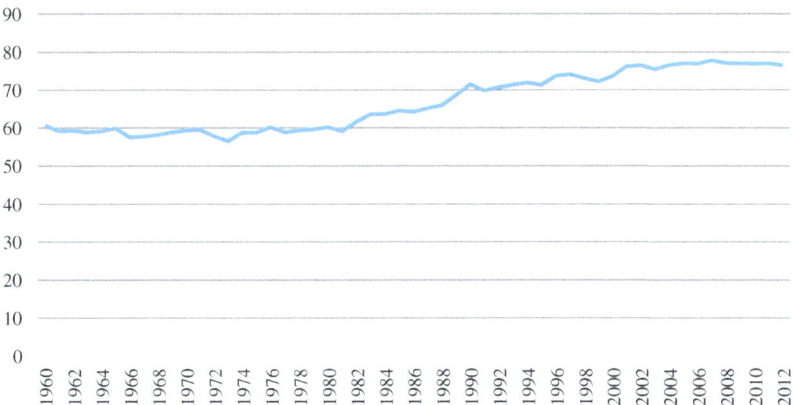

Fig. 5.2 Median Earnings of Women as Percent of Median Earnings of Men, Year-round, Full-time Workers, 1960–2012. *Source* United States Government, Bureau of the Census, Table P-40. Women's Earnings as a Percentage of Men's Earnings by Race and Hispanic Origin: 1960–2012. http://www.census.gov/hhes/www/income/data/historical/people/ (Retrieved June 15, 2014)

The Kennedy Commission report (United States Government, President's Commission on the Status of Women 1963) asserted that the pay gap between men and women in 1960 could be explained in large part by differences in occupation.

> Though women are represented in the highly paid professions, in industry, in business, and in government, most jobs that women hold are in low-paid categories. Some occupations—nursing and household work, for instance—are almost entirely staffed by women. The difference in occupational distributions of men and women is largely responsible for the fact that in 1961, the earnings of women working full time averaged only about 60 percent of those of men working full time. (United States Government, President's Commission on the Status of Women 1963, 28)

Women and men worked in different jobs in the 1960s, and although the extent of segregation declined in the 1970s and 1980s, it did not disappear. According to a 1998 study by Francine Blau, Patricia Simpson, and Deborah Anderson, in 1970, 78% of women worked in female occupations, 13% worked in male occupations, and 9.3% worked in integrated occupations. Seventy-eight percent of men worked in male occupations, 12% worked in female occupations, and 10% worked in integrated occupations. Only 10% of the total workforce was employed in "integrated" occupations.[3] By 1980, the percentage of women in female occupations had decreased to 69%, and the percentage of women in male occupations had climbed to 20% and the percentage of women in integrated occupations to 11%. The percentage of men in male occupations barely budged at 78% and 11% of the total workforce were employed in integrated occupations. By 1990, the percentage of women in female occupations had decreased to 65% and 14% of the total workforce were employed in "integrated" occupations (Blau et al. 1998).

Black[4] women did experience a shift in occupational distribution between 1960 and 1980 although they remained concentrated in female occupations. In 1960, more than a third of black women were employed as private household workers. By 1980, this percentage had declined to 6.2% (see Fig. 5.3). Only 8% of black women were employed in clerical work in 1960, a percentage that climbed to nearly 30% in 1980 (see Fig. 5.4). Black women's employment in blue-collar work also increased. This occupational shift contributed to an improvement in the earnings

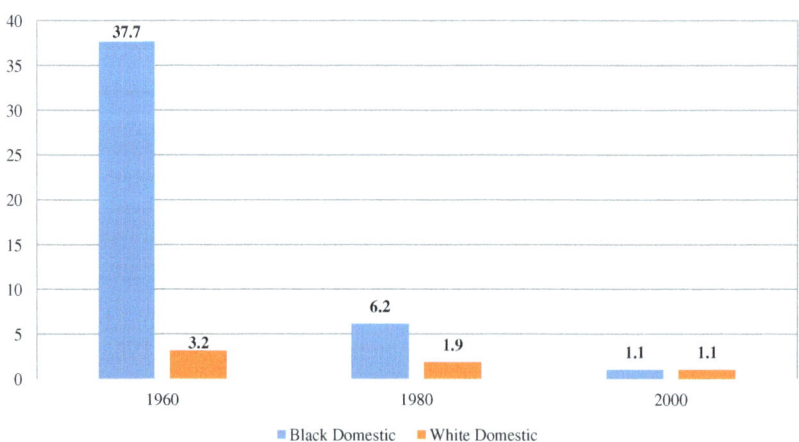

Fig. 5.3 Percentage of Women Employed as Private Household Workers by Race, 1960–2000 *Source* United States Government, U.S. Bureau of Labor Statistics, *Employment and Earnings*, January 2011 (for 2010), January 2002 (for 2000 data); January 1981 (for 1980 data); January 1961 (for 1960 data)

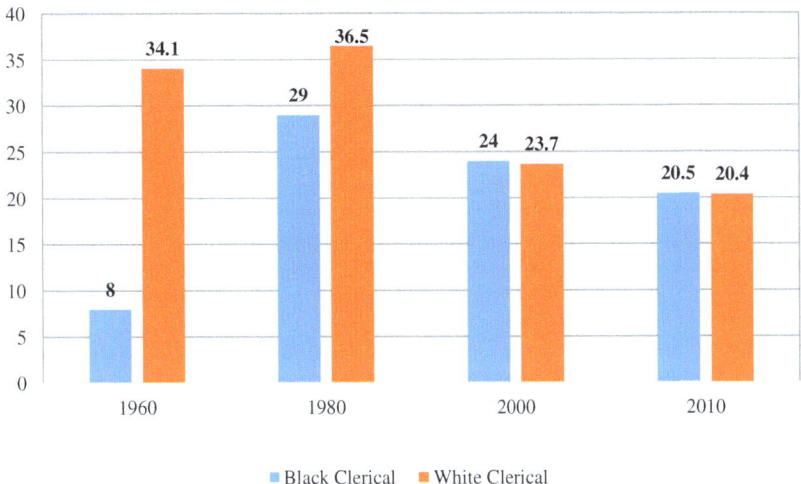

Fig. 5.4 Percentage of Women Employed as Clerical Workers by Race, 1960–2010 *Source*: U.S. Bureau of Labor Statistics, *Employment and Earnings*, January 2011 (for 2010), January 2002 (for 2000 data); January 1981 (for 1980 data); January 1961 (for 1960 data)

of black women relative to those of white men and women. The ratio of black women's median earnings to white women's median earnings (year-round, full-time workers) increased from 1955 to 1975, peaking at .96 in 1975 (see Fig. 5.5). The shift in occupations has been attributed both to a growth in educational attainment and to the enforcement of Equal Employment Opportunity laws and the federal contractor Affirmative Action requirements (Conrad 2005).

A second fact about women's economic status in the 1970s and 1980s was the growth in the labor force participation rate of married women. In 1960, less than a third of married women participated in the labor force (defined as either employed or actively looking for work). The labor force participation rate of black married women was higher, roughly 40%. By 1980, the labor force participation rate for married women of all races had climbed to 49.8% and by 1990 to 58.4% (see Fig. 5.6).

In the popular imagination, this growth in labor force participation rates reflected a change in social norms brought about first by the Rosie the Riveter experience of World War II and then accelerated by the women's movement in the 1960s and 1970s, but the empirical evidence

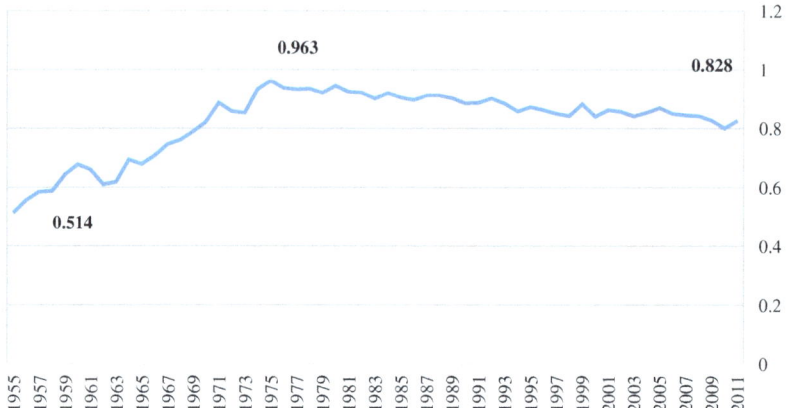

Fig. 5.5 Ratio of Black to White Median Earnings for Full-time, Year-round, Female Workers, 1955–2011 *Source* United States Government, US Bureau of the Census, https://www.census.gov/data/tables/time-series/demo/income-poverty/historical-income-people.html, Table P-35 (median income) for 1955–1966 and Table P-38 (median earnings) for 1967–2011. Retrieved June 25, 2017

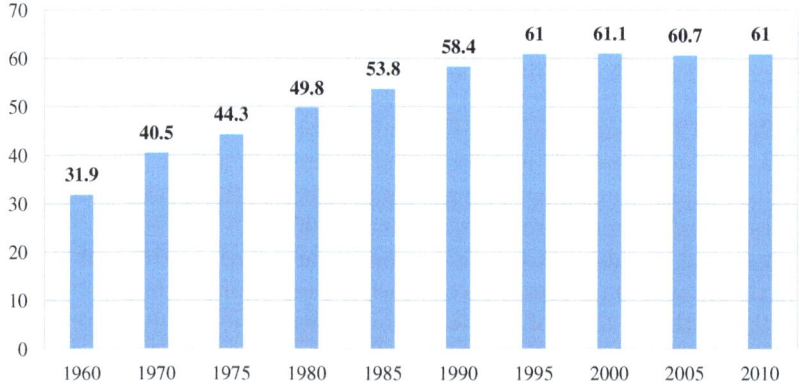

Fig. 5.6 Labor Force Participation Rate of Married Women, 1960–2010 *Source* United States Government, *Statistical Abstract of the United States* 2012 (131st Edition), Section 12: Labor Force, Employment and Earnings, Table 597. https://www.census.gov/library/publications/2011/compendia/statab/131ed/labor-force-employment-earnings.html. Retrieved June 25, 2017

suggests that it was a continuation of a trend begun in the 1900s, a trend temporarily slowed by the baby boom of the 1950s (Smith and Ward 1985; Goldin 1991). Goldin (1991) reports that the percentage of white married women gainfully employed increased by 15.5 points from 1930 to 1950 and continued to expand in the 1950s.

Economists worried about the impact of this increase in married women's labor supply on economic well-being. An article in the March 1958 issue of the *Review of Social Economy* opened with this lament,

> Woman, the masterpiece and crown of God's creation, has, by custom, culture, and nature, as her primary function and sublime mission, motherhood. And yet, America today is witnessing that majestic model of motherhood suffering from the schizophrenia of womanpower, the working woman. This sudden and shocking rise of womanpower in the work force of the United States may, if its rate of acceleration continues, have a more ominous effect on our culture and civilization than all the sputniks the Soviets can ever produce (Toner 1958).

Toner's comments sound extreme, but the general theme, that women's work has implications for families, was a concern shared by others. The Kennedy Commission report, noteworthy for its attention to the specific circumstances of black women, included a graphic entitled "Many Mothers, Especially Negroes, Must Work" to make the case for expanded child care and family services (United States Government, President's Commission on the Status of Women 1963, p. 20). Much of black married women had a long history of greater labor force attachment than white married women (see Fig. 5.7), explained in part but not wholly by the low incomes of black husbands.[5]

The third fact characterizing women's economic status in the 1960s and 1970s was the feminization of poverty. The term is slightly misleading as it refers neither to the growth in the percentage of the poor who are women nor to an increase in the poverty rate of women. The term refers to the percentage of poor persons (especially children) living in households headed by women.[6] Figure 5.8 depicts the trend in the proportion of poor children and the proportion of all children living in female-headed households. This feminization of poverty was the result of an increase in the proportion of persons (children) living in female-headed households not the result of an increase in the poverty rates of those households. The poverty rate of children living in

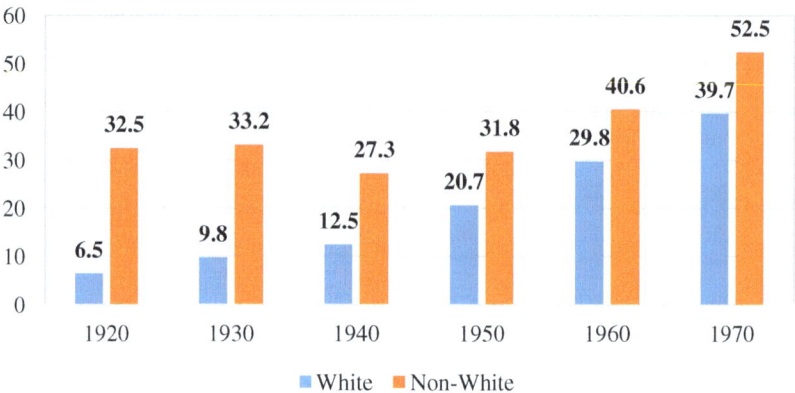

Fig. 5.7 Labor Force Participation Rate of Married Women by Race, 1920–1970 *Source* Goldin, Claudia. 1977. Female Labor Force Participation: The Origin of Black and White Differences, 1870 and 1880. *Journal of Economic History* 37(1): 88. Table 1 "Female Labor Force Participation Rates by Marital Status, Race, and Nativity, 1890 to 1970."

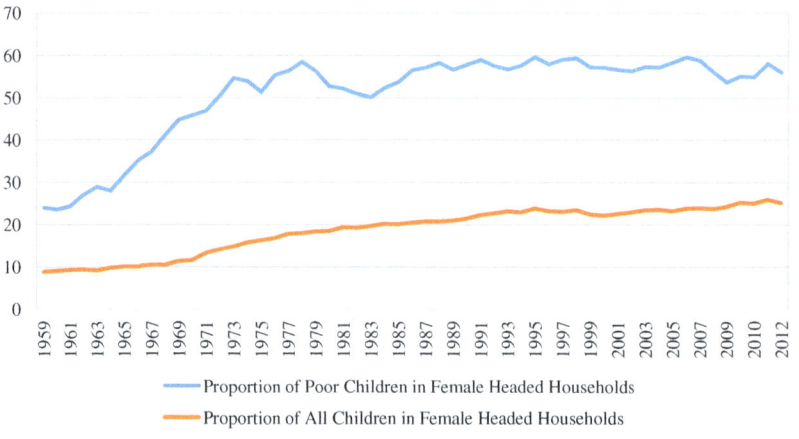

Fig. 5.8 Feminization of Poverty, 1950–2012 *Source* United States Government, US Bureau of the Census, https://www.census.gov/data/tables/time-series/demo/income-poverty/historical-poverty-people.html, Table Ten. Retrieved June 24, 2017

female-headed families actually decreased between 1959 and 1979. Hence, to understand the feminization of poverty, one must explore the low incomes of women relative to men.

Mainstream Economic Theory and the Economic Status of Women

Although the iconography of Second-Wave Feminism focused on the 59-cent wage gap, what most intrigued mainstream economists was the growth in the labor force participation of married women. Goldin (2006) cites work by Paul H. Douglas and Erika H. Schoenberg (1937) in the 1930s and Clarence Long (1958) in the 1950s on the relationship between labor supply of married women and the incomes of their husbands. In the 1960s, Jacob Mincer refined estimates of labor supply to resolve the seeming contradiction between a negative relationship between husbands' income and hours worked by women in cross-sectional studies and the positive relationship between husbands' income and hours worked by wives in time series data (Mincer 1962). Nobel prize winner Gary Becker, in several papers, developed a formal theory of the family to explain the supply of married women's labor.[7] Goldin claims that this interest in female labor supply gave birth to modern labor economics: "It would not be too much of an exaggeration to claim that women gave 'birth' to modern labor economics, especially labor supply" (Goldin 2006, 3).

Despite the interest in female labor supply, the volume of articles on the economic status of women published in the 1950s and the 1960s was low. A search of the ECONLIT database using the search terms, "gender," "women," "female," or "sex" yields only 22 articles out of a database of 15,970 articles for the period January 1950 to December 1959 and 48 articles out of a database of 26,698 articles for the period January 1960 to December 1969, a hit rate of 0.1–0.2%. The same search yields 476 from January 1970 to December 1979 out of 62,525 for a hit rate of 0.7% and 1872 from January 1980 to December 1989 out of 95,041, a hit rate of 1.9%, suggesting a slight uptick in interest. In a related analysis conducted in 1991, Albelda (1995) finds that 4.4% of articles in mainstream economics journals concerned women, children, families or feminist perspectives on economic analysis.

Indeed, interest in women's economic issues clearly grew in the late 1960s and early 1970s. Juanita Kreps, who later became the first women secretary of commerce under Jimmy Carter, published *Sex in the*

Marketplace: American Women and Work in 1971 (1971) and *Sex, Age and Work: The Changing Composition of the Labor Force* with Robert Clark in 1975 (1975). Other books included *The Economics of Sex Discrimination* (1973) by Janice Madden. Cynthia Lloyd's aforementioned edited volume (1975) and *A Time of Transition: The Growth of Families Headed by Women* (1975) by Heather Ross, Isabel Sawhill, and Anita R. Macintosh. Phyllis Wallace's *Equal Opportunity and the AT&T Case* (1976) described the economic research underlying that precedent-setting settlement to reverse race and sex discrimination. The *Industrial and Labor Relations Review* published a symposium on women in the labor force in 1968. In 1972, the papers and proceedings issue of the *American Economic Review* included three articles plus a discussion on economic equality for women. The papers' authors were Francine Blau (1972), Charlotte Phelps (1972), and Harriet Zellner (1972) with a discussion by Stephen Sandell (1972). This is not an exhaustive list.

Second-Wave Feminism contributed both directly and indirectly to the growth in economists' research on women. Second-Wave Feminism contributed directly by generating demand for this research from policymakers. Economists were hired as expert witnesses and researchers in legal cases pursued as a result of the new civil rights protections and contracted to produce background papers for presidential commissions and congressional hearings. Second-Wave Feminism contributed indirectly to the growth in economic research on women through its impact on the number of women in economics. The women's movement called attention to the underrepresentation of women in many professions, including economics where women represented only 4.6% of all tenured/tenure track faculty in PhD granting departments in 1972. In response to this activism, the American Economic Association (AEA) adopted a resolution in 1971 declaring that "economics is not a man's field" and created the Committee on the Status of Women in the Economics Profession (CSWEP) (Fels 1972). CSWEP's primary charge was to investigate conformity to the AEA's positive program to eliminate sex discrimination and to make recommendations for affirmative action (Fels 1972), but CSWEP defined its mission to include encouraging research on the role of women in the broader economy and sex discrimination with respect to wages and occupational segregation (Reagan 1977) and held a national research conference on occupational segregation with a grant from the Carnegie Foundation (Reagan 1975 and 1976). It organized sessions for the annual meeting of economists on the economic status of women, and a selection of these papers was published in papers and proceedings.[8] CSWEP's efforts to encourage the participation of women contributed to an increase in both women's participation (Reagan 1978) and the number of sessions on gender issues.

Second-Wave Feminism spurred an increase in both the representation of women in economics and the volume of economic analysis on women's economic status, but the resulting increase in representational diversity did not immediately produce a "feminist economics" analysis of women's economic status. Indeed, Albelda's 1992 survey of economists, less than one-third agreed that "mainstream economics would be enriched if it were to incorporate more feminist analysis." (Albelda 1992, p. 269) The first efforts to explain gender differences applied the standard tools of economic analysis, model building, and statistical analysis (econometrics), using the basic theoretical framework presented in Gary Becker's 1957 work "The Economics of Discrimination" (Becker 1957). Becker's theory, described in greater detail below, argued that individuals might discriminate, but over time, competitive markets did not. Becker's model provided a conceptual framework for the work of two economists, Alan Blinder (1973) and Ron Oaxaca (1973), co-credited with the introduction of a statistical technique to separate the portion of the wage gap due to differences in observable characteristics, like years of schooling, from the portion of the wage gap that is unexplained. The unexplained portion might be a measure of discrimination or it might be a measure of the impact of unobserved differences in productivity. The Blinder–Oaxaca decomposition analysis provides the basis for much of the economics research on both the racial wage gap and gender wage gap conducted since the 1970s. Economists who believe that discrimination would not persist under competitive market conditions tend to attribute the unexplained gap to unmeasured differences in productivity. Those who are not true believers tend to interpret the unexplained difference as evidence of market discrimination.

In a survey paper, Gunderson (1989) offers some general observations about findings from Blinder-Oaxaca decomposition studies of the male–female wage gap: (a) the greater the number of productivity-related variables included as controls, the smaller the unexplained differences; (b) most studies find some residual unexplained gap even after including an extensive list of control variables; and (c) men and women working in the same occupation in the same establishment tend to earn the same wage.

Competing Perspectives on the Male-Female Pay Gap

As described above, Second-Wave Feminism contributed to a surge of published work on the male–female pay gap in the 1970s. This flurry of papers and books published on the pay gap in the 1970s offered two competing narratives to explain the pay gap. The first narrative, labeled here as the "perfect market" narrative, explained the pay gap as an outcome of the competitive workings of the labor market. In the perfect market narrative, competitive market forces assure that each resource (including labor) is remunerated based on the value of its marginal product. Hence, women earn less than men on average because they produce less market value on average.[9] The second narrative, labeled here as the "discrimination" narrative, argues that discrimination—societal, individual, and statistical—constrains women's choices such that women lack the opportunity to pursue some jobs or occupations. Given these constraints, a woman may be underpaid relative to her potential productivity. This difference in explanations of the pay gap presaged the later development of a separate subfield of economics—feminist economics—but both narratives were outgrowths of Second-Wave Feminism. The "perfect market" narrative located the obstacles to women's advancement outside of the market economy; the second narrative identified at least some of the obstacles as within it.

In the perfect market framework, the existence of a pay difference between two workers reflects differences in marginal productivity. An individual's productivity is a function of innate talent, education, training, and work experience, but the value of the worker's marginal product will also depend on the nature of the work—the occupation or industry in which that worker is employed. According to this narrative, the average woman earns less than the average man because the average woman has less education, less work experience, and more discontinuous work experience than the average man, and because, on average, women choose occupations that best complement their housekeeping and childbearing roles. The emphasis is on individual choice. In the perfect market narrative, women are more likely to impose constraints on hours, geography, and working conditions than are men and this translates into lower pay. Under the assumption that the individual knows best, there is a presumption that the resulting economic outcomes are efficient and just.

In the perfect market narrative, the choices made by women about occupation and hours worked represent an efficient allocation of resources by individual households. Becker's theory of the family, work that contributed to his Nobel Prize in economics, recognized that production of goods occurs outside the market and within the household. In his model, an altruistic dictator makes decisions about the household resources so as to maximize the collective well-being of household members. In Becker's model, the allocation of hours to market work versus home production is based on comparative advantage. Women, both because they tend to have lower market wages than men and because of cultural norms, have a comparative advantage in nonmarket production and thus will supply less hours to the formal market than men.

The argument that women's tastes constrained their occupational choices later appeared in a landmark legal case. In the early 1970s, the Equal Employment Opportunity Commission (EEOC) charged Sears, then the nation's largest retailer, with discriminating against women and minorities in its hiring practices. Sears and the EEOC negotiated a settlement to the race discrimination case but not the sex discrimination case, and that case went to trial in September 1984 in the US District Court in Chicago (*EEOC v. Sears Roebuck* 1988). A major element of the government's case was the charge that Sears discriminated against women in hiring and promotion for high-paying commission sales jobs. Historian Rosalyn Rosenberg, a professor at Barnard College and author of *Beyond Separate Spheres: Intellectual Roots of Modern Feminism* (1982), testified in support of Sears claim that this statistical disparity resulted not from discriminatory hiring practices by Sears but from a lack of interest by women in the commission sales jobs.[10] The district court judge found Rosenberg's testimony more compelling than that of the EEOC witnesses, including the two economists—Eileen Applebaum and Janice Madden.

The perfect market narrative rejects labor market discrimination as a significant factor contributing to either the pay gap or occupational segregation. In alignment with Gary Becker's theory of discrimination, employers might have tastes for discrimination, a preference for hiring men relative to women, but given the profit-seeking behavior of firms and the competitive pressure of markets, these tastes do not translate into a long-term difference in wages. In Becker's analysis, tastes for discrimination on the part of fellow employees might lead to occupational segregation but would not result in a pay difference between workers with the same productivity. Only if consumers have tastes for discrimination, which is if consumers prefer a product produced by a man over a product produced by a woman, would a pay gap be sustained by market forces in Becker's model. True believers in this neoclassical model begin with a presumption that the pay differences between men and women are due to productivity differences and are reluctant to ascribe any differences to discrimination.

The second discrimination narrative reaches a different conclusion. It does not reject the argument that education, work experience, and training matter, but ascribes a significant role to discrimination as a contributor to the gender wage gap and to occupational segregation. In the second narrative, discrimination can have an effect on wages if labor markets are not perfectly competitive as might be the case in a local labor market for teachers or nurses or prison guards or if there is imperfect information. In the case of imperfect information, employers might rely on gender as a predictor of other productivity-related traits, as the likelihood of turnover, and relegate women to jobs where the cost of turnover is low. By judging an individual on the basis of the perceived average for a group, employers may engage in statistical discrimination and may be less willing to hire a woman because he/she perceives that a woman has a higher probability of quitting than a similarly qualified man (Edmund Phelps 1972; Lundberg and Startz 1983). Theories such as the efficiency wage model (Akerlof and Yellen 1986) could explain persistent unemployment[11] and with it the persistence of discrimination in employment. Bergmann's crowding model (1971) establishes that occupational segregation, based either on social custom or on discrimination by fellow workers,[12] could depress women's pay.

Adherents to the discrimination narrative generally believe that occupational segregation is not purely the result of women's choices, but also results from social custom and societal discrimination. The restrictions on hours worked or geography result from decision making within households that is also distorted by the effects of discrimination. Reskin and Hartmann's report for the National Research Council provides evidence to support this perspective (1986). Critics of the idea that households allocate resources efficiently cite the empirical observation that women devote greater time to housework than men even if they earn higher wages and work equivalent hours, most notably in households with an unemployed spouse. They also point to the fact that the introduction of labor-saving appliances in the 1950s and 1960s, which in theory should have decreased hours spent in home production and increased hours worked in the formal labor market actually increased the time spent doing related household tasks; for example, the time spent on laundry increased after the introduction of the automatic washer.[13] Both facts suggest that decisions about hours work are not purely driven by relative efficiency.

DUELING ECONOMISTS

Second-Wave feminist activism stimulated demand for the services of economists as expert witnesses before congressional panels and in legal cases involving allegations of sex discrimination. The testimonies of these expert witnesses vividly dramatize the contrast between the perfect market and discrimination narratives. A starting example is the testimony of economists at a hearing before the Joint Economic Committee of Congress held in 1973 (Economic Problems of Women, Part I, 1973). The focal point of the hearing was the Council of Economic Advisors' analysis of the economic role of women. The council, in a first, devoted a chapter of its 1972 annual report to the economic role of women. The report clearly reflected the perfect market narrative. Acknowledging the low representation of women in "positions of responsibility," the report observed, "Exactly how much of this situation has been imposed on women because of prejudice and how much of it derives from a voluntary adjustment to a life divided between home responsibilities and work remains obscure" (United States Government, Executive Office of the President, Council of Economic Advisors 1972, 100). The report reviewed various ways in which discriminatory attitudes or statistical discrimination might contribute to the approximately 20% of the earnings differential between men and women that remains even after adjusting for factors such as education, work experience by year, and lifelong work experience, but ultimately concluded "It is not now possible to distinguish in a quantitative way between the discrimination that bars women from jobs solely because of their sex, and the role differentiation whereby women, either through choice or necessity, restrict their careers because of the demand of their homes" (United States Government, Executive Office of the President, Council of Economic Advisors 1972, 107). The report's authors thought that most of the 20% unexplained differential could be explained by sex-role differences in the home.

The chair of the Council of Economic Advisers, Herb Stein, and council member Marina Whitman represented the perfect market narrative. In their testimony, Stein and Whitman attributed the gap in pay between men and women to differences in work experience, both cumulative years of experience and, citing work by Mincer and Polachek (1974), continuity of work experience. Whitman testified, "Years out of the labor market are not neutral in their effect on earnings; they have a negative effect. Skills depreciate during that time and the more education a woman has, the greater the rate of depreciation during the time spent at home" (Economic Problems of Women, Part I, 1973, Testimony of Marina Whitman, 36). Both Whitman and Stein minimized the role of occupational segregation and of labor market discrimination.

Representative Griffiths, who chaired the hearing, criticized the council's failure to recommend an economic policy to promote women's employment. In his reply, Stein defended the council's efforts: "Well, of course, we think that women are part of this country, and that the policy which we have recommended for increasing employment in total has served very substantially to increase the employment of women" (Economic Problems of Women, Part I, 1973, Testimony of Herb Stein). Though prodded by Griffith to address the issue of discrimination, Stein sidestepped the issue with the statement that "law enforcement was not the function of the Council."

The next witness panel included Barbara Bergmann and Nobel Prize-winning economist Paul Samuelson, who presented the discrimination narrative. Contrasting her views with those of Stein and Whitman, Bergmann identified occupational segregation resulting from employers' sex-typing of jobs as a major cause of the inferior position of women and explained:

> Overcrowding in the few women's occupation translates into lower wages and higher unemployment rates for women. The demand for women's labor is kept artificially low because of their virtual exclusion from certain fields—medicine, law, engineering and dentistry, supervisory and executive positions, the crafts—and the supply of women to the few fields where they are welcomed is artificially increased thereby. I would venture to say that the ideal of equal pay for equal work cannot be achieved without a far broader acceptance of women into jobs from which they have been excluded by discrimination. Under the current discriminatory employment and promotion practices, the law of supply and demand forbids equal pay for men and women, and the law of supply and demand is stronger than the Equal Pay Act (Economic Problems of Women, Part I, 1973, Testimony by Barbara Bergmann, 51).

Paul Samuelson's testimony asserted that social custom, law, and discrimination confined women to a limited number of jobs and focused his testimony on the economic costs of the failure to fully utilize the productive capacity of women: "If because of the dead hand of custom and discrimination half of our population have a quarter of their productive potential unrealized—and that may be an understatement—then by simple arithmetic a gain of between 10 and 15% in living standards is obtainable, by ending these limitations and discriminations" (Economic Problems of Women, Part I, 1973, Testimony of Paul Samuelson, p. 59). Samuelson's testimony contrasted sharply with the report's conclusion that it was difficult to evaluate "the full extent to which women's capabilities have actually been underutilized by society" because women college graduates "who reduce their outside work to care for small children clearly place a high value on the care they provide" (United States Government, Executive Office of the President, Council of Economic Advisors, 1972, p. 107).

Ten years later, Barbara Bergmann was again a witness at a hearing on women's economic status. She testified at a hearing before the Joint Economic Committee of the first session of the 98th US Congress in November of 1983. Her adversary this time was economist June O'Neill. The Census Bureau produced a report on *American Women: Three Decades of Change* that was agnostic on discrimination (United States Government, Bureau of the Census 1983). In her testimony, June O'Neill, who had been a staff member for the Council of Economic Advisors in 1972, emphasized that the wage gap between men and women could be explained by many factors other than discrimination. First, referring to the 59¢ button (Fig. 5.1), O'Neill cited evidence that full-time male workers work longer hours than full-time female workers arguing that the true ratio is probably 69¢ (*American Women: Three Decades of Change* 1983, Testimony of June O'Neill, 52). O'Neill then cited studies suggesting that the gap was much smaller than 31¢ once researchers account for differences in productivity as proxied by work experience, job tenure, and schooling and for differences in plant size. She then rhetorically asked "are the remaining, unaccounted for differences a measure of discrimination in the labor market?" Her answer was probably not. At the same hearing, Bergmann took a very different perspective: "Now, my friends from the Census Bureau tell us they are agnostic on discrimination, and when you ask them what are the factors that keep this huge gap between men and women's pay, they are very cautious and do not mention discrimination. But, I have no such inhibition, and I tell you discrimination is still extremely important. ... We heard mention of the concentration of women in low-paying occupations. Well, women are not stupid. They do not flock to low-paying occupations. They are excluded from high-paying occupations, and very little has been done to enforce the law against that exclusion" (American Women: Three Decades of Change, 1983, Testimony of Barbara Bergmann, 32).

For the 2000 congressional hearing on gender-based wage discrimination, the dueling economists were O'Neill v. Hartmann. O'Neil, testifying first, took a familiar stance:

> The simple differential in wages between women and men is frequently assumed to be the result of labor market discrimination. However, such conclusion, I believe would be wrong because it does not take into account gender differences in skills and work-related characteristics that would create differences in wages even in the absence of any gender bias. The most important nondiscriminatory factors affecting the pay gap stem from deeply rooted differences in the roles that are assumed by women and men in the family (Gender Based Wage Discrimination 2000, Testimony of June O'Neill, p. 19).

Hartmann responded,

> The economists that are testifying in this panel believe that, if there ever was any discrimination, it has been eliminated by now and anyway, all the remaining differences can be explained by legitimate factors. They argue, in essence, that women choose to work less hours than men and they chose lower earning careers. Obviously, I belong to the other school of thought. I believe that there is great part of the wage differences between men and women that cannot be explained by other factors, that is likely due to discrimination, and I further believe that some of the differences that are explained between men and women's wages actually are a result of discrimination. For example, if you know as a woman that you are going to go out there and face a lower wage in the labor market, you may invest less in your training. You may invest less in your career. So just the fact that we observe that maybe women do have less training and education does not mean that that is not the result of discrimination in the labor market (Gender Based Wage Discrimination 2000, Testimony of Heidi Hartmann, 44).

The policy implications emerging from the two narratives are clearly quite distinct. Subscribers to the perfect market narrative see the need for government intervention only to keep labor markets competitive.

Adherents to the discrimination narrative advocate a more activist agenda. The perfect market narrative argues that the gains made by women since the 1960s were largely the result of market forces, augmented by government deregulation, including the elimination of protective legislation. Their prescription for further improvement is more of the same—address market imperfections and then let the market be. Policies to break down barriers such as equal access to educational opportunity (Title IX), outreach programs to encourage women to consider nontraditional career paths, and mentoring programs are also acceptable roles for government within the perfect market narrative of how the world works.

The discrimination narrative argues that the gains made by women happened at least in part because the enforcement of Equal Opportunity laws and Affirmative Action opened opportunities for women workers in supervisory roles and in traditionally male jobs. To illustrate the potency of equal opportunity enforcement, they point to the watershed case of the consent decree reached between the EEOC, the Department of Labor, the Department of Justice, and AT&T, then the nation's largest private employer.[14] Under the decree, AT&T agreed to eliminate discriminatory recruiting, hiring, and promotion practices against women and minorities and provided pay increases for women and minorities whose advancement in the Bell system had been hampered by discrimination. The most visible impact of this agreement was the appearance of women as telephone repairpersons and men as telephone operators. A noteworthy aspect of this case was that AT&T was a regulated monopoly. Even in Becker's work, an employer with market power could discriminate in the long run. Hence, even orthodox economists might acknowledge the need for government action to remedy discrimination, but they did not.

A particular flashpoint among economists is comparable worth policy. Comparable worth, also known as pay equity, is a policy to legislate equal wages for jobs that appear similar in terms of skills required, level of responsibility, and working conditions. Implementation of the policy relies on job evaluation systems that assess the attributes of each position and creates weights so that jobs with different attributes may be compared with each other. An example made famous in *County of Washington v. Gunther*, 452 US 161 (1981), is the case of female matrons who worked in the female section of a county jail and male guards who worked in the male section of the jail. The female matrons earned 70% as much as the male guards even though a job evaluation study suggested that matrons should earn 95% as much.

Comparable worth challenges a fundamental precept of neoclassical economics—that labor markets assign a wage rate based on the value of the worker's product. Perhaps because of the challenge it poses to the invisible hand of the market, the attention given to the policy in the economics literature seems far in excess of its political viability. The large majority of labor economists (83%) soundly reject the idea of widespread implementation of comparable worth (Whaples 1996).

Not surprising, adherents to the perfect market narrative vociferously object to comparable worth policies. In the perfect market narrative, an increase in the wages of matrons above the market price of matrons would reduce the demand for matrons and reduce the number hired. At the same time, the higher wage would attract more women to the occupation. With fixed wages, there would be unemployment. Furthermore, comparable worth would encourage women to remain in traditionally female jobs.

Many economists who subscribe to the discrimination narrative and support active enforcement of Equal Employment Opportunity are queasier about comparable worth. For example, in a newspaper interview (Kleiman 1986), Francine Blau noted that there were pros and cons of comparable worth and expressed concern that comparable worth would create unemployment for women workers:

> It [comparable worth] has the potential to raise the wages of women and reduce, but not eliminate, the wage gap. But it could have some negative effects. Economists are concerned that if you increase wages for workers in a particular field, you could reduce the demand. And that would mean fewer jobs for women.

Other adherents to the discrimination narrative are more supportive of comparable worth. They argue that women are shunted into different jobs with similar work and skill requirements as those occupied by men, but are paid less because of crowding or because of social custom and discriminatory preferences. Comparable worth, by this line of reasoning, redresses this inequity. For example, Deb Figart and June Lapidus estimate that a comparable worth policy would reduce both gender and race inequality and alleviate poverty among women (1998).

Advocates of the "perfect market" narrative tend to share a common theoretical perspective on how labor markets work—the neoclassical model. Adherents to the discrimination narrative are not a monolithic group. For some adherents of the discrimination narrative, their disagreement with the perfect market narrative is primarily an empirical dispute—a difference in interpretation of the unexplained portion of the gender gap in the earnings, the gap that remains after adjustment for observable productivity-related attributes. In the face of empirical findings that are inconsistent with the predictions of the neoclassical model,[15] they propose alternative assumptions and derive a new set of predictions. For example, the neoclassical model assumes perfect competition. Economist Janice Madden at the University of Pennsylvania has offered a theory (1977) that assumes that women face imperfectly competitive labor markets. If markets are not perfectly competitive, then a wage gap due to discrimination does not erode over time. The neoclassical model assumes perfect information; if information is not perfect, then a different set of outcomes are predicted. Imperfect information can lead to statistical discrimination or stereotyping (Edmund Phelps 1972; Lundberg and Startz 1983). Because information is imperfect, employers may not know that two workers are equally productive and may make judgments based on historical precedents or stereotypes. For example, faced with two recent college graduates with identical resumes, an employer's belief that a woman is more likely to shorten her tenure because of family responsibilities might reduce the attractiveness of the female candidate relative to the male candidate. Neither of these alternative models fundamentally challenge the central precepts of mainstream economic thinking, and they largely adhere to its methodological form and language. For example, a statistical discrimination model retains the core assumption of self-interested individual actors acting to maximize individual happiness in the face of institutional and resource constraints, and hence, are not radical departures from mainstream economics.

The Emergence of Feminist Economics

For others, Second-Wave Feminism prompted a broader critique of mainstream economic theory than represented by the discrimination narrative. The limitations of the mainstream model were seen not only in its inability to explain the persistence of wage discrimination but also its failure to grapple with power dynamics within the household. Bergmann, a frequent protagonist in debates about women's labor market status, also offered a scathing critique of Becker's theory of the family (1995). Marilyn Waring's *If Women Counted* (1990) criticized mainstream economics' omission of women's work in national income accounting. Second-Wave Feminism's influence in economics extended beyond creating a demand for research on women to spurring the development of fundamentally new economic theories—a feminist economics.

In the 1980s, a group of mostly women economists coalesced around an electronic listserve to disseminate and discuss research on women's economic status and to debate the efficacy of mainstream economics and the implications of the feminist theory emerging in other disciplines for the field of economics. Although the pay gap was a point of entry for many participants, there was a recognition that sophisticated explanations for the pay gap had to go beyond an analysis of employer behavior to understand household nonmarket production and decision making. There was also a strong interest in addressing the feminization of poverty both in the USA and globally.

In 1990, the opportunity for an in-person gathering came at a session at the AEA annual meeting organized by Diana Strassman, entitled "Can Feminism Find a Home in Economics?" This session provided a catalyst for the formation, 2 years later, of the International Association for Feminist Economics. The organization defines itself as "an open, diverse community of academics, activists, policy theorists, and practitioners from around the world" with a "common cause to further gender-aware and inclusive economic inquiry and policy analysis with the goal of enhancing the well-being of children, women, and men in local, national, and transnational communities" (IAFFE 2014). This mission statement creates a big umbrella that includes participants of many different ideological stripes, some who might consider themselves mainstream economists[16] and others who self-consciously identify with one of the heterodox schools of thought.

Feminist economists shared the skepticism of institutional economists and Marxian economists, critiques that preceded concern about gender inequality and about the basic mechanics of wage determination. Institutional economics posited that labor markets were not as flexible as assumed by the neoclassical model, but were governed by rules, cultural norms, and specific institutional arrangements within firms and by external barriers to competition. Marxian economics posed an alternative model in which wages are determined by the relative bargaining strength of workers and the owners of capital with a baseline set by the level of subsistence. A gender gap in wages might persist because it exploits existing social divisions to reduce the bargaining strength of workers as a group. Although these models offered explanations for the persistence of a gender wage gap, feminists argued that they were constructed with gender biases akin to those of neoclassical economics. For example, both the Becker and Marxian analyses of the family were subjected to a feminist critique (Bergmann 1995; Folbre 1982; Hartmann 1979 and 1981).

Feminist economics take a critical stance regarding the fundamental precepts and language of mainstream economics and adhere to a general set of principles. Drawing from multiple sources (Seiz 1995; Power 2010; Pujol 2013; Nelson 1995; Strober 1994), these principles of feminist economics may be summarized as follows:

- Human well-being should be the central measure of economic success with the recognition that human well-being depends upon nonmarket as well as market produced goods and services, unpriced goods and services including care, environmental quality and human agency. A purpose of economic analysis is to identify ways to improve human well-being, especially the well-being of economically marginalized groups.
- Ethical judgments are valid, inescapable and desirable parts of economic analysis. Feminist economists question not only the specific assumptions of the neoclassical model, but question why models with those assumptions were constructed. Feminist economics "questions the whole notion of objectivity and argues that what one chooses to work on and how one formulates theories and policy recommendations are dependent upon one's culture, one's position in society, and one's life experiences" (Strober 1994).
- Economists need to build richer models of behavior than homo economicus, models that "can encompass both autonomy and dependence, individuation and relation, reason and emotion, as they are manifested in economic agents of either sex" (Nelson 1995). Feminist economists reject the self-interested, autonomous economic agent as the defining feature of economic analysis.

IAFFE's journal, *Feminist Economics,* published its first issue in 1995 with Strassman as editor. The first issues contained articles that clearly defined a scope for feminist inquiry well beyond the gender pay gap: two articles offering a feminist epistemological critique of economics (Grapard 1995, Harding 1995), articles on gender in peasant economies (Deere 1995), caring labor (Folbre 1995), sexuality (Badgett 1995), childcare as a workplace (Strober 1995), family support policies in Europe (Duggan 1995), and several articles on the economics of the family (Bergmann 1995; Strober et al. 1995; Grossbard-Schectman 1995; Phipps and Burton 1995). Other issues in the first volume included a symposium on welfare reform, an article on race, class, and occupational mobility in service work (Power and Rosenberg 1995), and a feminist critique on economic efficiency (Barker 1995). The first issues included contributions from non-economists like Sandra Harding (1995) and from solidly mainstream economists like Rebecca Blank (1995).

IAFFE defined itself as inclusive of many different economic ideologies, but embedded in the principles above is a critique of mainstream economic practice. Standard economic textbooks define the purpose of economics as the study of how scarce resources get allocated among competing alternatives, not the study of ways to improve human well-being. Mainstream economists posit neoclassical theory as value-free and objective, not as laden with particular class, gender, and racial biases. Feminist economics defines a new approach to economic analysis that is still evolving, but has already provided new insights into women's economic status. For example, feminist economics has enriched the concept of work to include care labor, introduced the idea of gender-aware budgeting and policy analysis, and identified the data required to analyze how the distribution of assets among household members affects household decision making. Feminist economics is clearly one legacy of Second-Wave Feminism.

Feminist economists have been vocal participants in policy debates related to gender inequality, and they have advocated on issues that extend beyond the pay gap. Barbara Bergmann has testified about gender discrimination in pension plans and on women and social security. Heidi Hartmann has testified on parental and family leave, and the think tank that she cofounded, the Institute for Women's Policy Research, has produced policy-relevant research on topics ranging from paid sick leave to immigration and has helped to make topics such as increasing the minimum wage a women's issue. Heather Boushey, who has served as an economist for the Joint Economic Committee, testifies frequently before Congress and has authored policy-relevant research through her association with Washington, DC, think tanks—the Washington Center for Equitable Growth, the Center for American Progress, and the Economic Policy Institute. Feminist economists have been especially active on issues related to low-income women and the feminization of poverty. For example, Randy Albelda, Senior Research Fellow at the Center for Social Policy at the University of Massachusetts, Boston, has produced policy-related research to inform both state and federal policies and has testified at congressional hearings on welfare reform (Subcommittee on Twenty-first Century Competitiveness, Committee on Education and the Workforce, September 20, 2001). Nancy Folbre has not been active in giving testimony, but has been very active in communications aimed at the general public. She is a contributor to the *New York Times* Economix blog, the only economist to comment regularly on topics related to women and children. This may not seem like a large number of active participants in policy discussions, but it contrasts with the near absence of conservative economists as active commentators on these issues.

Participation in policy debates does not translate immediately into measured impact. Twenty-two states implemented comparable worth or pay equity policies, but the policy has little traction outside of state and local governments. The USA remains the only rich country without a mandated paid family leave and lags behind on other supports for working families.[17] Furthermore, it is not clear that the feminist economics perspective has been explicit in the testimony of feminist economists. E. Trzcinsk (1995), in analysis of discussion of paid family leave, argues that the terms of the debate are still framed within a neoclassical economic framework. Nevertheless, the presence of feminist economists in policy debates assures attention to critical issues that might otherwise not get voiced and offers a counterweight to the prevailing mainstream economic paradigm.

Second-Wave Feminism and Economists Who Are Feminists

Second-Wave Feminism has also had an influence through the work of economists who might not self-identify as feminist economists. Economists might be usefully arrayed along a continuum. At one end of the spectrum is an economist like June O'Neill, a frequent protagonist in congressional hearings on the status of women. O'Neill is a public proponent of the "perfect market" narrative and is regularly quoted by the Heritage Foundation. Nevertheless, O'Neill served on the Committee on the Status of Women in the Economics Profession and staffed the Council of Economic Advisors when it first acknowledged women's role in the economy. She might be categorized as a "conservative feminist." Richard Posner (1989) defines conservative feminism as "the idea that women are entitled to political, legal, social and economic equality to men, in the framework of a lightly regulated market economy."

Close to the O'Neill end of the spectrum is the 2013 president of the AEA, Claudia Goldin. Goldin, a labor economist and economic historian, is best known for her analysis of long-term trends in women's economic status. In her work on the changing labor market status of women, she challenges the populist understanding of the growth in labor force participation rates of married women as reflecting social norms, emphasizing the importance of market forces and changes in technology that decreased demand for physical strength and increased in demand for dexterity in industrial work and, more recently, technological change in the form of "the pill" that allowed women more control over reproduction. Greater control over reproduction led women to make different investments in human capital, increasing their productivity in market work that has contributed to a narrowing of the pay gap with men. Goldin is on record with a statement that discrimination has impacted women's status (Covert 2014), but she does not emphasize the role of contemporary discrimination in her work.

Between the neoclassical economists who are conservative feminists and the solidly feminist economists are two categories: economists whose work might put them on what David Colander calls the "edges" of mainstream economics, who have no public presence in the feminist economics community, but who do work that seems in alignment with feminist economic principles, and economists who use the language and methods of mainstream economics but who have a public presence in the feminist economics community (Colander 2004). An example of the first category might be George Akerlof, whose joint work with Janet Yellen on efficiency wages was cited by Julie Nelson as an example of the richer model to which feminist economics should aspire (1995), and Esther Duflo, a behavioral economist whose work on women's empowerment aligns with many ideas of feminist economists, but has been criticized in an IAFFE blog as decidedly neoclassical (Kabeer

2013). In the second category are economists like Joyce Jacobsen, a self-proclaimed "fence-sitter" (2003) with respect to feminist economics who was elected president of IAFFE in 2014, and Francine Blau, coeditor of a textbook (2013) with a feminist economic stalwart, the late Marianne A. Ferber.

Economists who do not self-identify as feminist economists and who are located closer to the neoclassical end of this spectrum are more likely to occupy positions of prestige and influence within the economics profession, to be a member of the economics faculty at a top-twenty doctoral-granting institution, or to be published in or be a member of the editorial board of the most highly ranked economics journals. Feminist economists are not well represented in these institutions[18] or in these publications.[19] Nevertheless, some of the ideas of feminist economics have infiltrated mainstream economic analysis, even if not always credited. Examples include the inclusion of women in empirical research, a general acceptance of the need to account for the value of nonmarket goods in assessing economic impacts, and a recognition that gender may influence intra-household resource allocations.

FEMINIST ECONOMICS: TIDAL WAVE OR BARELY A RIPPLE?

Economics, more so than any other discipline, is dominated by a single paradigm—neoclassical economic theory. As a challenge to that paradigm, feminist economics is likely having a bigger impact outside of economics than within as feminist economists continue to participate in policy advocacy on behalf of women's advancement.

However, Second-Wave Feminism has also had an impact within the discipline of economics. By focusing public attention on the gender gap in earnings, Second-Wave Feminism helped create demand for economic research on women. The persistence of both a racial and gender gap in earnings, publicized by the Civil Rights and women's movements, forced greater scrutiny of neoclassical economic models and ultimately to the development of alternative theories of wage determination and household behavior. These alternative models, though rarely identified as feminist, are infiltrating mainstream economic theory. Colander, Holt, and Rosser (2004) argue that the face of mainstream economics has changed. I argue that Second-Wave Feminism contributed to this change. Feminist economic thought has an influence, perhaps a stealth influence, on both the discipline of economics and on public policy to reduce gender inequality.

In terms of the theory and practice of economics, the legacy of Second-Wave Feminism is more than a ripple but less than a tidal wave.

Notes

1. The chapter does not attempt to review the contributions of feminist economic thought to economic development policy or to other gender issues outside of the USA.
2. In the King James version, Leviticus 27: 1–8, the quotation is "thy estimation shall be of the male ... fifty shekels of silver ... if it be female, then thy valuation shall be thirty shekels." That translates into a ratio of 0.60.
3. Blau, Simpson, and Anderson (1998) define an occupation as male in any year t if "$p_{it} < (P_t - 0.10)$ and female if $p_{it} > (P_t + 0.10)$, where p_{it} is the proportion that women comprise of occupational employment and P_t is the proportion that women comprise of the labor force as a whole (equal to 0.380 in 1970, 0.425 in 1980, and 0.457 in 1990). The remaining jobs are classified as integrated."
4. Until 1970, all nonwhite women were grouped into a single category. Hispanic women were classified as white.
5. Barbara A. Jones synthesizes the research on the labor force participation of black married women up to the 1990s in a special issue of the *Review of Black Political Economy* (Jones 1985–1986). Another good resource is Phyllis Wallace's book, *Black Women in the Labor Force* (1982).
6. I use the antiquated census term *household head* here to be consistent with the statistical reporting practices before 1990. If an adult, able-bodied male were a member of the household, it could, by definition, not be classified as female-headed. Harriet Presser (1998) discussed the feminist mobilization in the 1970s that led to the elimination of this concept before the 1980 US Census.
7. Becker's book, *A Treatise on the Family*, encapsulates this body of work (Becker 1993).
8. CSWEP continues to organize sessions for the annual meetings, but they are split between gender-related sessions and sessions in another field of economics.
9. After Becker, the neoclassical model recognizes the value of home production. The presumption is that women choose not to work as many hours as men because the value of the nonmarket goods exceeds the value of what they could produce in the market.
10. Jellison (1987) describes the role of academic historians in this case, but there were also two economists who testified. Both narratives offer a policy prescription to advance the social and economic status of women and achieve gender equality. Feminist economics is a big umbrella, but it is

useful to describe a continuum of economists who have produced influential work on the economic status of women. At one end of spectrum are economists who might be reasonably labeled as feminist from a social or political perspective—a commitment to advancing equality of men and women, but who adhere strongly to the neoclassical framework in their research. Economists like June O'Neill, who served on the Committee on the Status of Women in the Economics Profession and who staffed the Council of Economic Advisors when it first acknowledged women's role in the economy, might be categorized as a "conservative feminist." Richard Posner (1989) defines conservative feminism as "the idea that women are entitled to political, legal, social and economic equality to men, in the framework of a lightly regulated market economy." O'Neill has been the most frequent proponent of the "perfect market" narrative in the public arena among economists and is regularly quoted by the Heritage Institute.
11. The gender wage gap was one of several statistical observations that challenged neoclassical orthodoxy in the 1970s. The others included the racial gap in wages and "stagflation"—persistence of high rates of unemployment coupled with inflation.
12. Becker's theory of discrimination posited that discriminatory tastes on the part of white male workers might lead to occupational segregation but not to a wage inequality.
13. This point is made in Julie Matthaei's book, *An Economic History of Women in America* (1982).
14. The chief economist at the EEOC was Phyllis Wallace, an African-American woman who later became a faculty member at MIT.
15. The neoclassical model struggled to explain the racial gap in wages as well as the gender gap. Econometric studies in the 1970s routinely found evidence of a difference in the wage gap between black men and white men that could not be explained by differences in schooling and work experience, but could be partially explained by differences in occupation and industry. The "tastes" argument that had been utilized to explain occupational segregation by gender and the gender wage gap was not as persuasive when applied to two groups of men. And it was difficult to appeal to market forces to explain the wholesale exclusion of black men from industrial work in the South. Also, given the history of high labor force attachment of black women to the labor force, it was also difficult to argue that black women were less willing to invest in job training because they did not anticipate a long-term commitment to the labor market.
16. For example, Joyce Jacobsen, a member of the IAFFE board, is a self-proclaimed "fence-sitter" with respect to feminist economics (2003).

17. Feminist economists are not entirely unified on paid family leave. Bergmann (1998) argues that mandatory family leave will enshrine the gender gap in labor market status.
18. Feminist economists are sometimes located outside of the economics department. For example, Myra Strober was at Stanford in the School of Education.
19. Ferber and Nelson analyzed citation patterns for three significant books: Bergmann's *The Economic Emergence of Women* (1986); Ferber and Nelson, *Beyond Economic Man* (1993); Folbre, *Who Pays for the Kids* (1994), and found that the books are cited more outside of economics than within. Woolley's (2005) analysis of citations of the journal *Feminist Economics* also finds greater impact outside of economics. Economics citations are less than 50% of overall citation impact with the greatest impact in interdisciplinary economics.

REFERENCES

Akerlof, George A., and Janet L. Yellen (eds.). 1986. *Efficiency Wage Models of the Labor Market*. Cambridge: Cambridge University Press.

Albelda, Randy. 1995. The Impact of Feminism in Economics—Beyond the Pale? A Discussion and Survey Results. *Journal of Economic Education* 26 (3): 253–273.

American Women: Three Decades of Change, Joint Economic Committee, 98th Congress. 1983. Testimony of June O'Neill.

American Women: Three Decades of Change, Joint Economic Committee, 98th Congress. 1983. Testimony of Barbara Bergmann.

Badgett, M.V.Lee. 1995. Gender, Sexuality and Sexual Orientation: All in the Feminist Family? *Feminist Economics* 1 (1): 121–139.

Barker, Drucilla. 1995. Economists, Social Reformers, and Prophets: A Feminist Critique of Economic Efficiency. *Feminist Economics* 1 (3): 26–39.

Becker, Gary. 1957. *The Economics of Discrimination*. Chicago: University of Chicago Press.

Becker, Gary. 1993. *A Treatise on the Family*. Cambridge, MA: Harvard University Press.

Bergmann, Barbara R. 1971. The Effect on White Incomes of Discrimination in Employment. *Journal of Political Economy* 79 (2): 294–313.

Bergmann, Barbara. 1986. *The Economic Emergence of Women*. New York: Basic Books.

Bergmann, Barbara. 1995. Becker's Theory of the Family: Preposterous Conclusions. *Feminist Economics* 1 (1): 141–150.

Bergmann, Barbara. 1998. Watch out for 'Family Friendly' Policies. *Dollars & Sense*, January 1. http://dollarsandsense.org/archives/1998/0198berg.html. Accessed June 2014.

Blank, Rebecca. 1995. Teen Pregnancy: Government Programs are not the Cause. *Feminist Economics* 1 (2): 47–58.
Blau (Weiskoff), Francine. 1972. 'Women's Place' in the Labor Market. *The American Economic Review* 62 (1–2): 161–166.
Blau, Francine D., Patricia Simpson, and Deborah Anderson. 1998. Continuing Progress? Trends in Occupational Segregation in the United States over the 1970s and 1980s. *Feminist Economics* 4 (3): 29–71.
Blau, Francince D., Anne E. Winker, and Marianne Ferber. 2013. *The Economics of Women, Men, and Work*, 7th ed. Upper Saddle River, NJ: Prentice Hall.
Blinder, Alan. 1973. Wage Discrimination: Reduced Form and Structural Estimates. *Journal of Human Resources* 8 (4): 436–455.
Colander, David. 2004. The Changing Face of Mainstream Economics. *Review of Political Economy* 16 (4): 485–499.
Conrad, Cecilia. 2005. Changes in the Labor Market Status of Black Women, 1960–2000. In *African Americans in the US Economy*, ed. Cecilia Conrad, John Whitehead, Patrick Mason, and James Stewart. New York: Rowman and Littlefield.
County of Washington v. Gunther, 452 US 161 (1981).
Covert, Bruce. 2014. The Gender Gap is Ugly. So is the Right-Winged Effort to Deny it. *New Republic*, April 29. http://www.newrepublic.com/article/117550/gender-pay-gap-and-77-cents-claudia-goldin-says-its-real.
Deere, Carmen Diana. 1995. What difference Does Gender Make?: Rethinking Peasant Studies. *Feminist Economics* 1 (1): 53–72.
Dimand, Robert W. 2005. Economists and the shadow of 'The Other' Before 1914. *American Journal of Economics and Sociology* 64 (3): 820–827 (July).
Douglas, Paul H., and Erika H. Schoenberg. 1937. Studies in the supply Curve of Labor: The Relation in 1929 Between Average Earnings in American Cities and the Proportions Seeking Employment. *Journal of Political Economy* 45 (1): 45–79.
Duggan, Lynn. 1995. Restacking the Deck: Family Policy and Women's Fall-back Position in Germany before and after Reunification. *Feminist Economics* 1 (1): 175–194.
Economic Problems of Women, Part I. Hearing before the Joint Economic Committee 1973. 93rd Congress.
EEOC v. Sears, Roebuck & Co. 628 F. Supp. 1264 (N.D. Ill. 1986), aff'd, 839 F.2d 302 (7th Cir. 1988).
Feiner, Susan, Edith Kuiper, Notburga Ott, Jolande Sap, and Zafiris Tzannatos (eds.). 2013. *Out of the Margin: Feminist Perspectives on Economics*. London and New York: Routledge.
Fels, Rendig. 1972. Minutes of the Annual Meeting December 28, 1971 New Orleans, Louisiana. *American Economic Review* 62 (1–2): 470–474.
Ferber, Marianne, and Julie Nelson (eds.). 1993. *Beyond Economic Man: Feminist Theory and Economics*. Chicago: University of Chicago Press.

Ferber, Marianne, and Julie Nelson (eds.). 2003. *Feminist Economics Today: Beyond Economic Man*. Chicago: University of Chicago Press.

Figart, Deborah, and June Lapidus. 1998. Remedying 'Unfair Acts': US Pay Equity by Race and Gender. *Feminist Economics* 4 (3): 7–28.

Folbre, Nancy. 1982. Exploitation Comes Home: A Critique of the Marxian Theory of Family Labour. *Cambridge Journal of Economics* 6: 317–329.

Folbre, Nancy. 1994. *Who Pays for the Kids?* London: Routledge.

Folbre, Nancy. 1995. Holding Hands at Midnight: The Paradox of Caring Labor. *Feminist Economics* 1 (1): 73–92.

Gender Based Wage Discrimination. Senate Committee on Health, Education, Labor and Pensions. 2000. 106th Congress. Testimony of June O'Neill.

Gender Based Wage Discrimination. Senate Committee on Health, Education, Labor and Pensions. 2000. 106th Congress. Testimony of Heidi Hartmann.

Goldin, Claudia. 1977. Female Labor Force Participation: The Origin of Black and White Differences, 1870 and 1880. *The Journal of Economic History* 37 (01): 87–108.

Goldin, Claudia. 1991. The Role of World War II in the Rise of Women's Employment. *American Economic Review* 81 (4): 741–756.

Goldin, Claudia. 2006. The Quiet Revolution That Transformed Women's Employment, Education, and Family. *American Economic Review* 96 (2): 1–21.

Grapard, Ulla. 1995. Robinson Crusoe: The Quintessential Economic Man? *Feminist Economics* 1 (1): 32–52.

Grossbard-Schectman, Shoshana. 1995. Do not Sell Marriage Short: Reply to Strober. *Feminist Economics* 1 (1): 207–214.

Gunderson, Morley. 1989. Male-Female Wage Differentials and Policy Responses. *Journal of Economic Literature* 27 (1): 46–72.

Harding, Sandra. 1995. Can Feminist Thought Make Economics More Objective? *Feminist Economics* 1 (1): 7–32.

Hartmann, Heidi. 1979. The Unhappy Marriage of Marxism and Feminism: Towards a More Progressive Union. *Capital and Class* 3 (2): 1–33.

Hartmann, Heidi. 1981. The Family as the Locus of Gender, Class and Political Struggle: The Example of Housework. *Signs* 6 (3): 366–394.

International Association for Feminist Economics (IAFFE). 2014. *Mission Statement*. http://www.iaffe.org/pages/about-iaffe/miss/.

Jacobsen, Joyce. 2003. Some Implications of the Feminist Project in Economics for Empirical Methodology. In *Toward a Feminist Philosophy of Economics*, ed. Drucilla Barker and Edith Kuiper, Vol. 21. London: Routledge.

Jellsion, Katherine. 1987. History in the Courtroom: The Sears Case in Perspective. *Public Historian* 9 (4): 9–19.

Jones, Barbara A. 1985–1986. Black Women and Labor Force Participation: An Analysis of Sluggish Growth Rates. *Review of Black Political Economy* 14 (2–13): 11–31.

Kabeer, Naila. 2013. Esther Duflo on 'Women's Empowerment and Economic Development': A Must-Read for Feminist Economists. *Blogpost*, 12/19/2013. http://feministeconomicsposts.iaffe.org/2013/12/19/esther-duflo-on-womens-empowerment-and-economic-development-a-must-read-for-feminist-economists/. Accessed June 2014.

Kleiman, Carol. 1986. No Matter What You Call It, Pay Equity Is Quietly Growing. *Chicago Tribune*, August 4. http://articles.chicagotribune.com/1986-08-04/business/8602260101_1_comparable-wage-gap-francine-d-blau. Accessed June 2014.

Kreps, Juanita. 1971. *Sex in the Marketplace*. Baltimore: Johns Hopkins University Press.

Kreps, Juanita M., and Robert L. Clark (eds.). 1975. *Sex, Age, and Work: The Changing Composition of the Labor Force*. Baltimore: Johns Hopkins University Press.

Lloyd, Cynthia (ed.). 1975. *Sex, Discrimination and the Division of Labor*. New York: Columbia University Press.

Long, Clarence D. 1958. *The Labor Force under Changing Income and Employment*. Princeton, NJ: Princeton University Press.

Lundberg, Shelly, and Richard Startz. 1983. Private Discrimination and Social Intervention in Competitive Labor Markets. *American Economic Review* 73 (3): 340–347.

Madden, Janice. 1972. The Development of Economic Thought on the 'Woman Problem'. *Review of Radical Political Economics* 4: 21.

Madden, Janice Fanning. 1973. *The Economics of Sex Discrimination*. Lexington: University Press of Kentucky.

Madden, Janice. 1977. A Spatial Theory of Sex Discrimination. *Journal of Regional Science* 17 (3): 369–380.

Matthaei, Julie. 1982. *Economic History of Women in America: Women's Work, the Sexual Division of Labor, and the Development of Capitalism*. New York: Schocken.

May, Ann Mari. 2002. The Feminist Challenge to Economics. *Challenge* 45 (6): 45–69.

Mincer, Jacob. 1962. Labor Force Participation of Married Women: A Study of Labor Supply. In *Aspects of Labor Economics*, ed. H. Gregg Lewis, 63–97. Princeton, NJ: Princeton University Press.

Mincer, Jacob, and Solomon A. Polachek. 1974. Family Investments in Human Capital: Earnings of Women. *Journal of Political Economy* 82 (2): S76–S108.

Nelson, Julie. 1995. Feminism and Economics. *Journal of Economic Perspectives* 9 (2): 131–148.

Oaxaca, Ron. 1973. Male-Female Wage Differentials in Urban Labor Markets. *International Economic Review* 14 (3): 693–709.

Peterson, Janice, and Margaret Lewis. 1999. *The Elgar Companion to Feminist Economics*. Northampton, MA: Edward Elgar Publishing.

Phelps, Charlotte. 1972. Is the Household Obsolete? *American Economic Review* 62 (1–2): 167–174.
Phelps, Edmund S. 1972. The Statistical Theory of Racism and Sexism. *American Economic Review* 62 (4): 659–661.
Phipps, Shelley, and Peter Burton. 1995. Social/Institutional Variables and Behavior Within Households: An Empirical Test Using the Luxembourg Income Study. *Feminist Economics* 1 (1): 151–174.
Posner, Richard. 1989. Conservative Feminism. University of Chicago Legal Forum 191. http://chicagounbound.uchicago.edu/journal_articles/1826/. Accessed June 2014.
Power, Marilyn. 2010. Social Provisioning as a Starting Point for Feminist Economics. *Feminist Economics* 10 (3): 3–19.
Power, Marilyn, and Sam Rosenberg. 1995. Race, Class and Social Mobility: Black and White Women in Service Work in the United States. *Feminist Economics* 1 (3): 40–59.
Presser, Harriet. 1998. Decapitating the US Census Bureau's 'Head of Household': Feminist Mobilization in the 1970s. *Feminist Economics* 4 (3): 145–158.
Pujol, Michelle. 2013. Into the Margin! In *Out of the Margin: Feminist Perspectives on Economics*, ed. Susan Feiner, Edith Kuiper, Notburga Ott, Jolande Sap, and Zafiris Tzannatos. London: Routledge.
Reagan, Barbara. 1975. Report of the Committee on the Status of Women in the Economics Profession. *American Economic Review*. Papers and Proceedings of the 87th Annual Meeting of the American Economic Association (May) 65 (2): 490–501.
Reagan, Barbara. 1976. Report of the Committee on the Status of Women in the Economics Profession. *American Economic Review*. Papers and Proceedings Of The 88th Annual Meeting of the American Economic Association (May) 66 (2): 509–20.
Reagan, Barbara. 1977. Report of the Committee on the Status of Women in the Economics Profession. *American Economic Review*. Papers and Proceedings of the 88th Annual Meeting of the American Economic Association (May) 67 (1): 460–64.
Reagan, Barbara. 1978. Report of the Committee on the Status of Women in the Economics Profession. *American Economic Review*. Papers and Proceedings of the 90th Annual Meeting of the American Economic Association (May) 65 (2): 484–99.
Reskin, Barbara, and Heidi Hartmann (eds.). 1986. *Women's Work, Men's Work: Sex Segregation on the Job*. Washington, DC: National Academies Press.
Rosenberg, Rosalind. 1982. *Beyond Separate Spheres: Intellectual Roots of Modern Feminism*. New Haven, CT: Yale University Press.
Ross, Heather, and Isabel Sawhill. 1975. *A Time of Transition: The Growth of Families Headed by Women*. Washington, DC: The Urban Institute.

Sandell, Stephen. 1972. Discussion. *American Economic Review* 62 (1–2): 175–176.
Seiz, Janet A. 1995. Epistemology and the Tasks of Feminist Economics. *Feminist Economics* 1 (3): 110–118.
Smith, James P., and Michael P. Ward. 1985. Times Series Growth in the Female Labor force. *Journal of Labor Economics* 3 (1, pt. 2): S59–S90.
Strassman, Diana. 1994. Feminist Thought and Economics; Or, What Do the Visigoths Know? *American Economic Review* 84 (2): 153–158.
Strober, Myra. 1994. Rethinking Economics Through a Feminist Lens. *American Economic Review* 84 (2): 143–147.
Strober, Myra. 1995. Do Young Women Trade Jobs for Marriage: A Skeptical View. *Feminist Economics* 1 (1): 197–205.
Strober, Myra, Suzanne Gerlach-Downie, and Kenneth Yeager. 1995. Child Care Centers as Work Places. *Feminist Economics* 1 (1): 93–119.
Toner, Jerome L. 1958. Married Working Women. *Review of Social Economy* 16 (1): 44–56.
Trzcinski, Eileen. 1995. The Example of Family and Medical Leave in the United States. In *Out of the Margin: Feminist Perspectives on Economics*, ed. Edith Kuiper and Jolande Sap, 231. London: Psychology Press.
United States Government, Bureau of the Census. 1983. *Special Demographic Analyses, CDS-80-8*. American Women: Three Decades of Change. US Government Printing Office.
United States Government, Executive Office of the President, Council of Economic Advisors. 1972. *Economic Report of the President*. US Government Printing Office.
United States Government, President's Commission on the Status of Women, 1963. *American Women*. US Government Printing Office. http://www.dol.gov/wb/American%20Women%20Report.pdf. Accessed 21 June 2014.
United States Government, Bureau of the Census, Table P-40. Women's Earnings as a Percentage of Men's Earnings by Race and Hispanic Origin: 1960–2012. http://www.census.gov/hhes/www/income/data/historical/people/. Retrieved June 15, 2014.
United States Government, US Bureau of Labor Statistics. 2011 2002 1981 1961. *Employment and Earnings*. January. United States Government Printing Office.
United States Government. US Bureau of the Census. 2012. *Statistical Abstract of the United States* 131st Edition. https://www.census.gov/library/publications/2011/compendia/statab/131ed/labor-force-employment-earnings.html. Retrieved June 25, 2017.
United States Government, US Bureau of the Census. 2016. Tables P-35 and P-38. https://www.census.gov/data/tables/time-series/demo/income-poverty/historical-income-people.html. Retrieved June 25, 2017.

Wallace, Phyllis (ed.). 1976. *Equal Employment Opportunity and the AT&T Case.* Cambridge, MA: MIT Press.

Wallace, Phyllis (ed.). 1982. *Black Women in the Labor Force.* Cambridge, MA: MIT Press.

Waring, Marilyn. 1990. *If Women Counted: A New Feminist Economics.* New York: HarperCollins.

Welfare Reform: An Examination of Effects: Hearing Before the Subcommittee on 21st Century Competitiveness of the Committee on Education and the Workforce. 2001. 107th Congress, First Session (20 September). Testimony of Randy Albelda.

Whaples, Robert. 1996. Is There Consensus among American Labor Economists? Survey Results on Forty Propositions. *Journal of Labor Research* 17 (4): 725–734.

Woolley, Frances. 2005. The Citation Impact of *Feminist Economics*. *Feminist Economics* 3 (3): 85–106.

Zellner, Harriet. 1972. Discrimination against Women, Occupational Segregation and the Relative Wage. *American Economic Review* 62 (1–2): 157–160.

CHAPTER 6

The Gender Gap as a Tool for Women's Political Empowerment: The Formative Years, 1980–1984

Susan J. Carroll

Abstract Suffragists argued that women would vote differently from men and use their votes to bring about policy-related change. Nevertheless, persistent and widespread differences in the voting choices of women and men only became evident after the emergence of the contemporary women's movement. What is now referred to as the "gender gap" in voting first came to public attention following the election of President Ronald Reagan in 1980. Scholars, mostly political scientists, have conducted considerable research on the gender gap, most of it quantitative and focusing on possible explanations for the gender gap. In this chapter, Susan Carroll explores both the politics surrounding the gender gap and the deployment of the gender gap as a political tool. Organizations and activists involved in the Second Wave of the women's movement were critical in identifying and publicizing the gender gap in the early 1980s.

The original version of the book was revised: Final corrections have been incorporated. The erratum to this chapter is available at https://doi.org/10.1007/978-3-319-62117-3_11

S.J. Carroll (✉)
Rutgers University, New Brunswick, USA

© The Author(s) 2018
A. Maxwell and T. Shields (eds.), *The Legacy of Second-Wave Feminism in American Politics*, https://doi.org/10.1007/978-3-319-62117-3_6

Eventually though the gender gap became an important tool in the final push to ratify the Equal Rights Amendment and in their efforts to secure a female candidate on the Democratic presidential ticket in 1984. Similarly, the gender gap became a tool in the political right's attempts to undermine feminism in the 1980s. Forces on the right of the political spectrum argued, for example, that the gender gap was a temporary phenomenon and/or that it was not the gender gap, but rather the marriage gap, that was important. Today, the gender gap continues to play a central part of electoral strategies, no candidate can afford to ignore gender differences in support, and women are successfully elected to state and national offices. In addition to improving equality, the gender gap clearly remains one of the important legacies of Second-Wave Feminism.

The authors of a widely read 312-page textbook on public opinion, published in 1980, devoted just two paragraphs and one table to a discussion of "Sex and Political Opinions," arguing: "Differences in the political attitudes of men and women are so slight that they deserve only brief mention .... In political attitudes and voting, people are seldom different because of their sex."[1] The authors did acknowledge the existence of a few differences between women and men on political issues, with women reacting "to some political issues in what might be called a more 'tender minded' fashion than men" and showing on social issues "what apparently is a more 'puritanical' streak." Nevertheless, they concluded, "Even these differences ... can hardly be called significant."[2]

A few years—even a few months—later, this description of gender differences seemed as antiquated as the pony express. With the discovery of the so-called gender gap in voting in the aftermath of the 1980 elections, the way that politicians, activists, the press, the populace, and even political scientists viewed gender differences changed quite dramatically in response to an altered political landscape. The women's movement worked to keep the gender gap in the public eye and to use it strategically to further movement goals. Political leaders and candidates for office had to figure out how to deal with the gender gap whether by embracing it, downplaying its significance, or addressing the gap symbolically even if not substantively. Soon after its discovery, ignoring the gender gap became a nonviable political option.

Political scientists and other scholars have devoted considerable attention to analyzing the possible causal factors and dynamics underlying the gender gap. Consequently, a vast literature focusing on explanations for the gender gap, based mostly on statistical analysis of survey data, now exists.[3] Nevertheless, the politics surrounding the gender gap has remained largely uninvestigated.[4] As a result, we lack an understanding of the political consequences of one of the major changes to have occurred in the electoral environment since the New Deal realignment of the 1940s.

This essay begins to fill this gap by focusing on the political strategies surrounding the gender gap and its deployment as a political tool in its earliest years, 1980–1984. The gender gap is clearly one of the important legacies of so-called Second-Wave Feminism, and this chapter highlights its relationship to the organized feminist movement of that era. I investigate the origins of the gender gap, the struggle over its political meaning and consequences, and the strategies deployed by both the feminist political community and the Reagan White House and reelection campaign as they attempted to take advantage of and counter, respectively, the gender gap in the early 1980s. Organizations and activists involved in the women's movement were critical in identifying and publicizing the gender gap, and the gender gap became a critical tool in both their last-ditch effort to ratify the Equal Rights Amendment and their campaign to have a woman added to the Democratic presidential ticket in 1984. As a result of feminist efforts to publicize the gender gap and utilize it to advance their agenda, political parties, the presidential administration, and presidential candidates were forced to develop strategies to respond to the gender gap in their attempts to win elections in the early 1980s.

METHODS

In examining the gender gap during its early years, I rely on an exhaustive examination of articles published in the *Washington Post* and the *New York Times*. Using the ProQuest Historical Newspapers archives for both the *Washington Post* and the *New York Times*, I searched for and examined all articles and editorials from November 1980 to December 1984 that included the words "gender gap" and either "election" or "politics." As Fig. 6.1 shows, in every year the gender gap received more coverage in the *Washington Post* than the *New York Times* with a total of 169 articles in the *Post* and 113 in the *Times*. Nevertheless, similar trends in coverage are evident. There was little to no coverage in 1980 and 1981. The number of articles and editorials on the gender gap increased heading into the 1982 midterm elections and picked up considerably in the aftermath of those elections.

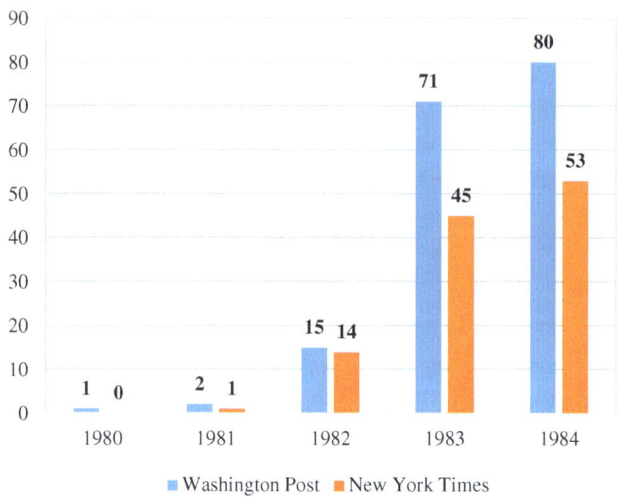

Fig. 6.1 Number of Gender Gap Articles Published by Year, 1980–1984

Coverage more than tripled in the *New York Times* and more than quadrupled in the *Washington Post* from 1982 to 1983 (Fig. 6.1). Coverage increased again in 1984, a presidential election year, but only slightly over the 1983 figures. For this chapter, I also draw upon other newspaper stories, magazine articles, and available documents, many of which I personally collected as a scholar at the Center for American Women and Politics who has frequently been called upon to speak about or comment on the gender gap.

The Gender Gap: Definition and Origins

The "gender gap" has been defined and measured in different ways over the years, sometimes as a deliberate strategy to maximize or minimize the apparent size of the gender difference and sometimes as a result of imprecision on the part of journalists or activists. In this chapter, the gender gap will be defined as the difference between the proportion of women and the proportion of men who support a particular politician, party, or policy position. This definition is consistent with the way the term was used when it first came into existence in the early 1980s.

With regard to the gender gap in presidential voting, in every presidential election since 1980, differences have been apparent in the proportions of women and men who voted for the winning candidate, ranging from a low of 4 percentage points in 1992 to a high of 11 percentage points in 1996. In each of these elections, women have been more likely than men to support the Democratic candidate.[5]

There can be little doubt that the National Organization for Women (NOW) and its campaign to have the Equal Rights Amendment (ERA) added to the Constitution of the United States were critical to the recognition of the gender gap in the early 1980s and the initial attention it received. As Anne N. Costain's work makes clear, women's groups largely emphasized sameness and equality of women and men in lobbying for legislation on the status of women throughout the late 1960s and early 1970s. Special interest arguments were not in fashion. For the Washington-based feminists of this era, Costain argues, "Gender difference was considered reformist and old-fashioned."[6] Nevertheless, by the late 1970s, with ERA ratification faltering and evidence mounting that equality-based legislation might not be sufficient to end discrimination, feminists began to question the effectiveness of an equality-based approach, and congressional action shifted more toward treating women as a special interest group with distinctive needs. This shift in feminist thinking helped create a climate receptive to the idea of an electoral gender gap. Costain argues, "it appears to have been necessary for leaders of women's organizations to accept and articulate the idea that women are politically different from men before a sustained [gender] gap was likely to emerge and be recognized."[7]

Occasional glimpses of gender differences in candidate preferences had been evident in presidential elections prior to 1980, with public opinion polls showing women more likely than men to support Dwight Eisenhower in the 1950s and less likely than men to support George Wallace in 1968, for example. However, there was no organization or movement at these times poised to recognize, publicize, and politically exploit these differences. In 1980, the situation was very different. The NOW, under the leadership of its president, Ellie Smeal, was spearheading the effort to have the ERA ratified by the requisite thirty-eight states before the extended ratification deadline of June 30, 1982. Kathy Bonk, who in 1981–82 coordinated the national media campaign for the ERA Countdown Campaign, credits Smeal with being the first person to publicly draw attention to the gender difference that appeared in exit poll data from the 1980 presidential race.[8] According to Bonk, Smeal noticed an important difference in the voting patterns of women and men in a table accompanying a *New York Times* analysis of election results written by Adam Clymer. While women had split their votes 46% for Ronald Reagan and 45% for Jimmy Carter according to the *New York Times*/CBS News Poll, men had cast 54% of their votes for Reagan, resulting in an 8 percentage-point difference between women and men.[9] Smeal and her NOW colleagues did not call this a "gender gap" but rather drafted a piece for the NOW newsletter with the headline, "Women Vote Differently Than Men, Feminist Bloc Emerges in 1980 Elections." This article, in edited form, also appeared on the editorial pages of the *Chicago Sun Times* and the *Chicago Tribune* under Smeal's byline. As Bonk explains, the real target audience for these editorials was Illinois state legislators who would be voting to ratify the ERA in the coming months.[10]

While Smeal and NOW were determined to use the gender differences apparent in the 1980 exit poll result to their political advantage, the exit poll was not the first poll to show gender differences in candidate preferences and Smeal was not the very first to take note of them. In the weeks leading up to Election Day, the presidential campaigns began to appeal explicitly to women voters in a way not characteristic of previous presidential campaigns. Presumably the campaigns were responding to gender differences which they were seeing in their own internal polling. Regardless, candidates and reporters were aware that gender differences in presidential preferences were part of the dynamic of the 1980 race before any voting actually took place. As early as January 1980, Leslie Bennetts observed in an article in the *New York Times*, "As the Presidential campaigns took shape in the fall, several contenders, including President Carter, gave early priority to the so-called women's vote." Despite the presidential candidates' attention to women, two political scientists that Bennetts interviewed insisted that women do not vote as a bloc, and even Ellie Smeal talked about the possibility of a "feminist vote" by both men and women rather than a women's vote. However, the final political scientist interviewed, Marjorie Lansing, proved prescient, arguing that a women's vote would become evident in the 1980s "because the effect of 10 years of the women's movement has been to educate women about what their needs are—and those needs are best resolved through the ballot box."[11]

Although scientific opinion polls had their origins in the mid-1930s and exit polling came into existence in the 1960s, fewer public opinion polls were conducted in 1980 than we have become accustomed to during elections in the twenty-first century. Nevertheless, polls conducted by both the *Washington Post* and the *New York Times* released shortly before Election Day revealed gender differences that were noted by reporters. For example, a national *New York Times*/CBS News poll showed Reagan with an 11-point advantage among men while Carter held an 8-point lead among women.[12] Similarly, a poll of voters in eight key states conducted by the *Washington Post* in October found that Reagan had a 5-point lead among men while Carter enjoyed a 7-point advantage among women. Betty Heitman, co-chair of the Republican National Committee and president of the National Federation of Republican Women, offered two explanations for these gender differences in candidate preferences. First, according to Heitman, "The message out of the convention was that the Republican Party had repudiated the ERA because the governor did not support it. A lot of women view the ERA as a symbol and felt that it was a put-down of women." As a second factor, she pointed to Carter's success "in painting Gov. Reagan as trigger-happy and a warmonger," which scared many women voters.[13]

In response to gender differences like these in polling results, Ronald Reagan in mid-October 1980 pledged to appoint a woman to one of the first Supreme Court vacancies that occurred during his administration. In addition, presenting himself as a man of peace who would use armed force only as a last resort, Reagan claimed that his lack of support among women was due not to his opposition to the Equal Rights Amendment, but rather to "the false charges made by the president and others that I might be prone to turn to war."[14]

Feminist and progressive columnists derided the actions and statements of Reagan, accusing him of political pandering. Richard Cohen noted how the first woman justice would have to be anti-abortion, opposed to the ERA, in favor of women staying at home, and a nonbeliever in evolution.[15] Judy Mann observed that "It's less than three weeks until Election Day and Ronald Reagan has discovered women," referring to him as a "born-again feminist."[16] Ellen Goodman mocked the "wooing" of women by both presidential candidates: "There was Ronnie last week down on bended knee" suggesting "If we would only say 'yes' this November, he would give us our very own Supreme Court justice." And then "Jimmy came a-wooing after years of taking us for granted.

Land's sake, if he hadn't been paying enough attention to our little old Equal Rights Amendment, he would fix all that."[17]

Even if Ellie Smeal and the National Organization for Women were not the first to take notice of gender differences in the 1980 elections, nevertheless they do seem responsible for the name that is most commonly used in referring to these differences—a name that has endured for decades. The actual term *gender gap* appears to have come about with little forethought. According to Bonk's account, it was first used when in 1981 NOW staffers were preparing a chart of poll results for a meeting of the Democratic National Committee and needed a way to highlight the differences between women and men in Reagan's approval ratings. They labeled the column heading for these differences "Gender Gap."[18] The chart was then included in a booklet issued by NOW called *Women Can Make the Difference*.[19]

Judy Mann picked up on the term gender gap and repeated it in a column in the *Washington Post* on October 16, 1981, as she reported on this pamphlet and NOW's intent to use its findings in the final push for ERA ratification. This appears to have been the first usage of the term in print media. Mann observed:

> The pamphlet is a stunning compilation of major polls .... While bits and pieces of the polls received some attention at the time they were done, they take on much more significance when they are massed together and examined chronologically: The inescapable conclusion from the total package is that there is a growing women's vote that could have major repercussions in the next election.[20]

NOW's findings on the gender gap became an important tool over the next few months as NOW waged the last stages of its campaign to win ratification of the ERA before the June 1981 deadline. As Ellie Smeal explained:

> Throughout 1981–82, ERA campaign media director Kathy Bonk and I discussed NOW's findings again and again with the press. We regularly updated the gender gap information and provided it to reporters throughout the country. During this same period, we also supplied polling data to political leaders.[21]

Thus, the gender differences in voting and public opinion apparent in the early 1980s emerged in a very different political environment than any gender differences that may have been statistically apparent in the 1950s or 1960s. One change was that women were voting at higher rates than they had in the past. Women voted at lower rates than men following the achievement of suffrage in 1920, but they gradually and incrementally caught up. In 1964 for the first time the number of women who voted outnumbered the men who voted, and in 1980 women's rate of voter turnout finally matched, and even slightly surpassed, men's turnout rate.[22]

The fact that increased numbers of women were voting enhanced their potential political clout. However, the major difference in the political environment between the 1950s and 1960s and 1980 was the existence of a vital women's movement. As Ruth Mandel explained in a 1982 article in *Working Woman*, "The last 15 years of feminism may have taught women to see their own deeply held values in practical political terms, to translate their issues into the world of real politics (parties, candidates, platforms), and to be more outspoken about their political judgments."[23] An especially critical feature of the altered political environment was the existence of an organization within the women's movement, engaged at the time in a historical struggle over the Equal Rights Amendment, which not only took note of the existence of gender differences but also attempted to publicize and use these differences to promote its own political agenda.

Ellie Smeal went so far as to suggest, "without the existence of a major movement for women's rights, there would be *no* gender gap in voting."[24] While on the surface this may seem a contestable assertion, far less contestable is the contention that without a major movement for women's rights, gender differences in voting may have gone unnoticed and certainly would have received far less public attention. For this reason, even if for no other, Smeal's claim seems to have some validity. For while there was an observable gender difference in votes for Reagan in 1980 and his presidential approval ratings in the aftermath of that election, the "gender gap" was a construction that gave political meaning to what otherwise was simply a statistical polling observation. The construction of the gender gap gave potential political power to women voters that they otherwise would not have had, and also led to battles over the interpretation and significance of the gap, as well as over strategies for dealing with it, that have continued for more than three decades.

THE WOMEN'S MOVEMENT ADVOCATES FOR THE ERA AND FERRARO

The ERA was a major political initiative of the Second-Wave women's movement. If the timing had been right, no doubt feminists would have used the gender gap as a weapon in their effort to ratify the amendment, arguing that women would vote to defeat anti-ERA legislators. However, the extension of the deadline for ratification of the ERA passed on June 30, 1982, more than four months before the first major election following the "discovery" of the gender gap in the 1980 election data. Thus, even if the gender gap could have been used as a tool for electing legislators who would vote for the amendment in unratified states, the timing was simply too late. However, NOW and other pro-ERA forces continued to work through the summer and fall of 1982 to send a message to legislators in unratified states and beyond by targeting particular races. According to NOW, women doubled their numbers in the Florida and Illinois senates, with eight of the nine senators in Florida and seven of the eight in Illinois supporters of the ERA. All four of the congressional candidates NOW endorsed in North Carolina won as well.[25]

The electoral successes claimed by pro-ERA forces in the 1982 elections as well as uncertainty about the extent to which the ERA and other women's issues were responsible for the appearance of the gender gap helped set the stage for the reintroduction of the ERA into Congress in January 1983. It was the first order of business for the new Congress, introduced as HJ Res1, with a majority of House members as cosponsors. However, the momentum behind the ERA was short-lived as the legislation failed in mid-November by six votes to achieve the two-thirds majority needed to pass a constitutional amendment. It was brought to the floor for a vote under suspension of the rules that severely limited debate and allowed for no amendments to the legislation. Although proponents generally favored this political maneuver because it meant opponents could not attach crippling amendments, it gave members of Congress who opposed the ERA a convenient excuse. They could claim that they voted "no" not because of the substance of the amendment, but rather because of the irregular procedure.[26]

Although the ERA appeared roadblocked, the gender gap still held considerable promise as a political tool for women's movement leaders to use in promoting feminist objectives. This was particularly true in the aftermath of the 1982 elections where the gender gap was evident across a large number of races and seemingly decisive in several. Adam Clymer of the *New York Times* reported that "in 73 of the 85 Election Day polls the three television networks conducted among voters who had just cast ballots in statewide races, women voted for Democrats more than men did." Moreover, "losses among women appear to have cost them [Republicans]" the governorships of "New York and Texas, and perhaps Michigan and Connecticut, as well."[27] Moreover, in some close contests won by Republicans, polls showed that women voters actually preferred the Democratic candidate.[28]

Both before and after the 1982 elections, the women's movement focused attention on sustaining the gender gap and enhancing the influence of women voters. Women's organizations held "gender gap conferences," such as the one sponsored by the League of Women Voters Education Fund in June 1983 in Washington, DC, where academic experts, political women, and leaders of major women's organizations came together to learn from existing research, examine the effects of coalition and organizational efforts to mobilize the women's vote in the 1982 elections, and discuss strategies for the 1984 elections. Leaders of women's organizations also began to strategize among themselves. In the summer of 1982, a number of leaders of women's organizations, academics, politicians, and feminist activists gathered at the Vermont home of Frances and Norman Lear to discuss how to advance women in the political process. One offshoot of this informal meeting was the creation of the Women's Roundtable, consisting of representatives of several women's organizations, which met in September to develop a public relations campaign to encourage women to vote in the 1982 elections. Following these elections, the Roundtable established a Women's Vote Project aimed at increasing the registration and turnout of women voters for subsequent elections. By the time of the 1984 elections, the Women's Vote Project had seventy-six member organizations and had registered 1.8 million women to vote.[29]

With the ERA derailed, feminist leaders soon found another cause they could rally around as they headed into the 1984 elections—the idea of a woman on the ticket, perhaps even at the head of ticket. Multiple conversations about the possibility of a woman on the ticket began to take place within the Washington-based women's political community, including among the women who had met in Vermont and organization leaders involved in the Women's Vote Project. As Evans Witt explained in a lengthy Associated Press story published just after Ferraro was selected as Mondale's running mate in July 1984, Ferraro's selection was "the culmination of a movement, an orchestrated effort that began in the political backrooms of Washington in early 1983."[30] Initially the hope was to pave the way for one or more women to run for president in the 1988 elections. Few activists or observers thought that a woman would or could be on the ticket in 1984. But over the course of discussions among feminist activists and organizational leaders, the idea emerged to push for the selection of a woman as a vice-presidential candidate in 1984 as "an attention-getting device" to build on the momentum generated by the gender gap and "keep women's issues on the front burner of American politics and that meant the front pages of the newspapers and on the evening TV news shows."[31]

The idea of a woman on the ticket as a vice-presidential nominee picked up steam in the fall of 1983. At a conference on the gender gap sponsored by the Democratic National Committee in late September, two women lieutenant governors, Marlene Johnson of Minnesota and Martha Griffiths of Michigan, advocated for the selection of a woman vice-presidential nominee as a way to help win women's votes and ensure a Democratic victory in 1984.[32] Shortly thereafter, Democratic National Committee vice chairman Lynn Cutler and Senator Ted Kennedy publicly endorsed the idea.[33] And in early October six Democratic presidential candidates, eager to capitalize on the gender gap, appeared before the annual convention of the National Organization for Women and pledged that they would consider a woman as their running mate.[34]

The idea of a woman as the Democratic vice-presidential candidate was clearly a matter of public discussion and debate by early 1984. A March article in the *New York Times* focused on this subject, proclaiming that:

> Feminist groups around the country have taken up the call for a woman on the national ticket. And the men who dominate the party's structure, looking at national polls showing President Reagan's popularity with women is relatively low and at the growing number of women voters, seem intrigued by the notion.[35]

The eight male Democratic candidates were repeatedly asked in the first few months of 1984 if they would pledge to choose a woman as a running mate. Only Jesse Jackson, the sole black contender who was considered by most observers to have little chance of winning the nomination, agreed to do so although others replied that they would consider women for the position. Several women were mentioned as possible nominees, including Maryland Senator Barbara Mikulski, Kentucky Governor Martha Lane Collins, Louisiana Representative Lindy Boggs, Colorado Representative Patricia Schroeder, San Francisco Mayor Dianne Feinstein, and New York Representative Geraldine Ferraro. All the women mentioned as serious possibilities in press coverage were white even though a number of black women were equally prominent and well positioned.[36] In spite of the fact that a black man was one of the contenders for the Democratic presidential nomination, the idea of a woman of color on the ticket was apparently a bridge too far.

Feminist leaders based their argument for a woman vice-presidential candidate on two claims: one factual and the other hypothetical. The factual claim was that women constituted a majority of the voting electorate and that a candidate who overlooked their potential political clout risked electoral peril. For the first time since receiving the franchise in 1920 women, who constitute a majority of the general population, turned out to vote at a higher rate than men in 1980; 5.5 million more women than men reported voting in that election according to the US Bureau of the Census.[37] A report that NOW prepared for the Democratic Party in early 1984 argued, "With 6 million more women than men expected to vote in 1984, the idea of a woman on the presidential ticket has become a matter for serious consideration."[38]

The second argument made by feminist activists in favor of a woman vice-presidential candidate—that a woman candidate would attract more women voters to the ticket and perhaps propel a Democratic presidential candidate to victory—was more debatable. Because there had never been a woman on either party's ticket, no one really knew what the actual impact, if any, would be on the party's election prospects. As the idea of naming a woman as the vice-presidential nominee circulated publicly, various polling firms asked questions designed to measure the effect on possible presidential voting choices of adding a woman to the ticket. Results varied markedly. Several polls showed voters in favor of the general idea of naming a woman to the ticket,[39] and some pollsters suggested that a woman on the Democratic ticket would attract voters, especially women voters. However, other polling experts expressed skepticism based on their findings. Perhaps most notably the findings of a study commissioned by the National Women's Political Caucus

(NWPC), one of the leading women's political organizations, and conducted by the polling firm Yankelovich, Skelly & White, Inc. suggested that adding a woman to the ticket might not make a difference. The study found that a woman's issue stances and her experience weighed more heavily than the simple fact of being a woman. Florence R. Skelly, president of the polling firm, concluded that "this study shows they can't just name any woman to that ticket and have it work… Even with sisterhood and the gender gap, you can't automatically attract women's votes with a woman candidate."[40] Some prominent feminists, perhaps most notably NOW founder Betty Friedan, were skeptical as well. As Friedan told a *New York Times* reporter, "A lot of women would not vote for a woman just because she is a woman … . I've never thought a woman Vice President was the most important issue."[41]

Nevertheless, given contradictory polling evidence and no real-world precedent, most feminist leaders pressed forward with the argument that the selection of a woman as the vice-presidential nominee would attract support for the Democratic ticket and help defeat Ronald Reagan. They made this argument both before and after Mondale selected Ferraro as his running mate. Kathy Wilson, the Republican president of the NWPC, said of the Mondale–Ferraro ticket:

> This team has the ability to electrify the electorate …. The people who would be repelled by having a woman on the ticket would be in the Reagan camp anyway. [With his selection of Ferraro] Mondale has said you're going to be included, you're going to participate, you're going to help set this nation's agenda. I think that's exciting. It's incredibly motivating.[42]

Judy Goldsmith, president of NOW, claimed that the selection of a woman vice-presidential candidate was the single factor most likely to lead to Reagan's defeat.[43] Even Ferraro herself joined in, claiming, "I don't think Archie Bunker would ever vote for me …. But I bet Edith would."[44]

While this public campaign for a woman on the ticket was taking place, a more private campaign on behalf of Geraldine Ferraro was also taking place behind the scenes. A group of seven savvy Washington insiders, who had many years of experience and were well connected in both Democratic and feminist political circles, had reviewed the credentials of the women who might be vice-presidential candidates and had decided upon Ferraro. This group, known as Team A, met with Ferraro and convinced her to consider the idea and then set about maneuvering to help position her as the ideal choice. For example, in order to increase her visibility, they worked to have her selected to head the Platform Committee at the Democratic National Convention.

The two major women's political organizations, NOW and NWPC, had never endorsed a presidential candidate. However, in December 1983 NOW took the unprecedented step of endorsing Walter Mondale for the Democratic nomination and the presidency. The multipartisan NWPC did not follow suit. NOW president Judy Goldsmith campaigned for Mondale during the final weeks of the primary campaign season and was invited to a private meeting with him to discuss his possible choices for a vice-presidential candidate.[45] By early summer Mondale, who had amassed a sufficient number of delegates to become the Democratic nominee, began to interview prospective running mates. Dianne Feinstein, Martha Lane Collins, and Geraldine Ferraro were among those invited to meet with Mondale in Minnesota. In early July, Mondale spoke at NOW's annual conference, acknowledging that he was considering naming a woman to the ticket but refusing to commit himself to choosing a woman. The next day the NOW conference passed a resolution calling for the nomination of a woman for the vice presidency from the floor of the Democratic convention if necessary, thereby threatening to stage a floor fight if Mondale did not choose a woman as his running mate.[46]

Mondale was under pressure to name a woman not only from NOW and feminist activists, but also from a growing host of Democratic officeholders, including House Speaker Tip O'Neill, who was a strong advocate for Ferraro. Mondale also was badly trailing incumbent President Reagan in the polls; for example, a Gallup Poll taken in late June showed Reagan with a 19-point lead among registered voters.[47] Many observers at the time believed that Reagan's sizable lead factored strongly in Mondale's decision to make a historic and unprecedented choice. On July 12, 1984, Walter Mondale announced his selection of Geraldine Ferraro as his vice-presidential running mate.[48]

GOP and White House Responses to the Gender Gap

The efforts of Second-Wave feminists to use the gender gap to their political advantage were mirrored by attempts by the Republican Party, which controlled the White House in the early 1980s, to minimize any negative effects the gender gap might have on its electoral fortunes. Between the 1980 and 1984 elections, the White House and the Republican Party faced considerable pressure to respond to the gender gap in voting and the lower levels of support Reagan received from women than men. Reagan's presidential approval rating declined over the first two years in office, and polls continued to show that women were less likely than men to favorably evaluate his performance. The pressure to counteract the gender gap grew following the 1982 midterm elections when the Democrats, propelled in many cases by strong support from women, made major gains in congressional seats.

The response of the Republican White House and the Republican Party more generally to the gender gap was multilayered. On the one hand, considerable evidence suggests that the White House was concerned about the gender gap and that at least some of the White House staff and Reagan aides were well informed about its underlying causes and dynamics. On the other hand, public attempts both by Reagan and Republican leaders to deal with the gender gap were often contrary to that information and largely symbolic, rather than substantive, in nature. Even when the responses to the gender gap were rhetorically substantive, follow-through was usually lacking.

In an internal White House memo dated November 5, 1982, three days after the general election, Ronald H. Hinckley, a poll analyst in the Office of Planning and Evaluation, presented an in-depth analysis of the gender gap based on more than 20,000 interviews conducted for the Republican National Committee in the previous year, US Census data, and published research. Hinckley concluded that "New, bold, and creative ideas are necessary to deal with the gender gap." While in some instances "communicating what has actually happened (e.g., inflation) will be more important than developing a new policy or program;" Hinckley recognized that in others "far ranging and far reaching policies will have to be developed." In sum, Hinckley concluded the gender gap "indicates serious issues with which this administration should deal."[49] The fourteen-page memo was distributed to the White House Coordinating Council on Women and "Working Group" members with a cover suggesting it was "to reinforce much of what we heard today in the Roosevelt Room." The existence of this detailed memo and analysis suggests that there certainly were people in the White House who were well informed about the underlying dynamics of the gender gap.

In addition, Reagan's pollster, Richard Wirthlin, was reputed to have a sophisticated understanding of the gender gap and women voters. He supposedly divided women voters into sixty-four different subcategories and targeted ads at the groups he identified as most persuadable.[50]

Even President Reagan himself showed occasional signs that he understood some aspects of the situation. When asked what was causing the gender gap by *US News and World Report*, he responded: "I have a hunch that part of it's been inspired by the ERA movement. I had very few opportunities to talk with some of those people. My belief that a constitutional amendment was not the best solution to the problem—they translated that into prejudice against women."[51]

The White House and the Republican Party took what appeared to be serious steps to examine and engage the gender gap. While feminists frequently criticized the White House for cutting federal programs that provided economic assistance to women and weakening the enforcement of antidiscrimination laws, the Reagan administration did back other legislation aimed at improving women's economic status. Seemingly in response to the gender gap, the Reagan administration supported congressional legislation providing tax credits for child care, individual retirement accounts (IRAs) for homemakers, stronger enforcement of child-support payments, and pension reform to help wives collect under their husband's policies. Sonia Landau, national chairman in 1984 of Women for Reagan–Bush, noted that additionally, "The President has changed tax laws that penalized married couples, improved the estate taxes so survivors, who often are the wives, are not stripped of all possessions."[52] In 1983 the White House created the Working Group on Women under deputy chief of staff Michael Deaver's supervision. Elizabeth Dole, who was put in charge of publicizing the administration's efforts to improve the status of women, explained, "This was the first time we'd had a lot of assistants to the president working on women's issues—child care, dependent care, issues like enforcement of child-support laws."[53] The Republican Party sponsored a major conference on the gender gap in June 1983 aimed at mobilizing women to help Republicans overcome the Democratic advantage with women voters. Vice President George H. W. Bush was sent out to speak to groups such as the General Federation of Women's Clubs and the National Forum for Women State Legislators, sponsored by the Center for American Women and Politics.

However, these steps did not appease feminist critics. In the words of Bella Abzug, for example, "the White House reaction to the gender gap was a farcical mixture of alarm, denials, reshuffling of female advisers, token gestures, cosmetic cover-ups, foot-in-mouth statements from Reagan, and a stonewall refusal to change any of the substantive policies and actions to which women were objecting."[54] While Abzug's characterization is certainly exaggerated, White House and Republican Party operatives did perhaps more often attempt to deal with the appearance than the reality behind the gender gap.

Research on the gender gap conducted by scholars and others in the early 1980s echoed the findings of the Hinckley analysis—that the causes of the gender gap were substantive and that the gender gap was rooted in differences in policy preferences. Most analysts concluded that the ERA and abortion were not the key issues underlying the gender gap, in part because women and men held similar views on these issues, although research showed that women might give more weight to these issues than men in their voting calculus.[55] Rather, most analysts concurred that issues of war and peace, especially in 1980, and economic policies, especially in 1982, were critical to explaining and thus counteracting the gender gap.[56] In contrast to the 1976 presidential campaign, where most positions taken by the Republican and Democratic candidates were not starkly different, the 1980 presidential campaign presented voters with clear alternatives. Reagan offered policy proposals that contrasted sharply with the policies of then incumbent President Jimmy Carter. Reagan promised to cut back on the size of the federal government, greatly reduce government spending, increase the strength of the US military, and get tough with the Soviet Union. Only when offered such clear-cut alternatives did differences in preferences between women and men become apparent. Differences between women and men on issues of military involvement had long been evident in public opinion research, and men were drawn, much more than women, to Reagan's hawkish positions. Similarly, women were much more likely than men to be both the recipients of the benefits provided by government social service programs and the professionals employed by them; Reagan was committed to reducing the size and role of the federal government, particularly the welfare state.

To the extent these policy differences lay at the heart of the gender gap, the Reagan administration was predictably reluctant to reverse its policy positions in order to attract the votes of more women.

Instead, the Reagan administration and the Republican Party looked for other ways to try to address the gender gap. The major strategies they seemed to follow were showcasing women in high-visibility positions, denial and displacement onto other subgroups, and emphasizing lack of adequate communication and understanding of their policies.

As noted earlier, Reagan during the 1980 presidential campaign pledged to appoint a woman to the Supreme Court, and when the first vacancy occurred in 1981, he followed through on his promise by nominating Sandra Day O'Connor. Although feminist leaders continued to express disappointment that his other appointments to the federal judiciary included few women, the choice of O'Connor seems to have been an obvious response to the gender gap. So too may have been Reagan's appointment in 1981 of Jeane Kirkpatrick as his ambassador to the United Nations although Kirkpatrick was the only woman to receive a cabinet-level appointment in the first two years of the administration. As David Broder noted in March 1981, "Sub-cabinet and senior White House staff jobs for women have been as scarce as—you should forgive the phrase—hens' teeth."[57]

Following the trouncing Republicans received in the 1982 congressional elections and evidence from statewide exit polls that suggested the widespread appearance of gender gaps in statewide races across the country, Reagan made two more high-visibility appointments of women, both moderates and both to positions in his cabinet. Elizabeth Dole was chosen as Secretary of Transportation, and shortly thereafter Margaret Heckler was picked to head the Department of Health and Human Services. Although Dole dismissed as "ridiculous" the idea that the appointment of the two women was politically motivated, feminists and even White House officials were more convinced that these appointments were driven by political considerations. As Juan Williams reported, "The president is seeking to neutralize this 'gender gap' by including women in the upper reaches of his administration, according to White House aides."[58] The Reagan administration apparently hoped that these appointments would show that Reagan was committed to the advancement of women and that the support of these highly visible women would somehow lead to greater support among women voters.

In addition to the strategy of showcasing women, the Reagan administration and Republican Party leaders engaged in the strategy of denial and displacement. They either flat out denied that the gender gap was a problem, or suggested that it was limited to a few subgroups of women, or claimed that the gender gap was really a problem that the Democratic Party has with men. As an example of outright denial, Dee Jepsen, the president's liaison to women's groups, called the gender gap "overrated." According to Jepsen, "You see a lot of figures .... The gap is a myth."[59] Shortly after assuming the position of chair of the Republican National Committee in 1983, Frank J. Fahrenkopf expressed his view on the gender gap, one that combined denial and displacement, suggesting "it was a mistake to say that President Reagan 'has trouble with women.'" Rather, the problem is really "concentrated among those between 21 and 40, working women and single heads of families."[60] Phyllis Schlafly also denied and displaced, claiming that the gender gap is really "a code word for the gay gap."[61] Unnamed White House officials who assessed the gender gap problem concluded that only a very small part was due to the president's policies; rather, most of the gender gap is "attributable to intransigent opposition to all Republican candidates from Jewish women, black women, and feminists."[62] Finally, White House representatives tried to take the pressure off themselves by claiming that the gender gap was really a problem for the Democrats, not the Republicans. One official who stressed that Reagan was taking the male vote away from the Democratic Party explained, "We'd like to shift the public debate from the Republican gender gap to the Democratic gender gap."[63] Senator Paula Hawkins, the lone Republican woman senator at the time, claimed the "gender gap is really caused by men going over to Republican candidates" and asserted, "I don't believe the Republican party does have a problem with women voters."[64]

As a third strategy for dealing with the gender gap, the Reagan White House and the Republican Party placed the blame on inadequate communication about Reagan's policies and/or the failure of women to appreciate his policy successes. As David Hoffman reported in 1983, "the White House has maintained that the problem is one of image or perception rather than any fault in the president's basic policies." Hoffman quoted White House spokesperson Larry Speakes as suggesting, "I think we have to articulate the agenda. There is a misconception of what we are trying to do."[65] Similarly, shortly after the 1982 election, Richard Wirthlin, the president's pollster, told a meeting of Republican governors that the gender gap was caused largely by women who gave Reagan less credit than men did for reducing inflation and that the gap would diminish when women came around to recognize the administration's success in doing so.[66] Wirtlin's view seemed to reflect a commonly shared perspective on the part of Republicans heading into the 1984 election. They believed that women voters had been slow to appreciate the strength of the economic recovery, and once they did, any problem with the gender gap or women voters would disappear. As Sonia Landau, national chairman in 1984 of Women for Reagan–Bush, explained, Reagan's "handling of the economy, more jobs, lower interest rates, lower inflation rates, these are issues of vital concern to women."[67]

The Immediate Aftermath of the 1984 Election

Ronald Reagan easily won reelection in 1984, winning a majority of women's as well as men's votes. The exit poll conducted by CBS News/*New York Times* showed 56% of women and 62% of men voted to re-elect the president.[68] Clearly, the presence of a woman on the ticket was not able to save the Democratic Party and its lackluster presidential candidate from a stinging defeat. The Mondale–Ferraro ticket lost every state except for Mondale's home state of Minnesota.

With the largest feminist organization having endorsed a presidential ticket for the first time, the defeat represented a substantial setback for the women's movement. The feminist political community, which had been playing offense since 1981, suddenly found itself in a defensive posture. Just as the Washington-based women's movement had for several years focused most of its attention and resources on an unsuccessful campaign to add an Equal Rights Amendment to the Constitution, so too had it focused much of its attention for the previous two years on an effort to get a woman on the ticket. Unlike the ERA campaign, this effort was successful. But success had its costs. To achieve the goal of a woman nominee, the movements' leaders had overpromised, suggesting that the nomination of Geraldine Ferraro would mobilize new women voters and motivate independents and even some Republicans to vote for the Democratic ticket. That did not happen in numbers anywhere close to what was needed to produce a Democratic victory.

There were many reasons for the Democratic loss and Ferraro's inability to change the outcome. Voters tend to make their voting choice based on the names at the top of the ticket, not based on vice-presidential preferences, and 1984 was no exception. Reagan benefited from an economy on the upswing, and the Reagan re-election campaign smartly focused largely on economic issues. The initial boost that Ferraro gave to the Mondale campaign was quickly tempered when questions arose about Ferraro's husband's separately filed tax returns and his reluctance to release them, and Ferraro became bogged down in answering questions about what she knew about her husband's financial dealings. Moreover, as Ellen Goodman noted, "The Mondale camp played to the women's vote only at the end … . It was as if the Mondale people expected Ferraro to win women's votes based on mysticism."[69]

Feminist leaders attempted to explain away the defeat and to put a positive spin on the results. Both Reagan and Mondale were faulted. Ellie Smeal offered the following explanation:

> To win the women's vote, Reagan successfully blunted the differences between himself and Mondale on gender gap issues. In doing so he stepped away from his right-wing agenda. Meanwhile, Mondale's domestic issue focus on deficits and increased taxes did not enhance the women's vote.[70]

Bella Abzug and Mim Kelber concluded that women, like men, "voted for the top of the ticket," and were attracted to Reagan as a result of a "brilliantly manipulated national media campaign" that emphasized "reassuring themes of peace, prosperity and patriotism."[71] Gloria Steinem suggested that while Ferraro was only a small net plus in terms of votes, her candidacy was "a substantial net plus in activism," with Ferraro raising $4 million for the ticket and attracting 10,000 volunteers.[72] Similarly, an Associated Press story appearing in the *New York Times* two months after the election noted, "Despite the defeat of the first woman to run for Vice President on a major party's ticket, women's leaders declared Friday that they won a big victory in 1984 with millions of women registering and voting for the first time."[73] Joanne Howes, head of the Women's Vote Project, claimed that her organization had registered 1.8 million new women voters in advance of the 1984 election.[74]

A Lasting Legacy

The gender gap is one of the enduring legacies of Second-Wave Feminism. Its effects continue to be felt today in large part because activists and leaders within the women's movement in the early 1980s named it, publicized it, and recognized its potential as a tool for women's political empowerment.

In the short term, the failure of the gender gap and Geraldine Ferraro's nomination to save the Democrats from defeat in the 1984 presidential election set feminists back on their heels and dramatically slowed the momentum that they had built. But through their efforts, feminists had ensured that the gender gap would be a factor with which candidates and campaigns would contend for decades into the future.

We can never know what would have happened had Ellie Smeal and NOW not decided in 1981 to name the gender gap, publicize it, and utilize it as a tool to push forward a feminist agenda. However, one might imagine that differences between women and men in their voting behavior and political preferences would have been treated much the same way as differences based on age, education, marital status, and most other demographic characteristics—as interesting statistical observations to be noted, incorporated into voter targeting plans, sometimes written about, but almost never considered central to political organizing, campaign strategies, or election outcomes. Without a movement to mobilize behind and make use of the gender gap, the statistical differences between women and men most likely would have received little attention.

In using the gender gap to push their agenda, feminists faced persistent resistance from the Reagan White House, which privately recognized and yet often publicly denied the gender gap's potential to derail Reagan's presidency and remove him from office. In light of the White House's desire to minimize the significance of the gender gap, the achievements that can be attributed at least in part to feminist publicity and organizing around the gender gap are impressive. In her column in the *Washington Post*, Judy Mann detailed some of these achievements: "the gender gap was in large measure responsible for getting a woman on the Democratic ticket, for making child care a hot political issue in congressional campaigns, and for getting legislation passed in the last Congress to reform pension plans and to tighten child-support enforcement."[75] In addition, the gender gap seemed to play a critical role in achieving the appointment of the first woman justice to the United States Supreme Court, a woman as the US ambassador to the United Nations, and two other women (Dole and Heckler) to Reagan cabinet posts.

Three decades later, with the gender gap long considered an accepted and more permanent feature of electoral politics in the USA, the amount of media and political attention the gender gap received in its early years appears striking. In 1983 and 1984, more than 150 stories and columns on the gender gap were published in the *Washington Post* and almost 100 appeared in the *New York Times* (Fig. 6.1). For the most part, these stories were not relegated to the "style" section of the papers. Rather they far more often appeared in the front section of the papers, sometimes on the front page. Frequently they were written by major political reporters and leading columnists. By the end of 1984, then, leaders of the women's political community had succeeded in turning a statistical difference observed in public opinion polls into a political phenomenon that not only would be difficult for future presidential candidates to ignore, but also would influence campaign strategies, policy proposals, and election outcomes for years to come.

Indeed, a gender gap in voting has been evident in every presidential election since 1980 with women more likely than men to vote for the Democratic candidate. In 2012, Barack Obama was reelected with a 10-point gender gap, capturing the votes of 55% of women compared with only 45% of men.[76] Over the years, Democratic presidential candidates have generally worked to maximize their advantage with women candidates without alienating male supporters. Republican candidates have tried to attract as many women voters as possible while maintaining their stronger support among male voters. And across all the intervening presidential elections between 1980 and 2012, women's organizations and feminist activists have drawn public attention to the gender gap and used it to pressure candidates to be more responsive to the concerns of women voters. The legacy of the early Second-Wave feminists on electoral politics continues to be evident today in the dynamics surrounding the gender gap.

Notes

1. Robert S. Erikson, Norman R. Luttbeg, and Kent L. Tedin, *American Public Opinion: Its Origins, Content, and Impact*, 2nd ed. (New York: John Wiley & Sons, 1980), 186.
2. Ibid.
3. See, for example, Kathleen A. Frankovic, "Sex and Politics: New Alignments, Old Issues." *PS: Political Science and Politics* 15 (Summer 1982): 439–48; Daniel Wirls, "Reinterpreting the Gender Gap," *Public Opinion Quarterly* 50 (Autumn 1986): 316–30; Pamela Johnston Conover, "Feminists and the Gender Gap," *Journal of Politics* 50

(November 1988): 985–1010; Susan J. Carroll, "Women's Autonomy and the Gender Gap: 1980 and 1982," in *The Politics of the Gender Gap: The Social Construction of Political Influence*, ed. Carol M. Mueller (Newbury Park, CA: Sage, 1988); Elizabeth Adell Cook and Clyde Wilcox, "Feminism and the Gender Gap—A Second Look," *Journal of Politics* 53, no. 4 (November 1991): 1111–22; Jeff Manza and Clem Brooks, "The Gender Gap in U.S. Presidential Elections: When? Why? Implications," *American Journal of Sociology* 103, no. 5 (March 1998): 1235–66; Karen M. Kaufmann and John R. Petrocik, "The Changing Politics of American Men: Understanding the Sources of the Gender Gap," *American Journal of Political Science* 43 (July 1999): 864–87; Janet M. Box-Steffensmeier, Suzanna De Boef, and Tse-Min Lin, "The Dynamics of the Partisan Gender Gap," *American Political Science Review* 98, no. 3 (August 2004): 515–28; Paul M. Kellstedt, David A. M. Peterson, and Mark D. Ramirez, "The Macro Politics of a Gender Gap," *Public Opinion Quarterly* 74, no. 3 (Fall 2010): 477–98.
4. For exceptions, see Kathy Bonk, "The Selling of the 'Gender Gap': The Role of Organized Feminism," in *The Politics of the Gender Gap: The Social Construction of Political Influence*, ed. Carol M. Mueller (Newbury Park, CA: Sage, 1988); Susan J. Carroll, "Security Moms and Presidential Politics: Women Voters in the 2004 Election," in *Voting the Gender Gap*, ed. Lois Duke Whitaker (Urbana: University of Illinois Press, 2008); Susan J. Carroll, "Moms Who Swing, or Why the Promise of the Gender Gap Remains Unfulfilled," *Politics & Gender* 2 (2006): 364–76; Susan J. Carroll, "The Dis-Empowerment of the Gender Gap: Soccer Moms and the 1996 Elections," *PS: Political Science & Politics* 32 (March 1999): 7–11.
5. Center for American Women and Politics (CAWP), "The Gender Gap: Voting Choices in Presidential Elections," 2014, www.cawp.rutgers.edu/fast_facts/voters/documents/GGPresVote.pdf.
6. Anne N. Costain, "Women's Claims as a Special Interest," in *The Politics of the Gender Gap: The Social Construction of Political Influence*, ed. Carol M. Mueller (Newbury Park, CA: Sage, 1988), 156.
7. Ibid., 168.
8. Bonk, "The Selling of the 'Gender Gap,'" 85.
9. Adam Clymer, "Displeasure With Carter Turned Many to Reagan," *New York Times*, November 9, 1980. Proquest Historical Newspapers: The New York Times, 28. See accompanying table labeled "How Different Groups Voted for President."
10. Bonk, "The Selling of the 'Gender Gap,'" 86.
11. Ibid.

12. Adam Clymer, "Reagan and Carter Stand Nearly Even in Last Polls," *New York Times*, November 3, 1980. Proquest Historical Newspapers: The New York Times, D15.
13. Quoted in Edward Walsh, "Reagan Is Still the Women's Second Choice," *Washington Post*, October 16, 1980. Proquest Historical Newspapers: The Washington Post, A1–A3.
14. Lou Cannon, "Reagan Pledges He Would Name a Woman to the Supreme Court," *Washington Post*, October 15, 1980. Proquest Historical Newspapers: The Washington Post, A6.
15. Richard Cohen, "First Woman Justice Won't Be a Feminist," *Washington Post*, October 19, 1980. Proquest Historical Newspapers: The Washington Post, B1.
16. Judy Mann, "Reagan Woos Women With Same Old Line," *Washington Post*, October 17, 1980. Proquest Historical Newspapers: The Washington Post, B1.
17. Ellen Goodman, "Flattery Won't Get You Elected," *Washington Post*, October 25, 1980. Proquest Historical Newspapers: The Washington Post, A19.
18. Bonk, "The Selling of the 'Gender Gap,'" 89.
19. Eleanor Smeal, *Why and How Women Will Elect the Next President* (New York: Harper & Row, 1984), 12.
20. Judy Mann, "WOMEN," *Washington Post*, October 16, 1981. Proquest Historical Newspapers: The Washington Post, C1.
21. Smeal, *Why and How Women Will Elect the Next President*, 12.
22. Center for American Women and Politics, "Gender Differences in Voter Turnout," 2014, www.cawp.rutgers.edu/fast_facts/voters/documents/genderdiff.pdf.
23. Ruth B. Mandel, "How Women Vote: The New Gender Gap," *Working Woman*, September 1982, 131.
24. Smeal, *Why and How Women Will Elect the Next President*, 22.
25. Ibid., 13; Bella Abzug with Mim Kelber, *Gender Gap: Bella Abzug's Guide to Political Power for American Women* (Boston: Houghton Mifflin, 1984), 103.
26. See Judy Mann, "ERA Again," *Washington Post*, January 5, 1983. Proquest Historical Newspapers: The Washington Post, B1, and Judy Mann, "Moral Lapse," *Washington Post*, November 18, 1983. Proquest Historical Newspapers: The Washington Post, B1.
27. Adam Clymer, "Women's Election Role Is Disturbing to G.O.P.," *New York Times*, November 18, 1982. Proquest Historical Newspapers: The New York Times, B19.
28. Ruth Mandel, "The Power of the Women's Vote," *Working Woman*, April 1983, 108.

29. "Women's Vote Effort Lauded," *New York Times*, February 17, 1985.
30. Evans Witt, "What Started as a Gimmick and a Dream for the Future Became a Historic Breakthrough Thursday," *AP Online*, July 13, 1984.
31. Ibid.
32. AP, "Democratics Urged to Pick Woman as No. 2 in '84," *Washington Post*, September 27, 1983. Proquest Historical Newspapers: The Washington Post, A5.
33. Witt, "What Started as a Gimmick."
34. Bill Peterson, "6 Democratic Hopefuls Vow to Consider Woman as Running Mate," *Washington Post*, October 3, 1983. Proquest Historical Newspapers: The Washington Post, A3.
35. Barbara Basler, "Democrats Discuss Woman on Ticket," *New York Times*, March 13, 1984. Proquest Historical Newspapers: The New York Times, B9.
36. Dorothy Gilliam, "Left Out," *Washington Post*, June 11, 1984. Proquest Historical Newspapers: The Washington Post, D1, mentioned as unconsidered possibilities Shirley Chisholm, Barbara Jordan, Yvonne Burke, Patricia Roberts Harris, Katie Hall, Cardiss Collins, Eleanor Holmes Norton, and Constance Motley. Women of color were also unhappy that they were not included in the process that Mondale used to choose his running mate. See Alison Muscatine, "Women's Movement Test Just a Beginning," July 20, 1984. Proquest Historical Newspapers: The Washington Post, A14.
37. Center for American Women and Politics, "Gender Differences in Voter Turnout."
38. UPI, "Vote Surge Seen if Woman Is Nominated," *Washington Post*, January 12, 1984. Proquest Historical Newspapers: The Washington Post, A7.
39. Ibid.
40. Quoted in Barbara Basler, "Study Finds Sex Stereotypes Affect Voters at Polls," *New York Times*, February 12, 1984. Proquest Historical Newspapers: The New York Times, 34.
41. Quoted in Jane Perlez, "Women, Power, and Politics: The 'Gender Gap' Worries Both Parties As Presidential Candidates Woo Women Voters–with Mixed Results," *New York Times*, June 24, 1984. Proquest Historical Newspapers: The New York Times.
42. Quoted in Judy Mann, "Good Choice," *Washington Post*, July 13, 1984. Proquest Historical Newspapers: The Washington Post, B1.
43. Perlez, "Women, Power, and Politics."
44. T. R. Reid, "Political Bridges: Liberal Feminist Ferraro Builds on a Bedrock Conservative Base," *Washington Post*, July 13, 1984. Proquest Historical Newspapers: The Washington Post, A6.

45. "The Vice Presidency and the Future of NOW," *Washington Post*, July 2, 1984. Proquest Historical Newspapers: The Washington Post, C1.
46. Bill Peterson, "Floor Fight Threatened by NOW," *Washington Post*, July 1, 1984. Proquest Historical Newspapers: The Washington Post, A1.
47. David S. Broder, "Reagan Takes 19-Point Lead Over Mondale, Gallup Poll Finds," *Washington Post*, July 1, 1984. Proquest Historical Newspapers: The Washington Post, A2.
48. Geraldine A. Ferraro. *My Story*. (Chicago: Northwestern University Press, 1985).
49. Ronald H. Hinckley, "Gender Gap," Memorandum, November 5, 1982, 2.
50. Karen Paget, "The Gender Gap Mystique," December 19, 2001, *American Prospect*. http://prospect.org/article/gender-gap-mystique.
51. Quoted in Judy Mann, "ERA Again," *Washington Post*, January 5, 1983. Proquest Historical Newspapers: The Washington Post, B1.
52. Quoted in Barbara Basler, "G.O.P. Starting Campaign to Show 'Reagan Is Terrific on Women's Issues,'" *New York Times*, April 6, 1984. Proquest Historical Newspapers: The New York Times, A24. Of course, Kathy Wilson, chair of the NWPC, claimed, "All those initiatives the President takes credit for now, the tax changes, the child support enforcement issues, those are simply congressional efforts that Mr. Reagan supported only after it became clear that their passage was inevitable."
53. Quoted in Paget, "The Gender Gap Mystique."
54. Bella Abzug with Mim Kelber, *Gender Gap*, 133.
55. See, for example, Jane Mansbridge, "Myth and Reality: The ERA and the Gender Gap in the 1980 Election," *Public Opinion Quarterly* 49 (1985):164–78, and Ethel Klein, *Gender Politics* (Cambridge, MA: Harvard University Press, 1984).
56. See, for example, Frankovic; Steven P. Erie and Martin Rein, "Women and the Welfare State," in *The Politics of the Gender Gap: The Social Construction of Political Influence*, ed. Carol M. Mueller (Newbury Park, CA: Sage, 1998).
57. David S. Broder, "A Victory Women Can Cheer," *Washington Post*, March 11, 1981. Proquest Historical Newspapers: The Washington Post, A23.
58. Juan Williams, "President Names Ex-Rep. Heckler As Head of HHS," *Washington Post*, January 13, 1983. Proquest Historical Newspapers: The Washington Post, A1.
59. Quoted in Juan Williams, "Reagan's Cheerleader on Women's Issues," *Washington Post*, March 7, 1983. Proquest Historical Newspapers: The Washington Post, A9.
60. Quoted in "GOP Acts to Better State, County Units," *Washington Post*, March 25, 1983. Proquest Historical Newspapers: The Washington Post, A5.
61. Quoted in Williams, "Reagan's Cheerleader on Women's Issues."

62. Juan Williams, "Reagan's Aides Say Gender Gap is GOP Problem," *Washington Post*, September 19, 1983. Proquest Historical Newspapers: The Washington Post, A1.
63. Quoted in Juan Williams, "White House Sees Two Sides to Gender Gap," *Washington Post*, July 25, 1983. Proquest Historical Newspapers: The Washington Post, A1.
64. Quoted in Tom Sherwood and Molly Moore, "Va. Republican Leaders Warn of Overconfidence," *Washington Post*, June 2, 1984. Proquest Historical Newspapers: The Washington Post, B1.
65. David Hoffman, "Reagan's Efforts to Placate Women Suffer, Aides Say," *Washington Post*, August 28, 1983. Proquest Historical Newspapers: The Washington Post, A1.
66. Adam Clymer, "Women's Election Role Is Disturbing to G.O.P.," *New York Times*, November 18, 1982. Proquest Historical Newspapers: The New York Times, B19.
67. Quoted in Basler, April 6, 1984.
68. Center for American Women and Politics, "The Gender Gap."
69. Ellen Goodman, "Yes, Ferraro Made a Difference," *Washington Post*, November 8, 1984. Proquest Historical Newspapers: The Washington Post, A27.
70. Eleanor Smeal Report, Volume 2, No. 11, November 12, 1984, 3.
71. Bella Abzug and Mim Kelber, "Despite the Reagan Sweep, a Gender Gap Remains," *New York Times*, November 23, 1984. Proquest Historical Newspapers: The New York Times, A35.
72. Maureen Dowd, "Setbacks Leave Women Leaders Viewing Their Political Progress in Inches," *New York Times*, November 8, 1984. Proquest Historical Newspapers: The New York Times, A22.
73. AP, "Women's Vote Effort Lauded," *New York Times*, February 17, 1985. Proquest Historical Newspapers: The New York Times.
74. Ibid.
75. Judy Mann, "Assessing the Women's Vote," *Washington Post*, November 9, 1984. Proquest Historical Newspapers: The Washington Post, C3.
76. Center for American Women and Politics, "The Gender Gap."

CHAPTER 7

Latina Mobilization: A Strategy for Increasing the Political Participation of Latino Families

Christina E. Bejarano and Valerie Martinez-Ebers

Abstract The Second-Wave feminists attempted to create a clear path for female political leaders. Caucasian women clearly benefited most substantially from the movement, and African American women have made some progress, particularly at the state level. In this chapter, Christina E. Bejarano and Valerie Martinez-Ebers expose the perceived disparate impact among the Latina community in which visible female political leaders are extremely rare, and the vast majority of Latinos are unable to name even a single important Latina political leader. Bejarano and Martinez-Ebers contend that Second-Wave Feminism did, in fact, impact Latinas, but the efforts of Latinas in the movement have not been well

---

The original version of the book was revised: Final corrections have been incorporated. The erratum to this chapter is available at https://doi.org/10.1007/978-3-319-62117-3_11

C.E. Bejarano (✉)
University of Kansas, Lawrence, USA

V. Martinez-Ebers
University of North Texas, Denton, USA

© The Author(s) 2018
A. Maxwell and T. Shields (eds.), *The Legacy of Second-Wave Feminism in American Politics*, https://doi.org/10.1007/978-3-319-62117-3_7

documented or publicized by scholars or the media. Rather, their successes have been overshadowed by their male counterparts. Bejarano and Martinez-Ebers demonstrate how Latinas' increased community participation provides them with stronger civic skills and stronger ties to their community/institutions, which, in turn, can also be linked to their higher political participation levels and high success rates as political candidates. In an effort to see the broad legacy of Second-Wave Feminism, Bejarano and Martinez-Ebers claim that it is critical to recover this history of Latina activism and to focus on Latinas as catalysts of political change, since women are perceived to be the key to mobilizing Latino families and communities.

In this chapter, we will explore and highlight the various roles of Latinas in mobilizing the Latino[1] community since the Second Wave of the women's movement. During this time frame, Latina activism was often overlooked or overshadowed by the more dominant actors in the women's movement and Chicano movement. However, Latinas have increasingly served as key figures in Latino political activism. There is now evidence of the growing political influence of Latinos in politics, as well as the growing distinctiveness of Latinas in their partisanship and participation rates (Bejarano 2014).

The growing Latina population in the USA has been an integral segment in Latino community involvement and political participation. The Latina share of the female population in the USA will increase from 16.4% in 2013 to 25.7% by 2050 (Jackson 2013). Latinas are also making significant strides in educational attainment, political influence, and overall health; however they still face significant racial and ethnic disparities (Jackson 2013, 1).

Who Are the Latino Leaders?

We have seen various groups contest leadership within the Second Wave of the feminist movement, and this has also played out within Latino community activism. Both outside observers and Latinos themselves have wondered if there is a potential Latino leadership vacuum. Many questions remain over who will lead the growing Latino population in the USA. Latinos had several key influential figures leading their communities during the Civil Rights and Chicano movements in the 1960s and 1970s. Since then, Latinos are unsure who to look toward for leadership.

In fact, a 2013 Pew Hispanic poll asked Latinos, "who is the most important (Hispanic/Latino) leader in the country today?" and over 60% of the Latinos polled answered that they "don't know" who their Latino leader is today (Lopez 2013). Instead, only a few Latinos were actually able to provide a name of a potential Latino leader: which included Sonia Sotomayor, Marco Rubio, Antonio Villaraigosa, and Luis Gutierrez.

Keep in mind that this short list of possible Latino leaders included a majority of Latino males, rather than females. Adelina Nicholls, the executive director of the Georgia Latino Alliance for Human Rights (GLAHR), summed up this gendered phenomena. She said,

> You always hear people say "Where are the Latino leaders?" If they're women, they're not recognized … Women have taken on an important role, maybe because of the nature of this fight that's in defense of the family, in defense of children—to end the deportations that take away our spouses, our parents, our brothers and sisters, our friends. (Rosello 2013)

Women are often not recognized for their leadership roles. However, the increased presence of Latina officeholders can have multiple effects on the political environment, especially in terms of their leadership style and emphasis on certain types of public policies. Previous research by Fraga et al. revealed that Latina state legislators tend to "place greater emphasis on representing the interests of multiple minority groups, promoting conflict resolution, and building consensus in both the legislature as a whole and within the Latino caucus" (2006, 122). In addition, the Latina legislative style differed from the Latino men, where Latinas were "more likely than Latino men to introduce and successfully pass legislation that addresses the issue agenda held by both Latina and Latino legislators" (122).

Latina Activism and the Chicano Movement

Latinas have a long history of community activism and are often seen as key community organizers (Hardy-Fanta 1993; Gutierrez et al. 2007). However, Latinas often had to tackle obstacles related to gender and race/ethnicity, intersectionality obstacles, especially as they fought to bring about greater equality and social justice during the Chicano movement in the 1960s–1970s. The Chicano movement was actually comprised of multiple reform efforts, including ones that sought land restitution, farm workers' rights, and political, gender, and educational equality in the USA. In countless ways, it was Latinas who built and sustained the Chicano movement, and continue to lead its modern incarnations today. Yet their contributions are too seldom acknowledged (Flores 2014).

Prime examples are Helen Chávez and Delores Huerta, who helped César Chávez form the United Farm Workers of America (UFW). It was Helen who first convinced her husband César to get involved in grassroots organizing as a member of the Community Service Organization (CSO), an early Hispanic civil rights organization. Helen and César were equally committed to civil rights and both volunteered extensively for the CSO. When César resigned from the CSO in 1962 to devote his time to establishing a labor union for farm workers, Helen also resigned to help her husband with the administrative duties of the fledging National Farm Workers Association (later renamed United Farm Workers of America or UFW). During the formative period of the UFW, Helen was a constant presence in the internal deliberations of the union as well as many of the external demonstrations and protests (Flores 2014). Yet she receives little if any mention in the history of the Farm Workers movement.

Delores Huerta began her grassroots organizing efforts in the early 1950s when she helped found the Agricultural Workers Association and then served as a vice president in the AFL-CIO affiliated Agricultural Workers Organizing Committee. Neither of these organizations had much success, so Huerta went to work for the local CSO chapter in 1955. As one of the few women in the organization with a college education, Delores quickly rose in the ranks to a leadership position in the California CSO office. However, she chose to resign from the group around the same time as Helen and César Chávez when CSO refused to make farm workers' rights a priority. Huerta was a key leader in the formation and political battles of UFW. She participated in practically every protest and strike and was the chief negotiator in meetings with growers' representatives. In sharp contrast with popular perceptions of Mexican women as submissive and quiet, Huerta's negotiating style with the growers' representatives was very direct and forceful (Flores 2014). She earned the moniker Dragon Lady, despite her small stature, for her fierce determination in the face of long odds (Gorman 2014). Huerta is also the author of the famous slogan "*Si se Puede*!"—properly translated as "yes, it can be done"—but better known as "Yes We Can!" This saying has been effectively used by multiple organizations and candidates, including President Obama and not always with the attribution Huerta deserves (Rodriquez 2014).

Today, at the age of 84, Huerta is still one of the most influential and esteemed Latina activists known for her tireless efforts for unions and laborers' rights. She also is a longtime activist for women's rights, working with the Feminist Majority and other organizations in an effort to get more Latinas to run for political office. Huerta was honored for her legacy of activism with the 2012 Medal of Honor, given to her by President Obama. However, public recognition of Huerta's contributions pale in comparison to the accolades given to César Chávez.

The Chicano movement preached equality and an end to oppressive systems of power, but its almost exclusively male leadership frequently resulted in unjust situations with women sidelined and their issues dismissed, yet they performed most of the organizational work and the men received the credit for it (Gutierrez et al. 2007). Eventually, Chicanas resorted to forming their own organizations.

One of the first Chicana organizations was the Comisión Femenil Mexicana Nacional (CFMN), created in 1970. The CFMN was founded in Sacramento, California, during the National Chicano Issues Conference when a group of attending Chicanas became frustrated that their concerns were not adequately addressed at the conference. The women met outside of the conference and drafted a founding resolution. Francisca Flores was selected as the first president. Flores was a Chicana activist already well experienced and highly regarded for her many decades of community works. Recognizing that there were few organizations that met the needs of Latina women, nine resolutions were presented to the group calling for the establishment of a Chicana/Mexicana women's commission. The resolution called for a commission that could direct its efforts toward organizing and networking women so that they might assume leadership positions within the Chicano movement and in the community. The commission would also disseminate news and information regarding the achievements of Chicana/Mexican women, and promote programs that provide solutions for women and their families (Guide to CFMN Archives 2003).

The inequality between the women and men in the movement particularly bothered feminist Chicanas who were initially called sell-outs, or *vendidas*, for advocating an end to male superiority in the movement and in the Mexican American culture in general (Chicana Feminism-History, n.d.). The first national Chicana conference (Mujeres Por La Raza Conference) was held in May of 1971 in Houston, Texas. Over 600 Chicanas attended the conference to discuss equal access to education, legalization of abortion, formation of childcare centers, the oppression of the Catholic Church, and other issues. Attendees could not agree on actions to resolve these issues and as a result divided into two groups as to what should be the emphasis of their organizational efforts. One group, called the "loyalists," felt ending race/class domination should remain their first priority. The other group, referred to as the "feminists," saw male domination within Mexican American culture as the primary problem. Interestingly, a survey taken at this conference showed that 84% of the women there felt as though they were not encouraged to seek professional careers and education was not considered important for Chicanas; 84% thought that there was not equal pay for equal work; 72% felt as though there was discrimination toward them in La Raza; and 84% agreed with the statement that "there is a distinction between the problems of the Chicana and those of other women." (Vidal 1971). One of the organizers of the conference was Elma Barrera. Her statement from the conference reveals the frustrations of many of the "feminist" attendees with the Chicano men and the Chicano movement:

> I have been told that the Chicana's struggle is not the same as the white woman's struggle. I've been told that the problems are different and that ... the Chicana's energies are needed in the barrio and that being a feminist and fighting for our rights as women and as human beings is anti-Chicano and anti-male. But let me tell you what being a Chicana means in Houston, Texas. It means learning how to best please the men in the Church and the men at home, not in that order. (Barrera 1971)

Meanwhile, the growing movement of Second-Wave Feminism, led by mostly middle-class, Anglo-American women, also did not provide common or hospitable ground for Chicanas speaking out about the unique oppressions they faced as working women and members of La Raza (Marino 2012). The struggles of Chicanas/Latinas were, and continue to be, different from those of Anglo women in the USA.

In terms of contemporary political activism, Latinas are now often seen in leadership roles in prominent Latino national organizations. There have recently been several Latina leaders of Latino national civil rights organizations: National Council of La Raza (NCLR): Janet Murguia; League of United Latin American Citizens (LULAC): Margaret Moran; Mexican American Legal Defense and Education Fund (MALDEF): Charlene Aguilar; and Puerto Rican Legal Defense and

Education Fund (PRLDEF): Indrani Franchini. Latinas have also led several immigrant rights organizations, such as the Coalition of Latino Leaders with America Gruner.

Latina Political Representation

Women have made large gains in political representation since the Second-Wave movement. This includes more recent gains made by racial/ethnic minority women in elective office in the last 20 years. Latinas first attained national electoral office in Congress in 1989 and have gained increased representation in state legislatures since the 1990s. The first Latina elected to Congress was Ileana Ros-Lehtinen in 1989, a Cuban American from Florida (Garcia-Bedolla et al. 2005). Over the course of the 1990s, Latina representation in Congress increased 500% (from one to six) and their representation in state offices increased 280% (from 16 to 61) (Fraga and Navarro 2004, 4; Bejarano 2013, 3). Latina officeholding grew more modestly at the county, municipal, and school board levels, but at each level of government "Latina increases far outpaced increases in Latina/o representation overall" (2004, 4; 2013, 3).

As of 2005, women of color at the state and national level made up a larger proportion of their minority delegation compared to their respective minority male counterparts, than white women compared with their white male counterparts (Garcia-Bedolla et al. 2005, 166). In 2014, women made up 99 total seats in Congress, with 79 in the House and 20 in the Senate. White females were 75.8% of the female delegation, or 75 seats. In comparison, there were 14 black females, 1 Asian female, and 9 Latina females in Congress.

As of 2014, Latinas made up 9 out of the 28 Latino members of the US Congress (in California, Florida, New Mexico, New York, and Washington). This included 7 Democratic and 2 Republican Latina members of Congress. In 2014, 1,789 women state legislators served nationwide, with 375 or 21% being women of color, and of those 87 were Latinas (CAWP 2014). The Latina state legislators in 2014 included 19 Latinas in the state senate and 68 in the lower house; with the majority, 72, serving as Democrats and 15 as Republicans. Overall, Latinas have increased their political presence across a wide variety of state legislatures and "at a rate that outpaces overall gender representation" (Fraga et al. 2006, 129; Bejarano 2013, 5).

Latina Political Participation

In addition to leading various Latino national organizations and increasing their political representation, Latinas are also wielding increased political influence in their communities and at the ballot box. Previous research has provided several explanations for Latinas' key role in their communities. Latinas are socialized to have more civic skills than Latino males, which include more community involvement and increased responsibility within the family (Lopez 2003).

Previous research has also found that Latinas have a different view of political involvement than Latino men (e.g., Hardy-Fanta 1993; Garcia et al. 2008). Latinas generally have a more participatory vision of politics, where they focus on grassroots organizations and community work, while Latino males focus on electoral politics (Hardy-Fanta 1993; Pardo 1998; Jones-Correa 1998a; Garcia et al. 2008). Moreover, Latinas often view their political participation "as an extension of their daily lives, which informs their mobilization strategies and effectiveness with the Latino community" (Hardy-Fanta 1993, 2; Garcia et al. 2008; Bejarano 2014, 60).

Latinas are increasingly motivated to get involved in their communities, especially when there is an issue of importance at stake. Latinas are also likely to take the initiative and personally organize their communities. As a result of Latinas' gendered roles as primary caretakers, they often engage in more contact with governmental institutions and services (Jones-Correa 1998b; Hondagneu-Sotelo 1994). Moreover, Latinas often motivate other Latinos to participate in US politics, by organizing naturalization and voter registration drives and volunteering for local political campaigns (Jones-Correa 1998a). They apply their leadership and organizational skills to their political work on political campaigns, social movements, and community organizations (Garcia et al. 2008; Garcia and Sanchez 2008; Pardo 1998). As a result, Latinas are perceived to be the key to mobilizing Latino families and communities.

Overall, Latinas' increased community participation may very well provide them with stronger civic skills and stronger ties to their community and political institutions. In addition, Latinas' community involvement can also be linked to their higher political participation levels and high success rates as political candidates (Bejarano 2013). In terms of political participation rates, since 1996 there is evidence of a modern Latino gender gap with Latinas voting at higher rates than the Latino men (Bejarano 2014). In addition, Latinas also provide increased electoral support to Democratic candidates compared to Latino men. In the 2012 presidential election, Latinas overwhelming supported President Obama to Romney, by 76% compared to 23% (CNN 2012; Bejarano 2014). In comparison, Latino male support for President Obama was 65%, which provides an 11-point gender gap for President Obama. This was the largest gender gap among all the racial/ethnic groups in the 2012 presidential election. Meanwhile, the gender gap among whites and blacks was smaller at 7 and 9 points, respectively.

In terms of specific policy preferences, there are few gender differences for racial/ethnic minority preferences from 1990 to 2000 (Conway 2008). There is little previous evidence that Latino policy attitudes differ by gender, even on the politically salient issue of immigration (García-Bedolla et al. 2007; Wrinkle 1991; Binder et al. 1997). There was a growth in the Latino gender gap for some public opinion attitudes across the late 1990s; however, these gaps were generally small (Montoya 1996). In particular, Montoya found the most perceptible gender gap appeared in Latino views on "women's roles," with Latinas supporting more progressive gender roles than Latino males (1996). In addition, other more recent work has found some significant gender differences in Latinos' attitude toward the death penalty (Latinas less supportive) and "women's roles in the religious upbringing of their children" (Latinas more supportive) (García-Bedolla et al. 2007, 152). Previous explanations for the Latino gender gap have emphasized Latinas' "experiences of marginalization across multiple dimensions" that can result in different policy priorities and policy focus than Latino men (García-Bedolla et al. 2007, 166).

In terms of gender differences, there are also few major differences in the priority listing of the issues. In 2012, Latinas prioritized their top issues as the economy/jobs (49%), immigration (37%), education (16%), and health care (16%) (impre-media/Latino decisions 2012), while Latino males reported the economy/jobs (59%), immigration (25%), health care (9%), and education (7%) (impre-media/Latino decisions 2012). The polling of Latinos throughout the 2012 election also demonstrated there is a significant gender gap in support of the more liberal public policies (Bejarano 2014). Overall, Latinas demonstrate a slightly higher level of support compared to Latino men, with Latinos overall supporting women's equal pay (85% Latino total), women's easy access to birth control (81% Latino total), some legal recognition for same-sex couples (26% Latino total), government providing income support for those who need it (79% Latino total), and continuing the Affordable Care Act or Obamacare as law (66% Latino total) (Bejarano 2014). In addition, Latinas were also significantly more supportive of the Democratic Party and President Obama in the 2008 and 2012 elections, compared to Latino males.

THE LATINA STRATEGY FOR MOBILIZATION

Just as we have seen a broad spectrum of women's activism within the Second Wave of the feminist movement, we have also witnessed the indelible mark that Latinas have brought to the movement. Latinas bring a variety of unique perspectives and skills to the art of community mobilization. It is important to focus on Latinas as catalysts of political change, since they are perceived to be the key to mobilizing Latino families and communities. Latino political organizations and the major political parties are realizing the political impact of gender differences in Latino political participation. Latinas often serve as the key connection with the Latino community, in mediating roles between political parties and groups; therefore, they are often targeted for campaign and candidate training.

NALEO, the National Organization of Latino Elected/Appointed Officials, recently developed a "Latina Strategy" for their naturalization and get-out-the-vote efforts, which includes a campaign focused on mobilizing Latinas, especially those who are business owners (Vargas 2013). In particular, NALEO's research has found that Latinas are often "the most influential family members in convincing persistent non-participating Latinos to vote" (Vargas 2013). A second initiative, LatinasRepresent, by Political Parity and the National Hispanic Leadership Agenda worked to increase the number of Latina elected officials in the USA. Even though Latinas have a history of community activism, they are underrepresented at all levels of US political office. Therefore, LatinasRepresent is driving a national dialogue about the need for Latina representation. Members of this initiative argue that even though Latinas are one of the fastest-growing populations, there are not many Latina political leaders who can serve as mentors to the new generation and capitalize on this momentum to dramatically increase their political representation (LatinasRepresent March 2014). Moreover, it is often "difficult to recruit and retain Latina political leaders, who often believe they can do more good in community leadership roles, rather than political ones" (LatinasRepresent 2014).

In terms of women as political candidates, researchers are now discovering that female political candidates often underestimate their qualifications, and therefore only the highly qualified females are elected to political office (Anzia and Berry 2011; Fulton 2011; Fox and Lawless 2004). Moreover, minority females can benefit from their interactive identities of both race/ethnicity and gender, which can provide them with more crossover voter appeal gained from "their multiple community identifications" (Smooth 2006, 411; Bejarano 2013, 6). Therefore, Latinas can benefit from fewer electoral disadvantages and more readily attain electoral support (Bejarano 2013).

The LatinasRepresent initiative is working toward encouraging more advocacy and action toward Latina representation; sharing models of successful programs; promoting new alliances that will increase support for political candidates; and encouraging more Latinas to serve as elected representatives. The strategy includes identifying role models and peer stewards who can support Latinas as they run for political office, encourage incumbents to run for high-level office, and promote Latina elected officials to seek out successors for when they leave office. In addition, the strategy includes encouraging "national and state political parties to recruit and support Latina candidates, channel resources (both political and financial) into their campaigns, and more actively engage female and minority voters" (LatinasRepresent 2014).

Conclusion

We are reminded that all women can dream big and work to attain their goals. In addition, there is a universal need to recognize the rights and viewpoints of all people, including those that are often in the minority. One particular strength of this volume and its editors was the effort made to identify the important contributions from women of color, including those from Latinas.

We hope this chapter provides some recognition and acknowledgment of Latina contributions not only through the Second-Wave movement but also with a look to their future impact. Latinas are increasingly seen as key figures in Latino political activism, political representation, and political participation. As a result, more political organizations are taking notice and working to create more opportunities to attract and support Latinas in politics.

Note

1. In this chapter, the term "Latino," unless immediately followed by a "male" qualifier, refers to both women and men living in the United States who come from, or trace their ancestry to, regions in Spanish-speaking Latin America and the Caribbean.

References

Anzia, Sarah F., and Christopher R. Berry. 2011. The Jackie (and Jill) Robinson Effect: Why Do Congresswomen Outperform Congressmen? *American Journal of Political Science* 55: 478–493.

Barrera, Elma. 1971. *Statement of Alma Barrera*. Retrieved from http://library.duke.edu/rubenstein/scriptorium/wlm/chicana/.

Bedolla, Lisa Garcia, 2005. *Fluid Borders: Latino Power, Identity, and Politics in Los Angeles.* University of California Press.

Bejarano, Christina E. 2013. *The Latina Advantage: Gender, Race, and Political Success.* Austin: University of Texas Press.

Bejarano, Christina E. 2014. *The Latino Gender Gap in U.S. Politics.* New York: Routledge.

Binder, Norman, J.L. Polinard, and Robert Wrinkle. 1997. Mexican American and Anglo Attitudes Toward Immigration Reform: A View from the Border. *Social Science Quarterly* 78: 324–337.

Center for American Women and Politics (CAWP). 2014. Women of Color in Elective Office, 2014. Fact Sheet. New Brunswick, NJ: Eagleton Institute of Politics, Rutgers University.

Chicana Feminism—History. n.d. Retrieved from http://www.umich.edu/~ac213/student_projects05/cf/history.html.

CNN. National Exit Poll, 2012 President Election. 2012. Collected by Edison Research. http://www.cnn.com/election/2012/results/race/president#exit-polls. Accessed 10 Dec 2012.

Conway, M. Margaret. 2008. The Gender Gap: A Comparison across Racial and Ethnic Groups. In *Voting the Gender Gap*, ed. Lois Duke Whitaker, 170–183. Urbana: University of Illinois Press.

Flores, Lori. 2014, March 31. The Neglected Heroines of Cesar Chavez. Colorlines: News for Action. Retrieved from http://colorlines.com/archives/2014/03/the_neglected_heroines_of_cesar_chavez.html.

Fox, Richard L., and Jennifer L. Lawless. 2004. Entering the Arena?: Gender and the Decision to Run for Office. *American Journal of Political Science* 48: 264–280.

Fraga, Luis, and Sharon Navarro. 2004. Latinas in Latino politics. Prepared for delivery at the conference "Latino Politics: The State of the discipline," Texas A&M University, College Station, TX, April 30–May 1, 2003.

Fraga, Luis, Linda Lopez, Valerie Martinez-Ebers, and Ricardo Ramirez. 2006. Gender and Ethnicity: Patterns of Electoral Success and Legislative Advocacy among Latina and Latino State Officials in Four States. *Journal of Women, Politics, and Policy* 28: 121–145.

Fulton, Sarah. 2011. Running Backwards and in High Heels: The Gendered Quality Gap and Incumbent Electoral Success. *Political Research Quarterly* 65 (2): 303–314.

Garcia-Bedolla, Lisa, Katherine Tate, and Janelle Wong. 2005. Indelible Effects: The Impact of Women of Color in the U.S. Congress. In *Women and Elective Office: Past, Present, and Future*, ed. Sue Thomas and Clyde Wilcox, 205, 152–175. New York: Oxford University Press.

Garcia, F. Chris, and Gabriel R. Sanchez. 2008. *Hispanics and the U.S. Political System*. Upper Saddle River, NJ: Pearson/Prentice-Hall.

Garcia, Sonya, Valerie Martinez-Ebers, Irasema Coronado, Patricia Jaramillo, and Sharon Navarro. 2008. *Politicas: Latina Trailblazers in the Texas Political Arena*. Austin: University of Texas Press.

García-Bedolla, Lisa, Jessica Lavariega Monforti, and Adrian Pantoja. 2007. A Second Look: Is There a Latina/o Gender Gap? *Journal of Women, Politics & Policy* 28: 147–171.

Gorman, Peter. 2014. Latina Dreamer: Dolores Huerta's Life Proves That Yes, You Can. *Fort Worth Weekly*, May 14. Retrieved from http://www.fwweekly.com/2014/05/14/latina-dreamer.

Guide to Commission Femenil Mexicana Nacional Archives, 1967–1997. 2003. Retrieved from http://www.library.ucsb.edu/sites/default/files/attachments/special-collections/cema/cfmn/cfmn_guide.pdf.

Gutierrez, Jose Angel, Michelle Melendez, and Sonia Noyola. 2007. *Chicanas in Charge: Texas Women in the Public Arena*. Lanham, MD: AltaMira Press.

Hardy-Fanta, Carol. 1993. *Latina Politics, Latino Politics: Gender, Culture, and Political Participation In Boston*. Philadelphia, PA: Temple University Press.

Hondagneu-Sotelo, Pierrette. 1994. *Gendered Transitions: Mexican Experiences of Immigration*. Berkeley: University of California Press.

impre-media/LatinoDecisions. 2012. Election Eve Poll [dataset]. November 6, http://www.latinovote2012.com/app/#all-national-all.

Jackson, Mareshah. 2013. Center for American Progress. Fact sheet: The state of Latinas in the United States. https://www.americanprogress.org/wp-content/uploads/2013/11/SOW-factsheet-Lat.pdf. Accessed Mar 2014.

Jones-Correa, Michael. 1998a. *Between Two Nations*. Ithaca, NY: Cornell University Press.

Jones-Correa, Michael. 1998b. Different Paths: Gender, Immigration and Political Participation. *International Migration Review* 32: 326–349.

Latinas Represent. 2014. Retrieved from www.latinasrepresent.org/.

Lopez, Nancy. 2003. *Hopeful Girls, Troubled Boys: Race and Gender Disparity in Urban Education*. New York: Routledge.

Lopez, Mark Hugo. 2013. *Three-Fourths of Hispanics Say Their Community Needs a Leader.* Washington, DC: Pew Hispanic Center, October 22. Retrieved from http://www.pewhispanic.org/2013/10/22/three-fourths-of-hispanics-say-their-community-needs-a-leader/.

Marino, Katherine. 2012. Liberating the Chicana Feminist Archive. *Gender News*, June 6. Retrieved from http://gender.stanford.edu/news/2012/liberating-chicana-feminist-archive.

Montoya, Lisa J. 1996. Latino Gender Difference in Public Opinion: Results from the Latino National Political Survey. *Hispanic Journal of Behavioral Sciences* 18 (May): 255–276.

Pardo, Mary. 1998. *Mexican American Women Activists, Identity and Resistance in two Los Angeles Communities.* Philadelphia, PA: Temple University Press.

Rodriquez, Roberto. 2014. Cesar Chavez: Conditions in the Field and the Struggle of Memory. *Truthout*, May 31. Retrieved from http://www.truthout.org/opinion/item/24049-cesar-chavez-conditions-in-the-fields-and-the-struggle-over-memory.

Rosello, Johanes. 2013. Guess Who's Leading Georgia's Latino Boom? Las Mujeres. *News Taco*, October 28. Retrieved from http://www.newstaco.com/2013/10/28/guess-whos-leading-georgias-latino-boom-las-mujeres/.

Smooth, Wendy G. 2006. Intersectionality in electoral politics: A mess worth making. *Politics & Gender* 2: 400–414.

Vidal, Mirta. 1971. *Chicanas Speak Out, Women: New Voice of La Raza.* New York: Pathfinder Press. Retrieved from http://library.duke.edu/rubenstein/scriptorium/wlm/chicana/.

Vargas, Arturo. 2013. Re: The Latina Strategy. Message to the author. June 14. E-mail.

Wrinkle, Robert D. 1991. Understanding Intra-Ethnic Attitude Variations: Mexican Origin Population Views of Immigration. *Social Science Quarterly* 72: 379–387.

CHAPTER 8

Black Women Lawmakers and Second-Wave Feminism: An Intersectional Analysis on Generational Cohorts Within Southern State Legislatures from 1990 to 2014

Nadia E. Brown, Guillermo Caballero, Fernando Tormos, Allison Wong and Sharonda Woodford

Abstract While the Second Wave of feminism opened doors for female political activism and for women to be seen as strong political leaders, the movement has been accused of focusing largely on the concerns of white women and generally avoiding the concerns of African American women—who live in a double bind of racial and gender discrimination. In this chapter, Nadia E. Brown, Guillermo Caballero, Fernando Tormos, Allison Wong, and Sharonda Woodford argue that despite criticism of Second-Wave feminists for ignoring the intersection of race and gender, the movement, when viewed in conjunction with the African American Civil Rights Movement proved influential for Black women

---

The original version of the book was revised: Final corrections have been incorporated. The erratum to this chapter is available at
https://doi.org/10.1007/978-3-319-62117-3_11

N. E. Brown (✉) · G. Caballero · F. Tormos · A. Wong · S. Woodford
Purdue University, West Lafayette, USA

© The Author(s) 2018
A. Maxwell and T. Shields (eds.), *The Legacy of Second-Wave Feminism in American Politics*, https://doi.org/10.1007/978-3-319-62117-3_8

who came of age during this period, launching a generation of female, African American state political leaders. Specifically, Brown and colleagues examine differences in class and generational cohorts among African American female state legislators from 1990 to 2014. They focus primarily on African American female state legislators in the South since that is where most African Americans live and where female African Americans have had the most electoral success. In order to explicate the ways in which race and gender function in tandem, Brown et al. profile two African American female state legislators from Maryland. From this in-depth case study, the authors are able to provide a more nuanced description of how these two legislators championed policies designed to help the most marginalized people in their community—an approach that allows African American legislators to establish common ground at the crucial intersection of race and gender, highlighting the complexity of Black feminism in the post-Second-Wave era.

Though Second-Wave feminism made significant political inroads promoting gender equity, the attempted solidarity of the women's movement often ignored the unique double marginalization faced by Black[1] women. Yet Black activists, political elites, and female politicians made exceptional efforts during this period, not only for their own generation but for the generation of women leaders who followed in their footsteps. In this essay, we disaggregate by race, gender, and generation to quantify and to expand the narratives regarding the failures and successes of Second-Wave Feminism. We turn our analysis to women serving in modern southern state legislatures to present demographic trend data and highlight the experiences of Black women Maryland state legislators to further explore differences between women political elites.

As of 2014, there are 242 Black women serving in forty state legislatures nationwide. African American women make up the largest number of the 377 women of color[2] state legislators (CAWP Fact Sheet 2014). While no women of color currently serve in the Alaska, Kentucky, North Dakota, and South Dakota state legislatures, Black women specifically do not currently hold seats in the Hawaii, Maine, Montana, Utah, Vermont, and Washington state legislatures. Because most African Americans reside in the South, it makes sense that there are more Black voters and elected officials in this region of the country (Bositis 2011). As such, we focus our attention on Black women elected to southern state legislatures. Black women, however, as a specific category of lawmakers, are gaining elected office at an all-time high. While Black men and White women are not represented in elite politics in proportion to their presence in the general population, Black women have attributed to the growth in both African American and women's political representation (Orey and Brown 2014; Smooth 2010; CAWP Fact Sheet 2014) (Fig. 8.1).

In this essay, we incorporate a generational analysis to argue that the Civil Rights Movement of the 1950s and 1960s along with the Voting Rights Act of 1965 (VRA) and Second-Wave Feminism has led to the increased numbers of Black women southern state legislators. First, the Voting Rights Act enforced the Fifteenth Amendment and extended suffrage to millions of African Americans who were disenfranchised through both legal and extralegal measures. The passage of the Voting Rights Act led to a monumental increase in Black elected officials, with fewer than 500 in 1965 to over 10,500 elected officials in 2011 (Joint Center for Political and Economic Studies). Indeed, the percentage of African American voters has also drastically increased during this same time period. Women, who make up 51% of the US population, have faced a similar trajectory. Prior

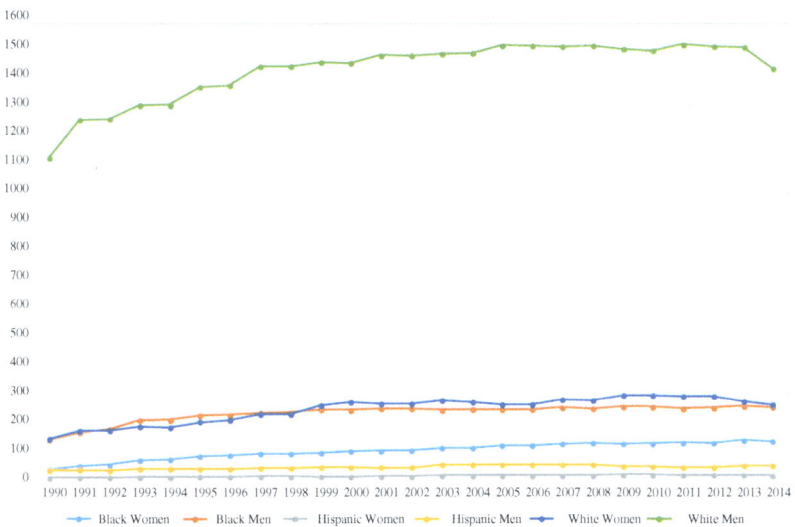

Fig. 8.1 All Southern Legislators by Race and Gender, 1990–2014

to the 1970s, scant few women occupied major elected positions in US political institutions. By 1979, women held only 10% of the state legislative positions nationwide (Fox and Lawless 2012). While several scholars have documented the importance of the Voting Rights Act and the Civil Rights Movement on increasing Black civic participation and elite politics (Andrews 1997; Davidson and Grofman 1994; Guinier 1991; Tate 1994) and the impact of the feminist movement in contributing to the number of politically engaged women and women elected to political office (Meyer and Whittier 1994; Taylor 1989; Whittier 1995), there has been a dearth of scholarship that has observed the effect of these movements on electing Black women to state legislatures.

Whereas both Linda Faye Williams (2001) and Nadia Brown (2014) have mapped generational differences onto the policy priorities of Black women state lawmakers, in departure from extant research, this study seeks to provide demographic information about Black women lawmakers to assess the growth of this population within southern state legislatures between 1990 and 2014. This contribution adds to our scholarly understanding of who these women are as well as compares the racial and gender diversity within modern southern state legislatures.

BLACK WOMEN LAWMAKERS AND THE LEGACIES OF SECOND-WAVE FEMINISM

Feminist activist efforts have challenged gender relations across various societal institutions and national borders (Nicholson 1997, 1). A robust body of literature confirms the successes and continuity of transnational and national women's movements (Esping-Andersen 2009; Khagram et al. 2002, 9; McBride and Mazur 2010; Mazur 2002; Moghadam 2005; Weldon 2002, 2006). Yet, until recently, the study of intersecting forms of oppression and how feminism has challenged them in the context of the USA remained understudied (Rosser-Mims 2011, 150).[3] Specifically, a marked gap still exists within the literature on political opportunities for women of color in state and local government in the USA.[4]

Black feminist scholars have also pointed to the obstacles that Black women face in ascending to leadership roles within activist-oriented organizations and particularly within civil rights and women's movements (Combahee River Collective 1977; Crenshaw 1991; Harris 2001; Rosser-Mims 2011, 15–18). Feminist and antiracist struggles tended to privilege the experience of men and White women while silencing the voices of women of color. The tendency to assume a unitary notion of women—essentialism—suppressed issues that live at the intersection of gender and race (Crenshaw 1991; Harris 1990). Both within civil rights and women's movements, feminist women of color have pushed advocacy groups to recognize differences among women and among people of color and to transform their political strategies and policy prescriptions accordingly. These efforts for recognition of intra-group difference have been heralded as the most important developments of Second-Wave Feminism (Nicholson 1997).

Take for example, the groundbreaking Black feminist text published by the Combahee River Collective in 1977, which decried the lack of inclusion of Black lesbian feminists in leadership positions within both the women's and Civil Rights movements. This statement, however, was not an attempt to break off from these movements, but rather, a claim for recognition, solidarity across differences, and inclusion within progressive movements. In order to overcome the multiple forms of oppression that many Black women experience, the members of the Combahee River Collective argued it was necessary to build and sustain coalitions with progressive organizations and movements. The Combahee River Collective advanced radical Black feminist politics as a way to end marginalization based on race, gender, class, sexual orientation, ability, and motherhood status. The advancement of Black women across dominant societal institutions was also seen as necessary for the ultimate goal of ending marginalization in all its forms.

The efforts of Black feminists inspired a reconceptualization of identity politics to recognize the claims of people marginalized by interlocking systems of oppression (Collins 1990; Crenshaw 1991). Black feminists also fought to create a structural form through which Black women's political leadership could emerge (Harris 2001; Rosser-Mims 2011, 15). These structures included the development of Black women's political organizations such as the National Council of Negro Women (NCNW), National Congress of Black Women (NCBW), and the National Black Feminist Organization (NBFO). Black feminists also held limited leadership roles in Civil Rights organizations, including the National Association for the Advancement of Colored People (NAACP), the Mississippi Democratic Freedom Party (MDFP), the Student Nonviolent Coordinating Committee (SNCC), and the Southern Christian Leadership Conference (SCLC) (Collins 1990; Rosser-Mims 2011, 12). However, women's exclusion from leadership positions in the Civil Rights Movement (Robnett 1996) based on intersections of race, class, and gender within the social movement led to powerful hierarchies that pushed Black women into other roles. Unlike their male counterparts, many Black women were not afforded the opportunities to gain formal political leadership skills through the Civil Rights Movement.

In conjunction with Black political and social organizations, Black feminist and civil rights activists worked to reform the US electoral system. Canon (1999, 340) argues that the most common political strategy within the Civil Rights Movement has been what Lani Guinier called the "Black electoral success strategy," which aimed to simultaneously enhance Black voting and the political representation of minority interests (Guinier 1991, 1081–1134). The VRA allowed for the creation of majority-minority districts that allowed for many African Americans to earn elected seats in legislative bodies. Research on the election of minority women candidates and the substantive representation of minority interests affirms the importance of majority-minority districts (Lavariega et al. 2009; Lublin et al. 2009).

Generational Differences

A generation is defined as a distinguishable group sharing birth years, age, and location and that experiences important life events at critical developmental stages (Kupperschmidt 2000). As an age cohort, generational groups share historical and social life experiences. The effects of these experiences are relatively stable over the course of their lives (Smola and Sutton 2002).

Incorporating generation, race, and political behavior, Gillespie's (2010) edited volume on Third-Wave[5] Black political elites illustrates that those born after 1960 distinctly differ from their predecessors. For starters, they were born or came of age after the Civil Rights Movement, and other parallels include their education—that is, they were educated in Ivy League and other White institutions and often attended law schools as they began to build their political careers. This group is also seen as having additional political potential; that is, they have more realistic chances to hold higher executive office than their predecessors (Gillespie 2010, 139). This younger generation seeks to move beyond the moods and methods of their predecessors toward cultivating Blacks' ability to live the American dream. Sadly, Gillespie's pathbreaking edited volume only includes one chapter on African American women political elites. In general, the work on generational differences among Black political elites pays little attention to African American women.

Linda Faye Williams (2001) shepherded the first study to analyze the political agendas of Black women state legislators disaggregated according to the Civil Rights and post-Civil Rights generation. Through the use of committee assignments and legislative priorities, the women of the New Deal (defined as those aged 65 years or older) and the women of the Civil Rights generations (defined as those 40–64 years old) were analyzed to examine the "thesis that the further we move from the Civil Rights–Black Power Era, the less important the long-term dual agenda of Africans Americans (ending racial discrimination and oppression *and* supporting social and economic justice for all Americans) would be centrally important to Black female elected officials" (Williams 2001, 322–323). In a multivariate analysis, Williams contended that Black women state legislators who came to political maturity during the New Deal or Civil Rights–Black Power eras are more prone to report a resilient obligation to civil rights and redistributive programs. She also found that the post-Civil Rights generation of Black women state legislators does not view redistributive and civil rights issues as having a primary importance, although women of the Civil Rights–Black Power era did.

Nadia Brown (2014) examines the policy priorities of Black women Maryland state legislators and their relationship to gender politics. She finds that Third-Wave Black women lawmakers are committed to race-gender issues, as demonstrated by their attention to domestic violence legislation. In sum, Brown argues that the Third-Wave Black women Maryland state legislators' understanding of political phenomena is altered by their generation's privileged background of benefiting from the Civil Rights and women's movements. The younger cohort of Black women political elites is reaping the benefits of the struggles that older Black women endured in both the feminist and Civil Rights movements. Hip-hop feminist Joan Morgan (1999) concludes that as daughters of the postfeminist, post-Civil Rights, post-soul hip-hop generation, younger Black women are uniquely poised to step into the legacy of activism and political achievements that older Black women have paved. Morgan theorizes that Black women of this generation are "college-educated, middle-class black girls, [who] are privileged because we now believe that there is nothing we cannot achieve because we are women, though sexism and racism might fight us every step of the way" (Morgan 1999, 59). The new generation of Black women legislators is aware of the difficulties and impediments they face as women of color, yet their individual educational and professional backgrounds prove that they have been advantaged when compared to predecessors.

While the terms Civil Rights–Black Power era for generational cohorts and post-Civil Rights and Third-Wave Black politicians' terminology can be mapped on top of one another, the waves of feminism are not easily mapped onto the above-described age cohort groups.[6] The wave analogy often associated with White feminist discourse is not only problematic but also not easily reassigned to Black feminists (Springer 2002). We assert that younger Black women state legislators have not only benefited from the VRA and the Civil Rights Movement, but also from the Second-Wave feminist movement during the 1960s through the 1980s that challenged gender inequality within politics, culture, and law.

In what follows, we present demographic data on Black women southern state legislators. We show that Black women who serve between 1990 and 2014 were largely born between 1935 and 1942 and thus came of age during the Civil Rights and feminist movements. These women were duly impacted by the success of these social-justice-oriented movements that may have led them to seek elected office once eligible. The women born between the late 1950s and 1970s are heirs to the successes of the movements.

Assessing Progress in State Legislatures

We collected biographical data on southern state legislatures from 1990 to 2014. These states are Alabama, Arkansas, Delaware, Florida, Georgia, Kentucky, Louisiana, Maryland, Mississippi, North Carolina, Oklahoma, South Carolina, Tennessee, Texas, Virginia, and West Virginia.[7] The information was retrieved from government-sponsored state websites, campaign websites, news articles, archives, Facebook pages, obituaries, and the website, Project Vote Smart (votesmart.org). We coded each legislator's race, gender, and date of birth. We chose to focus on a sample comprised of the Alabama, Florida, Maryland, Tennessee, and Texas state legislatures because these states had the most complete information in our dataset. The data that were collected on each southern state legislature were organized by the legislator's name, date of birth, race, gender, and year that he or she served in the state legislature. The data for this essay come from a large dataset. This data collection was sponsored by the National Science Foundation for principle investigator S. Laurel Weldon's project entitled, "Diversity and Inclusion: Implications for Science and Society."

We focus on the number of Black women who were born in a specific year or a range of years and who served in southern state legislatures from 1990 to 2014. We then organized the findings between three different generational cohorts 1930–1946 (the Greatest Generation), 1947–1964 (the Baby Boomers), and 1965–1984 (Generation X). Those born in the Greatest Generation and the beginning of the Baby Boom are those that lived through the Civil Rights and women's movements. Generation X'ers are the heirs to these movements.

The data used for the case study analysis are part of a sample collected between 2009 and 2011 with members of the Maryland state legislature.[8] Maryland was selected as the case study because of the comparatively large number of African American women state legislators and because of the structure of the legislature, which makes it easy to pinpoint how race and gender influence legislative behavior.[9] While still a new methodology in political science, feminist theorists across several academic fields of study have argued for the significance of locating and historicizing the lives of women (Bell and Nkomo 2001; Collins 1990). Feminist life histories were conducted with 18 of the 20 Black women Maryland state legislators between June and October 2011. The Black women state legislators crafted their narratives by drawing on their personal experiences to signify cultural mores that are natural to their own biographical, generational, cultural, historical/material, and geographical situations. The life histories allow the researcher to reveal a more nuanced consideration of how the lawmaker views and interprets her life course which would be inconceivable with quantitative research. Thus, this method is ideal for learning about a woman's experiences, how she views the world, and how she views herself.

A View from the Southern States

Below we present each state's individual graphs to illustrate the number of lawmakers born in each of the generational cohorts who served in each particular state's legislature between 1990 and 2014.

Figure 8.2 depicts the race, gender, and generational cohort for Alabama state legislators between 1990 and 2014. There were 84 Black women legislators born between 1930 and 1946, 48 born between 1947 and 1964, and 16 born between 1965 and 1984. Of the Black men lawmakers who served during this time, 308 were born between 1930 and 1946, 136 were born between 1947 and 1964, and 64 born between 1965 and 1984. Turning our attention to White women Alabama state legislators, we find that 48 were born between 1930 and 1946, 88 born between 1947 and 1964, and 4 born between 1965 and 1984. Lastly, of the White men lawmakers, there were 1,060 born between 1930 and 1946, 936 born between 1947 and 1964, and 236 born between 1965 and 1984. Figure 8.2 also illustrates that the majority of legislators who served in the Alabama state legislature between 1990 and 2014 were born between 1930 and 1946, with the exception of White women state legislators. Here we see that the number of Black women is proportionally smaller than any other demographic group in the Alabama state legislature. As such, the generational cohorts of Black women are much closer in age than the other racial/gendered groups of legislators.

The data represented in Fig. 8.3 illustrate the race, gender, and generational cohorts for those who served in the Florida state legislature from 1990 to 2014. The figure shows that the majority of Black women Florida state legislators were born between 1947 and 1964. These women were born during the Civil Rights and women's movements. Unlike their peers in the Alabama state legislature, the generational

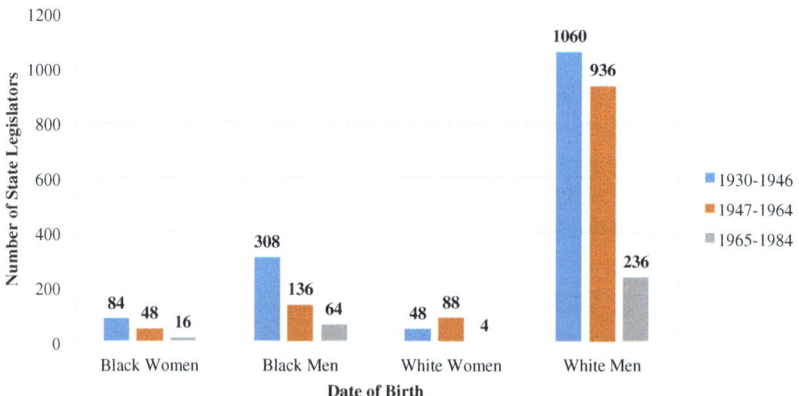

Fig. 8.2 Alabama State Legislature, 1990–2014: Race and Gender by Date of Birth

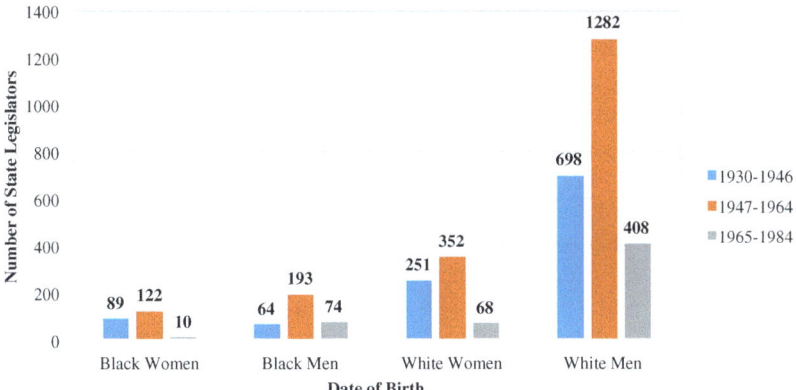

Fig. 8.3 Florida State Legislature, 1990–2014: Race and Gender by Date of Birth

cohorts of 1930–1946 and 1947–1964 for Black and White women lawmakers are proportionally similar. Turning to a detailed breakdown of the generational cohort, we observed that there were 89 Black women Florida state lawmakers born between 1930 and 1946, 122 born between 1947 and 1964, and 10 born between 1965 and 1984. That data for Black men legislators indicate that there were 64 born between 1930 and 1946, 193 between 1947 and 1964, and 74 between 1965 and 1984. The generational cohorts of White women lawmakers reveal that 251 were born between 1930 and 1946, 352 were born between 1847 and 1964, and 68 were born between 1965 and 1984. Lastly, the data specify that of the White male Florida state legislators 698 were born between 1930 and 1946, 1,282 were born between 1947 and 1964, and 408 were born between 1965 and 1984.

The span of Black women Florida state legislators is vast. There are 11 that were born in 1926, and there are 6 that were born in 1968. The majority of Black women who held office in the Florida state legislature between 1990 and 2014 were born in 1942 (30 Black females) and 1949 (30 Black females).

Figure 8.4 represents the race, gender, and generational cohorts of lawmakers within the Maryland state legislature between 1990 and 2014. The number of African American women lawmakers by generational cohorts reveals that 139 were born between 1930 and 1946, 132 were born between 1947 and 1964, and 16 born between 1965 and 1977. Turning our attention to Black men Maryland state legislators, we observe that 224 were born between 1930 and 1946, 223 were born between 1947 and 1964, and 48 were born between 1965 and 1977. The data on the generational cohorts of White lawmakers for this state demonstrate that 421 were born between 1930 and 1946, 316 were born between 1947 and 1964, and 44 were born between 1965 and 1977. The number of White men lawmakers by generational cohort illustrates that 915 were born between 1930 and 1946, 1,274 were born between 1947 and 1964, and 288 were born between 1965 and 1977. The data denote that Black women and men Maryland state legislators are similarly proportioned for the generational cohorts born between 1930–1947 and 1947–1964. However, we see that the Black men lawmakers in this state nearly double that of the generational cohort of Black women born between 1965 and 1977, the generation of heirs to the Civil Rights and women's movements.

Turning our attention to the Tennessee state legislature, the data in Fig. 8.5 illustrate the race, gender, and generational cohorts of the lawmakers in this state who served between 1990 and 2014. The data demonstrate that of the Black women lawmakers' generational cohorts, there were 106 who were born between 1930 and 1946 and 38 who were born between 1947 and 1964. There are no younger Black

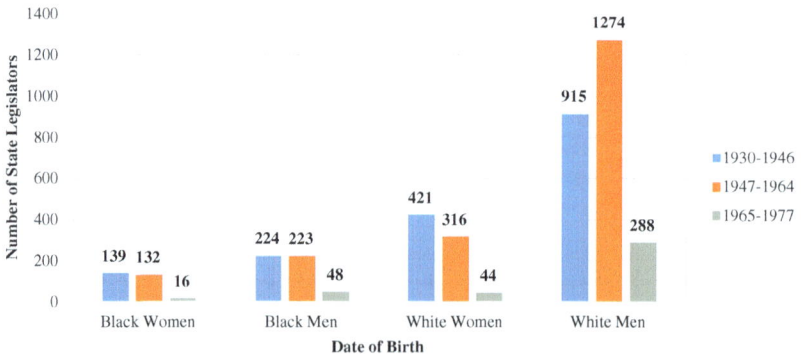

Fig. 8.4 Maryland State Legislature, 1990–2014: Race and Gender by Date of Birth

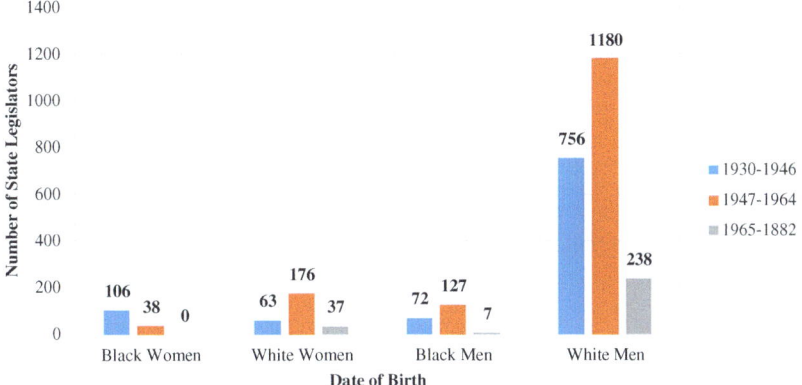

Fig. 8.5 Tennessee State Legislature, 1990–2014: Race and Gender by Date of Birth

women, those born between 1965 and 1984, who served in the state legislature between 1990 and 2014. For Black men Tennessee state legislators, there were 72 born between 1930 and 1946, 127 born between 1947 and 1964, and 7 born between 1965 and 1984. The data indicate that there were 71 White women lawmakers born between 1930 and 1946, 176 born between 1947 and 1964, and 37 born between 1965 and 1984. Lastly, of the generational cohorts of White men Tennessee state legislators we find that 756 were born between 1930 and 1946, 1,180 were born between 1947 and 1964, and 246 were born between 1965 and 1984.

Lastly, Fig. 8.6 illustrates race and gender for those who served in the Texas state legislature from 1990 to 2014 by generational cohorts. Of the Black women Texas state legislators in our sample, 89 were born between 1930 and 1946 and 28 were born between 1947 and 1964. Similar to the Tennessee state legislature, there are no Black women born between 1965 and 1984 serving in the Texas state legislature. Of the generational cohorts of Black men lawmakers, the data reveal that 78 were born between 1930 and 1946, 129 were born between 1947 and 1964, and 14 were born between 1965 and 1984. Turning our attention to White women Texas state legislators, we observe that 201 were born between 1930 and 1946, 282 were born between 1947 and 1964, and

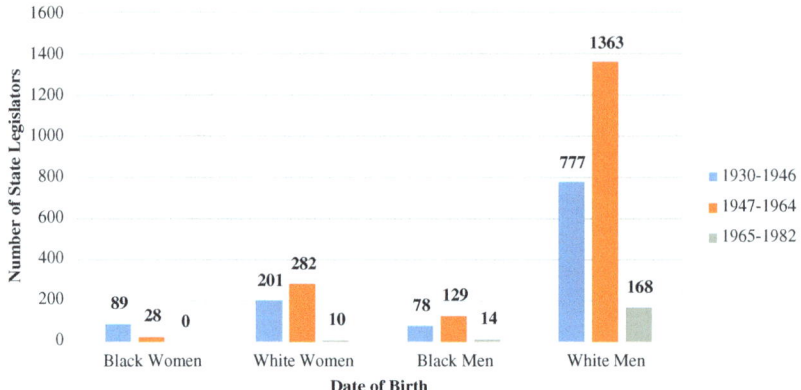

Fig. 8.6 Texas State Legislature, 1990–2014: Race and Gender by Date of Birth

10 were born between 1965 and 1984. Of the generational cohorts of White men lawmakers, we find that 777 were born between 1930 and 1946, 1,363 were born between 1947 and 1964, and 168 were born between 1965 and 1984.

An examination of data from all five states in our in-depth sample demonstrates that the generational cohort of Black women southern state legislators who were born between 1965 and 1984 is paltry. This younger generation, heirs to the Civil Rights and women's movements, of Black women are not well represented in southern state legislatures. This is surprising given the fact that all other race/gendered groups of state legislators have representatives of this generational cohort. Indeed, we observe that for White women of this generational cohort were 2–3 times more likely than Black women to serve in southern state legislatures between 1990 and 2014. Unsurprisingly, we find that White men serve at disproportionally higher rates in southern state legislators than all other race, gender, and generational cohort groups.

The data represented in Fig. 8.7 illustrate the number of Black women southern state legislators by generational cohort. Here we see that the majority of Black women lawmakers were born between 1939 and 1948. As such, this group of southern state legislators would have been between the ages of 20–35 years old during the Civil Rights

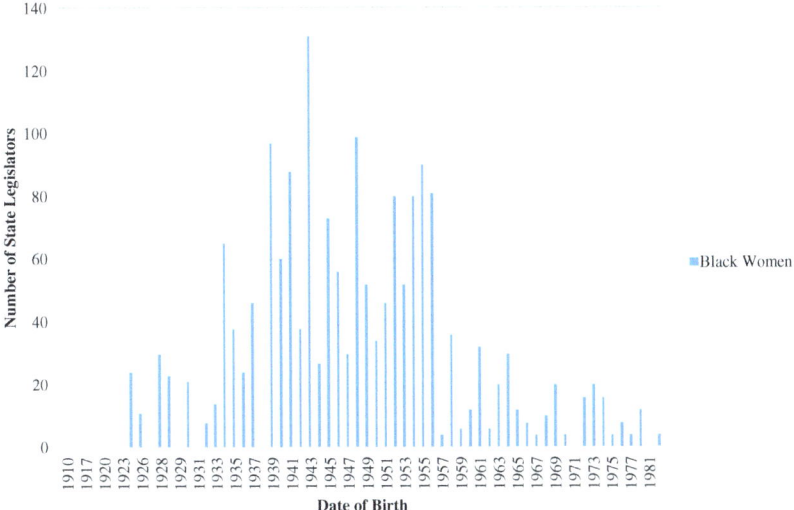

Fig. 8.7 Southern State Legislatures, 1990–2014: Black Women by Date of Birth

Movement and between 30 and 40 years old during the Second-Wave feminist movement.

Figure 8.8 compares the generational cohorts of Black women and men southern state lawmakers. The data show that Black males who were in office from 1990 to 2014 in the South were born earlier than Black females who were in office during that time period. African American men state legislators also have a larger range of generational cohorts than do their female counterparts.

The data in Fig. 8.9 present a comparison between the generational cohorts of Black and White women southern lawmakers who served between 1990 and 2014. The data reveal the Black women southern state legislators were born during years more closely to one another, while White women lawmakers were born within a wider range of years than their African American counterparts.

Finally, through the data presented in Fig. 8.10 we observe that the largest differences among generational cohorts are found between Black women and White men southern state legislators. From these data, it is clear that the presence of White males in southern state legislatures

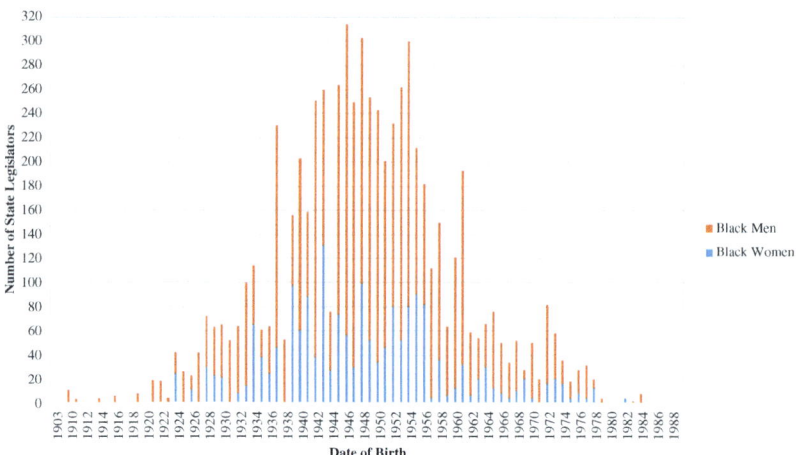

Fig. 8.8 Southern State Legislatures, 1990–2014: Black and Gender by Date of Birth

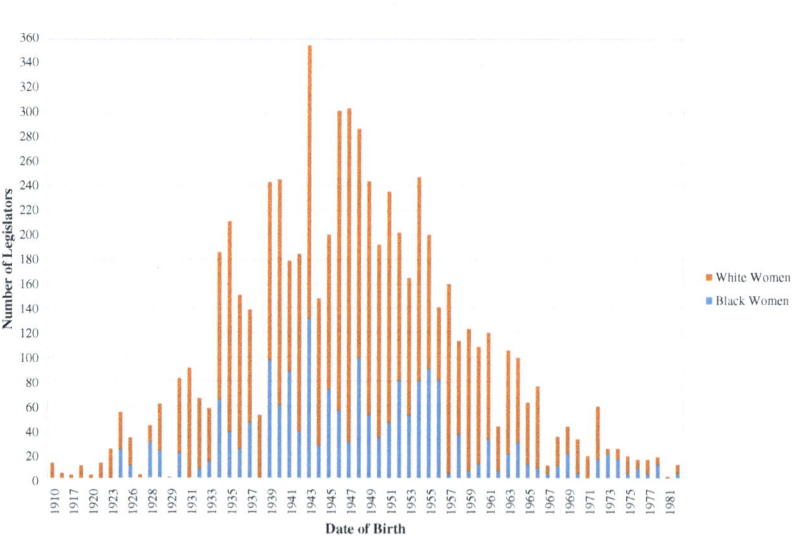

Fig. 8.9 Southern State Legislatures, 1990–2014: Race and Women by Date of Birth

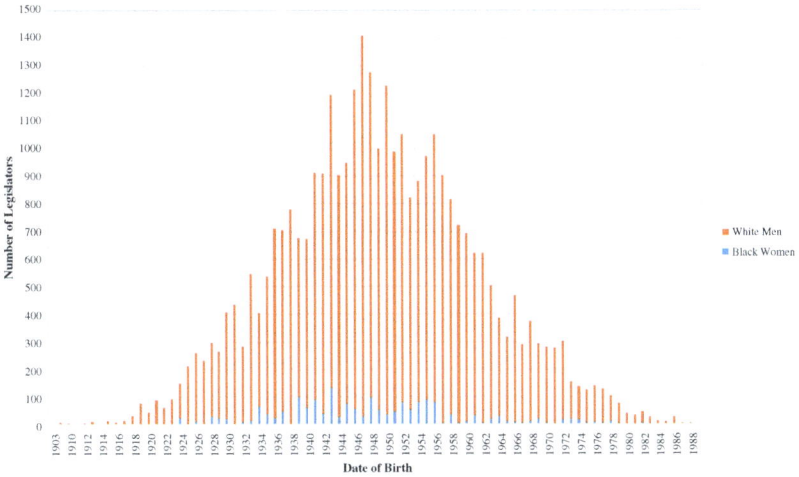

Fig. 8.10 Southern State Legislatures, 1990–2014: Black Females and White Males by Date of Birth

greatly overshadows the presence of Black females. However, the data indicate that there were fewer differences among generational cohorts of White men southern state legislators in office beginning in 1973 and extending to 2014.

Generational Cohort Case Study Analysis: Two Black Women Maryland State Legislators

In the section below, we present two narratives from Black women who served in the Maryland House of Delegates in 2011.[10] These women's narratives are exemplary of the generational differences articulated by the lawmakers in the study. The younger woman, Delegate Fatima Coleman, expresses benefiting from the women's and the Civil Rights movements. Both the racial and gendered empowerment of the 1960s has impacted Delegate Coleman's political ambition. However, Delegate Justine Anderson, who was 64 at the time of her feminist life history, did not provide a distinctly gendered analysis nor articulate how the feminist movement influenced her political career. For Delegate Anderson,

Martin Luther King, Jr. and the Civil Rights Movement had the larger effect on her nascent political career.

Delegate Fatima Coleman, a younger member of the Maryland House of Delegates, was 42 years old when her feminist life history was conducted. She grew up in the primarily Black, Washington, DC, suburb of Maryland, Prince Georges' County, and came of age in the 1980s. Delegate Coleman credits her undergraduate experience at the University of Maryland as exposing her to identity politics, race-based discrimination, and gender politics. Growing up in a primarily all-Black community Delegate Coleman learned about the Civil Rights Movement and advancements that African Americans had made in her community. However, it was not until her town elected its first Black woman mayor that a young Delegate Barnes began to think about politics. "My mother suggested that I consider (Mayor) Vivian M. Dodson as my role model" (Personal Interview, July 29, 2011). Delegate Coleman used her interest in politics at the University of Maryland to advocate on behalf of Black student athletes who she felt should be paid for representing their school in athletics. She organized sit-ins during the University of Maryland basketball games. This action, inspired by the coalition building and politicking she witnessed Mayor Dodson foster in her administration, catapulted the young Delegate Coleman into a world of student politics.

However, it was not until her first women's studies course at the University of Maryland that Delegate Coleman thought about a gendered identity: "This was also the first time that I met an open lesbian, I didn't know what 'gay' meant until I was a junior in college. College was the time when I got a lot of exposure to the world" (Personal Interview, July 29, 2011). It was in this women's studies course that Delegate Coleman married her love of politics, the embodiment of Mayor Dodson's spirit, and her newfound knowledge of gender identity into a cohesive political identity and calling. In her senior year of college, she volunteered on the political campaign of an older sorority sister who was running for the Maryland House of Delegates at the time. Delegate Coleman used her experiences and first-hand knowledge of working with a Black woman candidate to shape her views on formal politics. During her senior year of college, Delegate Coleman decided that she wanted to run for office and to become a politician. Having benefited from the feminist and Civil Rights movements, Delegate Coleman used her exposure to Black women's political activism and experiences growing up in a politically engaged Black community to reach her goal of becoming an elected official. In this capacity, Delegate Coleman would use her voice in the Maryland state legislature to champion issues of the Black lesbian, gay, bisexual, and transgender communities. Indeed, Delegate Coleman was the first Black representative from Prince George's County to cosponsor marriage equality legislation. Her political activism is a direct byproduct of the tenets of the Combahee River Collective who sought to build coalitional politics and end advanced marginalization.

Unlike Delegate Fatima Coleman, Delegate Justine Anderson came of age in the late 1960s in Prince George's County, Maryland. During her feminist life history, Delegate Anderson fondly remembered Dr. Martin Luther King, Jr. as the impetus for her political action. Delegate Anderson was seventeen when Dr. King was assassinated, and his death left an indelible mark on her. Most notably, Delegate Anderson was moved by Dr. King's instance on equality for all people, particularly working-class African Americans. Her grandmother, a stable figure in the delegate's life, would often remind Justine Anderson of the importance of economic security and opportunities for Blacks in the inner city. This ideological stance helped to shape Delegate Anderson's first career choices as she later helped to unionize the then-segregated Prince George's County hospital. She first went to work at the hospital in 1969 and the union was not organized until 1974, all the while, Delegate Anderson was insistent that workers should be treated fairly. In the Maryland state legislature, Delegate Anderson is a tireless advocate for workers' rights and seeks to improve the lives of lower- and working-class Marylanders through legislation and direct government intervention.

A gendered identity is largely missing from Delegate Anderson's feminist life history. Her narrative is largely shaped by her racial identity and experiences of race-based discrimination. Delegate Anderson's only distinctly gendered identity is of having to drop out of college because she became pregnant at 18: "Back then, in 1968 you had to watch everything. You were supposed to be a virgin until you were married. Ha! That went out the window … I had to come home from college. You couldn't go to school pregnant in 1968. No one believed in abortion" (Personal Interview, October 10, 2011). Delegate Anderson would later return home to Maryland to raise her child with the help of her grandmother. As a single mother, Delegate Anderson worked hard to provide for her son. However, motherhood is not prominently displayed in her feminist life history nor is the feminist movement. Delegate Anderson's seemingly lack of gender consciousness may be an indicator of Black women shying away from the label of feminist or a failure to connect with the Second-Wave feminist movement. This is consistent with the majority of Black women who do not use this label (Anderson et al. 2009).

It is expected that members of minority racial and ethnic groups are reluctant to identify as feminists; these groups often perceive feminism as reflecting only the concerns of and resolutions for middle-class White American women. "Many black women view feminism as a movement that at best, is exclusively for women and, at worst, dedicated to attacking or eliminating men" (Collins 1990, 11). Alice Walker (1983) distinctively noted that feminism does not fully include the standpoints of African American women. Black women practice a form of feminism that is clearly unique from what is typically understood to be feminism, and in the process, renounce neither their status as women nor their race. Unquestionably, the work of Black feminism is permanently conducted from the intersectional vantage point of being both Black and female and is a commonly recognized phenomenon that develops from the experiences of African American women.

While modern Black feminism stems from Black women's discontent with the Civil Rights and women's movement of the 1960s and 1970s, Black women's politics remains centered on social justice and willingness to form coalitions with enthusiastic partners to end economic exploitation, racial discrimination, gender discrimination, and heterosexism (Collins 1990). An intersectional framework allows scholars to account for the ways in which Black women, who were largely excluded from formal leadership roles in the women's and Civil Rights Movement, have shaped political careers to advocate for those at the margins of society. Delegates Coleman and Anderson, whose ideologies were formed in their youth, are forceful defenders of social justice on all fronts. These women use their voice in the Maryland state legislature to support the most marginalized in their communities. Undeniably, both Delegates Coleman's and Anderson's narratives illustrate the complexity and beauty of how Black feminist practices actually operate.

Conclusion and Possible Future Directions

It was not until the late 1970s that mainstream Second-Wave Feminism began to actively pay attention to race relations and purposely include the perspectives of Black women activists and political leaders. Additionally, Black women were also excluded from several key leadership positions within the Civil Rights Movement. Both movements demonstrated an absence of an intersectional praxis informed by a racial/gendered perspective. As such, many Black women were not given leadership opportunities. However, the lack of formal leadership positions did not stop many Black women from becoming politically active.

The data presented in this essay dispel the notion that elected Black female southern state legislators achieved office through a one-dimensional social justice movement framework. We have demonstrated that the intersectional framework of the Civil Rights Movement and the feminist movement may account for the increase in elected Black female legislators. Indeed, the women who came of age during these political movements are heavily represented in southern state legislators. An overview of the data reveals that the generational cohort of those born between 1930–1946 and 1947–1964 had some of the largest numbers of women, especially Black women, who served in southern state legislatures between 1990 and 2014. Surprisingly, it is younger Black women, those who are heirs to the achievements gained through the Civil Rights and women's movements, who are not proportionally represented in southern state legislatures from 1990 to 2014.

The diversifying of state legislatures has connections to the work that was done by the generational cohorts who pushed for reforms through the Civil Rights and women's movements. The case study analysis of Delegates Coleman and Anderson of the Maryland state legislature reveals these connections. Both women are committed to social justice and draw from their experiences as Black woman to aid their work in the Maryland state legislature. However, the younger woman—Delegate Coleman—ties her political activism to the distinct legacy of Black women's struggles for antiracist and feminist work. Both women reject the notion of the "universal womanhood" and instead draw on their experiences as Black woman who seemingly prioritize a racial identity.

White and Black women acknowledge the role that gender plays in their experiences, while only Black women seem to provide a racialized analysis. Black women's divergent experiences within the feminist and

Civil Rights movements may have played a role in seeking political office. Furthermore, younger women who inherited the victories of these movements may view politics different from their predecessors who actively participated in these social-justice-oriented movements. Understanding this variance is necessary for analyzing how Black women political elites navigate American politics. While our intentions were not to assess these women's policy priorities, we view this line of inquiry as a worthy scholarly project. An intersectional approach to examining women political elites provides a more detailed picture of the women who serve the nation as policymakers. By further examining the narratives of Black women, we find that generational cohorts provide a meaningful lens to assess differences and similarities within groups. The legacies of Second-Wave Feminism had and continue to have implications for Black women serving in modern southern state legislatures.

Notes

1. The terms African American and Black are used interchangeably throughout this book. As such, the term Black is used as a proper noun in recognition of a specific cultural group. To that end, we have chosen to capitalize the "B" in the word Black. Currently, both terms are used to refer to people of African descent living in America.
2. By women of color, we are referring to Asian Pacific Islanders, Latinas, and Native American women.
3. There are various exceptions, including Strolovitch (2006), who applied an intersectional lens to the study of advocacy groups in the United States. Paxton et al. (2007) review work on women in politics both in the United States and worldwide.
4. Recurrent attacks on feminist and Black politics scholarship and their funding further complicate this problem. National Science Foundation funding for political science research has come under recent attacks (see Beth Mole's "NSF cancels political-science grant cycle" for more information: http://www.nature.com/news/nsf-cancels-political-science-grant-cycle-1.13501). The main proponent of cutting NSF political science research funding, Senator Tom Coburn (R-OK) argued that "unless the NSF Director certifies projects are vital to national security or the economic interests of the country," the NSF was "wasting federal resources on political science projects." Various studies on Black elected officials rely on data collected by the Joint Center for Political and Economic Studies, and it remains unclear whether the center will continue to have funds to operate (see Richard Prince's "A Leading

Black Think Tank Is Barely Scraping By" for more information on the center's financial situation, http://www.theroot.com/blogs/journalisms/2014/06/the_joint_center_for_political_and_economic_studies_is_broke.html).
5. The First-Wave of Black politicians achieved electoral success directly after the Voting Rights Act of 1965 during the time period 1965–1988. The Second Wave of Black politics is characterized by the prevalent use of a deracialized campaign strategy during the late 1980s and early 1990s, such as the mayoral races of David Dinkins (NYC), Norm Rice (Seattle), John Daniels (New Haven), Chester Jenkins (Durham), and Douglas Wilder for Governor of VA (Gillespie 2010, 142).
6. Third-Wave Feminism, which began in the 1990s, does not overlap with the above-mentioned terms. This particular wave of feminism is informed by postcolonial and postmodern thinking. Third-Wave feminists have challenged the stabilization of cultural constructions of gender, sexuality, hetero-normativity, the body, as well as the notion of universal womanhood.
7. We determined the southern states based on the US Census https://www.census.gov/popest/about/geo/terms.html.
8. The General Assembly includes 47 Senators and 141 Delegates elected from 47 districts. The Maryland legislature is comprised of part-time representatives who dedicate a ninety-day period annually to lawmaking. Maryland's short legislative session requires a structure that facilitates lawmaking at a relatively quick pace. The state legislature is structured to enable lawmaking; therefore legislators are given a degree of autonomy to maneuver legislation through the representative body. Maryland's political culture is regarded as individualistic, akin to that of a business, where individual legislators broker deals and orchestrate political favors (Elazar 1972). While the party structure is highly organized, legislators have the ability to act as individuals, especially regarding policy areas in which some have specialized knowledge (Smooth 2001).
9. The multimember district structure is ideal for examining the effects of race and gender identity on Black women's legislative decision making, since a majority of the African American women represent the same constituency. As a result, we can differentiate constituent wishes from other internal factors, such as identity, that drive legislators' decision making.
10. While the legislators were informed that their interviews were "on the record," we have replaced legislators' names with pseudonyms due to the candid nature with which some legislators engaged Nadia Brown in conversation. While it was impossible to remove all identifying information, we believe that the pseudonyms provide a healthy amount of anonymity for the legislators in this study.

Acknowledgements The authors wish to thank Alexandra Filandra of the University of Illinois, Chicago, for sharing the initial dataset used in this project. The authors acknowledge Valeria Sinclair-Chapman, Rosalee Clawson, S. Laurel Weldon, and Leigh Raymond of Purdue University for their guidance. This research has been supported by a generous grant from the Center for the Environment at Purdue University.

REFERENCES

Anderson, K.J., M. Kanner, and N. Elsayegh. 2009. Are Feminists Man Haters? Feminists' and Non-feminists' Attitudes Toward Men. *Psychology of Women Quarterly* 33: 216–224.

Andrews, K.T. 1997. The Impacts of Social Movements on the Political Process: The Civil Rights Movement and Black Electoral Politics in Mississippi. *American Sociological Review* 62 (5): 800–819.

Bell, E.E.L., and S.M. Nkomo. 2001. *Our Separate Ways: Black and White Women and the Struggle for Professional Identity.* Boston, MA: Harvard Business School Press.

Bositis, D.A. 2011. *Resegregation in Southern Politics?* http://jointcenter.org/research/resegregation-in-southern-politics. Washington, DC: Joint Center for Political and Economic Studies.

Brown, N. 2014. *Sisters in the Statehouse: Black Women and Legislative Decision Making.* New York: Oxford University Press.

Canon, D.T. 1999. Electoral Systems and the Representation of Minority Interests in Legislatures. *Legislative Studies Quarterly* 24 (3): 331–385.

Center for American Women and Politics. 2014. Fact Sheet. *Women of Color in Elective Office 2014: Congress, Statewide, and State Legislature.*

Collins, P.H. 1990. *Black Feminist Thought: Knowledge, Consciousness and the Politics of Empowerment.* New York: Routledge.

Combahee River Collective. [1977] 1995. A Black Feminist Statement. In *Words of Fire: An Anthology of African American Feminist Thought*, ed. Beverly Guy-Sheftall, 232–240. New York: New Press.

Crenshaw, K.W. 1991. Mapping the Margins: Intersectionality, Identity Politics, and Violence against Women of Color. In *Critical Race Theory: The Key Writings That Formed the Movement*, ed. K. T. Crenshaw, Neil Gotanda, and Gary Peller, 357–383. New York: New York University Press.

Davidson, C., and B. Grofman. (Eds.). 1994. *Quiet Revolution in the South: The Impact of the Voting Rights Act, 1965–1990.* Princeton, NJ: Princeton University Press.

Elazar, D.J. 1972. *Federalism: A View from the States*, 2nd ed. New York: Harper & Row.

Esping-Andersen, G. 2009. *The Incomplete Revolution: Adapting to Women's New Roles*. Cambridge: Polity Press.

Gillespie, A. 2010. *Whose Black Politics?: Cases in Post-Racial Black Leadership*. New York: Routledge.

Guinier, L. 1991. The Triumph of Tokenism: The Voting Rights Act and the Theory of Black Electoral Success. *Michigan Law Review* 89 (5): 1077–1154.

Harris, A. 1990. Race and Essentialism in Feminist Legal Theory. *Stanford Law Review* 42 (February): 581–616.

Harris, D. 2001. From The Kennedy Commission to the Combahee Collective: Black Feminist Organizing, 1960–1980. In *Sisters in the Struggle: African-American Women in the Civil Rights–Black Power Movement*, ed. Bettye Collier-Thomas and Vincent P. Franklin, 280–304. New York: New York University Press.

Khagram, S., J.V. Riker, and K. Sikkink. 2002. From Santiago to Seattle: Transnational Advocacy Groups. In *Restructuring World Politics: Transnational Social Movements, Networks, and Norms*, ed. Sanjeev Khagram, James V. Riker, and Kathryn Sikkink, 3–23. Minneapolis: University of Minnesota Press.

Kupperschmidt, B.R. 2000. Multigeneration Employees: Strategies for Effective Management. *Health Care Manager* 19: 65–76.

Lavariega Monforti, J.L., B. D'Andra Orey, and A.J. Conroy. 2009. The Politics of Race, Gender, Ethnicity and Representation in the Texas Legislature. *Journal of Race and Policy* 1 (5): 7–25.

Lawless, J.L., and R.L. Fox. 2012. *Men Rule: The Continued Under-Representation of Women in U.S. Politics*. Washington, DC: Women & Politics Institute.

Lublin, D., T.L. Brunell, B. Grofman, and L. Handley. 2009. Has the Voting Rights Act Outlived Its Usefulness? In a Word, 'No.'. *Legislative Studies Quarterly* 34 (4): 525–553.

Mazur, A.G. 2002. *Theorizing Feminist Policy*. Oxford: Oxford University Press.

McBride, D.E., and A.G. Mazur. 2010. *The Politics of State Feminism: Innovation in Comparative Research*. Pennsylvania: Temple University Press.

Meyer, D.S., and N. Whittier. 1994. Social Movement Spillover. *Social Problems* 41 (2): 277–298.

Moghadam, V.M. 2005. *Globalizing Women: Transnational Feminist Networks*. Baltimore: Johns Hopkins University Press.

Morgan, J. 1999. *When Chickenheads Come Home to Roost: My Life as a Hip-Hop Feminist*. New York: Simon & Schuster.

Nicholson, L. 1997. Introduction. In *Second Wave Feminism: A Reader in Feminist Theory*, ed. Linda Nicholson, 1–6. New York: Routledge.

Orey, B.D., and N.E. Brown. 2014. Black Women State Legislators: Electoral Trend Data 1995–2011. *National Political Science Review* 16: 143–147.

Paxton, P., S. Kunovich, and M.M. Hughes. 2007. Gender in Politics. *Annual Review of Sociology* 33: 263–284.

Robnett, B. 1996. African American Women in the Civil Rights Movement 1954–1965: Gender, Leadership, and Micromobilization. *American Journal of Sociology* 101 (6): 1661–1693.

Rosser-Mims, D. 2011. *How and Why Black Women Are Elected to Political Office*. New York: The Edwin Mellen Press.

Smola, K.W., and Charlotte D. Sutton. 2002. Generational Differences: Revisiting Generational Work Values for the New Millennium. *Journal of Organizational Behavior* 23 (4): 363–382.

Smooth, W.G. 2001. African American Women State Legislators: The Impact of Gender and Race on Legislative Influence. Dissertation Services, UMI.

Smooth, Wendy. 2010. Intersectionality and Women's Leadership. In *Gender and Women's Leadership: A Sage Series Handbook*, ed. Karen O'Conner, 31–40. New York: Sage.

Springer, K. 2002. Third Wave Black Feminism? *Signs* 57: 1059–1082.

Strolovitch, D.Z. 2006. Do Interest Groups Represent the Disadvantaged? Advocacy at the Intersections of Race, Class, and Gender. *Journal of Politics* 68 (4): 893–908.

Tate, K. 1994. *From Protest to Politics: The New Black Voters in American Elections*. Cambridge, MA: Harvard University Press.

Taylor, V. 1989. Social Movement Continuity: The Women's Movement in Abeyance. *American Sociological Review* 54 (5): 761–775.

Walker, A. 1983. *In Search of Our Mothers' Gardens: Womanist Prose*. New York: Harcourt, Brace Jovanovich.

Weldon, S.L. 2002. Beyond Bodies: Institutional Sources of Representation for Women in Democratic Policymaking. *Journal of Politics* 64 (4): 1153–1174.

Weldon, S.L. 2006. Inclusion, Solidarity, and Social Movements: The Global Movement against Gender Violence. *Perspectives on Politics* 4 (1): 55–74.

Whittier, N. 1995. *Feminist Generations: The Persistence of the Radical Women's Movement*. Philadelphia, PA: Temple University Press.

Williams, L.F. 2001. The Civil Rights-Black Power Legacy: Black Women Elected Officials at the Local, State, and National Levels. In *Sisters in the Struggle: African American Women in the Civil Rights-Black Power Movement*, ed. Bettye Collier-Thomas, and Vincent P. Franklin, 306–331. New York: New York University Press.

CHAPTER 9

Not in Conflict, But in Coalition: Imagining Lesbians at the Center of the Second Wave

Claire Bond Potter

Abstract Historical assessments of Second-Wave Feminism have often portrayed lesbian feminists as outsiders of the more popular organizations that have been, at least in scholarly accounts, depicted as the real driving forces behind the movement. The common narrative characterizes lesbian activists as forced into exile by heterosexual feminists attempting to appeal to a more general public. Such portraits are understandable given the openly homophobic views expressed by leaders such as Betty Friedan, who warned of the "lavender menace" and the threat lesbians presented to the success of the feminist movement. In this chapter, however, Claire Potter argues that lesbian feminists played a central role in the Second Wave by forcing key leaders and organizations to grapple with differences across race, class, and sexuality. For example, sexual freedom was an important component of the movement, and lesbian feminists represented women who were uniquely defining sexuality entirely on their own terms without male influence. Lesbian feminists,

---

The original version of the book was revised: Final corrections have been incorporated. The erratum to this chapter is available at https://doi.org/10.1007/978-3-319-62117-3_11

C.B. Potter (✉)
The New School, New York, USA

in this respect, posed a direct challenge to the homogenous view of womanhood and forced society, as well as heterosexual feminists, to face differences across and among women. In addition, Potter argues that existing scholarship often ignores the many lesbians who did indeed play a central role in the Second Wave, even ignoring lesbians who remained active within Friedan's National Organization of Women. Ultimately, Potter concludes that while lesbians certainly found conflict in the Second-Wave feminist movement, their very presence, and the way in which they challenged the assumptions of the movement, created a critical activist foundation crucial to the fights for gay marriage, gay motherhood, and gay rights in the decades that followed. Placing lesbians at the center of the Second-Wave movement brings their true legacy to light.

What would the history of the women's movement look like if we put lesbians, rather than conflicts over lesbianism, at the center of Second Wave Feminism? What if, instead of using "lesbian" as a modifier for feminism's most destructive political tendencies—lesbian feminism, lesbian separatism, lesbian culture—we also understood lesbians as agents of, and advocates for, feminism's most potent social justice agendas? What would this history look like if we scrutinized what lesbians—despite their frequent difficulties functioning as feminist insiders—wanted, and continued to want, from feminism after the founding of the National Organization for Women (NOW) a half century ago? Or if we extended that history to how lesbians linked feminism to gay liberation?

As this volume shows, lesbianism—the idea that women could lead healthy and happy lives without men—was one of many fault lines within a movement that sought, ambitiously, to position itself as an agent of universal reform. Because "women" was a category that embraced multiple differences, Second-Wave feminists believed they could succeed at creating sweeping changes that the peace and African American Civil Rights movements had been unable to achieve. Lesbianism was necessary to liberal feminism as a sign of feminists' ability to understand and successfully incorporate difference. By 1970, radical *lesbian* feminism, a feminism in which women worked principally with and for other women, had become a visible alternative to liberal feminist institutions that hoped to succeed by persuading men that they too would benefit from a social justice agenda grounded in gender equality.

For radical feminists, lesbianism was more than an erotic choice: it was a form of resistance to the larger structures of gender oppression that forced women into subservient roles. The sexual revolution that had been dominated by men, and the fulfillment of male desire, could be reignited to include "feminine socialization, beauty standards, sexual practices, experts' accounts of health, and the whole range of interpersonal dynamics between women and their sexual partners," historian Jane Gerhard writes: "In this light, sexuality mattered because feminists saw it as the raw material out of which standards of womanhood were forged….radical feminists came to see sexuality as the primary source of both women's oppression and liberation." Even among feminists who were less than radical, Heather Love observes, to be a lesbian was to put one's feminism into practice. The "conflation of lesbian activity and feminist consciousness" redefined lesbianism "as a personally beneficial, politically meaningful activity for women."[1]

Lesbianism had its pragmatic uses for the movement as well, making it distinct from the First Wave and injecting a heady excitement about feminism's task of articulating women as a class. But as a sexual practice condemned by psychiatry, religion and the law, lesbianism was also dangerous. Perhaps it was even this sense of the enormous potential power of sexuality as politics that also caused some heterosexual women in the movement, even radical feminists, to hesitate at the full incorporation of lesbian rights in a feminist agenda. Lesbian sisters identified these hesitations and fears early on; in true movement style, they were singled out for special criticism. Straight feminists, Radicalesbians charged in a 1970 manifesto, often went to "great lengths to avoid discussion and confrontation with the issue of lesbianism." The title of this manifesto, "The Woman-Identified Woman," reversed the equation of normalization: it was lesbians who were offering inclusion to straight women, not the other way around. Radicalesbians saw their erotic and political commitment to women, and the displacement of men from feminist community, as a real possibility for the revolution. Their insistence that straight women would have to face this as a logical goal of the movement demonstrates that many lesbians imagined themselves as central players in Second-Wave Feminism's history from the beginning. Although their straight sisters perpetually tried to steer conversations about lesbianism into "some broader issue," the authors charged, they would continue to refuse this diversion: lesbianism *was* the broader issue. At least, it was the broader issue if women were not to be perpetually defined by their relationships to men. "It is absolutely essential to the success and fulfillment of the women's liberation movement that this issue be dealt with," the writers affirmed.[2]

In fact, feminism's high focus on sexuality after 1969 may be one of the defining differences between so-called First-Wave Feminism, re-energized in 1966 as a nonpartisan political movement; and the swift evolution of a distinct "Second Wave" that was powered by Eros, theory-making, and New Left direct action tactics.[3] What it meant to "deal with" lesbianism after 1969 was a question that generated both excitement and conflict within the movement. Feminism's many different impulses barely held together in those four intellectually fertile years after 1969. Furthermore, after a decade of struggle in which liberal feminism had moved left and gay liberation had displaced homophile activism, lesbians had choices about where and how to pursue their political goals. Slowly, even as political feminism hedged on the subject of lesbianism, feminist collectives, new women's studies programs, and grassroots projects were founded and pursued on the assumption that lesbian issues *were* women's issues.

Like other feminists, lesbians began by writing themselves into existence. In 1973, the first mass-market edition of the Boston Women's Health Book Collective's (BWHBC) classic volume, *Our Bodies, Ourselves*, initially self-published, became a best-selling bible of women's sexual health. The chapter on lesbians embraced a homophobic epithet as a political identity: "In Amerika, They Call Us Dykes." In the spirit of the BWHBC's ethic of challenging established expertise with knowledge developed through feminist inquiry, lesbians wrote the chapter—but as a separatist endeavor, unlike the process that had produced the rest of the book. Although it remained one of the most controversial portions of the volume within the collective, as well as to external audiences in the USA and abroad, publishing "In Amerika, They Call Us Dykes" was a crucial step in 1973, and perhaps the first time that lesbians had spoken back authoritatively to the medical profession, and to a mass audience, about their desires. By nurturing conversation about lesbians, and printing those conversations, organizations like the BWHBC not only expanded feminism's social justice mandate, they expanded the reach of feminism as an anti-homophobic practice.[4]

Yet by necessity lesbians, like women of color, had to embrace a paradox that, as Joan Scott has argued, is a central theme of feminist political and intellectual work.[5] Lesbian politics in the Second Wave insisted on the importance of difference within feminism's universal "woman": this was a problem and a provocation for a movement that, in both its liberal and radical formations, sought to imagine women's politics as a class politics emerging from a set of unified interests. Yet, as all veterans of the New Left knew, class politics and feminism's identity-based analysis were often a poor fit. As Alice Echols evaluated these contradictions in 1984, a year when the movement was imploding over the question of pornography, sex and desire were persistently unresolvable vexations that confounded the sex-as-class paradigm. Shared womanhood might not be a useful basis for a political movement at all if women's differences about something as basic as sexual desire could not be reconciled.[6] The unresolvability of these struggles over sex, many of which were fought by and between lesbians, has been viewed by some veterans of the Second Wave as having killed the movement itself. I disagree. Instead, there is ample evidence that these bitter political battles over sex, battles that left some activists exhausted and alienated by the mid-1980s, set the stage for a feminist "Third Wave" beginning in the 1990s that presumed women's right to sexual freedom and sexual dissent. One feature of this revitalized feminism was the campaign to admit both lesbians and gay men to marriage and parenthood. A second, somewhat different phenomenon, was the maturing of alliances between lesbians and gay men, which had been pioneered in the 1970s and flowered after 1987 in feminist responses to the fight against AIDS.[7]

As this volume demonstrates, there is no simple history of Second Wave Feminism, and no feminist history that does not lead quickly to strong evidence of intra-movement conflict over racism, homophobia, and class privilege. Within this framework, the question of whether feminism ought to be concerned with men at all, and if so, how, was often a defining issue for feminists. Crucial moments in feminist history that illustrate explicit and implicit disagreements about men between lesbians and straight women are iconic in the history of the Second Wave: National Organization for Women (NOW) founder Betty Friedan's 1969 warning that there was a "lavender menace" within the organization; the exuberant disruption of the Second Congress to Unite Women by Gay Liberation Front lesbians on May 1, 1970; and the bitter, but ultimately successful, fight over the lesbian rights resolution at the National Women's Conference in Houston in November 1977.

But what happens if we displace events that describe conflict, and move other events and tendencies that emphasize coalition and compromise to the center? While this chapter addresses the history of division, it imagines another history of sexual politics as well, a history of lesbians and straight women coming together over two decades to experiment with and try to refine an inclusive feminist vision. Historians are beginning to understand, for example, how lesbians functioned in community organizing and political contexts where sexual injustice embraced reproductive and economic, as well as erotic, choice. They have begun to document the cross-fertilization of lesbian politics with the Second-Wave women's movement and gay liberation, as well as the effects of this political bridging on the rise of a feminist direct action politics during the AIDS epidemic. These efforts flowered in the 1990s, when the AIDS Coalition to Unleash Power (ACT UP) brought lesbians and gay men together in a project for sexual and social justice that demonstrates the impact of feminism on American social and political history more generally. If lesbian rights had not always been a priority for heterosexual feminist organizations, they became a priority within ACT UP as lesbian organizers functioned within the crisis of the HIV pandemic to make links between the challenges of AIDS; reproductive choice, such as abortion and access to birth control; economic oppression; and sexual freedom.

An under examined aspect of the lesbian community that emerged within Second-Wave Feminism is how heterogeneous it was. Many, if not most, lesbians had a heterosexual past, and it is a mistake to not consider that when imagining the diversity of their commitments within the movement. Even those lesbians who did not require reproductive services had been raised to be heterosexual, giving them critical insights into the links between reproductive justice and their own freedom to pursue desire freely and without fear. Questions about the right to mother, and the right to retain custody of one's children when challenged by male dominated courts as "unfit," emerged as an opportunity for lesbian activism as more women, emboldened by the movement, left their marriages, some to pursue intimate relationships with other women.

While some lesbians sought to separate from men as much as possible, others explored political and erotic commonalities (and sometimes dismaying new experiences with sexism) within new gay men's communities that were flourishing in the 1970s.[8] In turn, Second-Wave Feminism encouraged lesbians to imagine themselves as a distinct, rights-seeking group in a longer American social justice tradition. "By encouraging people to think critically about the sex roles that structured relations between men and women, and limited women's choices in life, work and love," George Chauncey writes, "feminism gave gay male and especially lesbian liberationists a framework for analyzing their oppression."[9] But the reverse is also true: when we center lesbians in the Second Wave, we see that the representation of difference across class and race may have also given feminism the opportunity to become the universal rights movement that it had imagined itself to be in the 1960s.

Lesbian/Feminism

Histories of Second-Wave Feminism do not ignore lesbians, but too often lesbians are seen only as the objects of oppression and homophobia; they appear in these histories less as feminist agents, than as objects of straight feminists' curiosity and discomfort. Perhaps the most frequently repeated example of this is NOW co-founder Betty Friedan's 1969 characterization of lesbians as a "lavender menace." For over a decade, Friedan made it clear in her writings that she believed prominent lesbians like Kate Millet, Rita Mae Brown and Ivy Bottini to be the Achilles heel of the movement, and their radical vision for "sex-class warfare" divisive.[10] But perhaps Friedan looms too large in these histories, and more influential than she was in a movement that primarily drew its energy from grassroots actions and organizing that was far more diverse. In addition, histories of 1970s feminism that emphasize a "gay-straight split" do so at the cost of ignoring socialist feminists and women of color—groups where divisions over sexuality were far less salient.[11]

Betty Friedan's homophobia, and the centrality of NOW to feminism's history, has had a huge impact on how lesbians are remembered as agents of fear and division in the movement, and as perpetually marginalized and in resistance when that was hardly the case, even in NOW. Friedan's fear of lesbian influence was at least partly rooted in her adherence to social science, particularly psychology, as a way of understanding gender. More importantly, she feared that the organization she had begun to nurture in 1966 would be crushed by attacks on its reputation, as McCarthyism—a not very distant memory in the early years of NOW—had crushed the feminist reform tradition of the 1940s and 1950s.[12]

The stigma of lesbianism—still linked to madness and criminality in the public mind and in the law well into the 1970s—should never, Friedan believed, be modified with the word feminist. "The attempt to equate feminism and the women's movement with lesbianism had always been a favorite device of those who wanted to discredit the women's movement—or frighten women away from it," Friedan wrote in 1976.

It was for this reason that, when younger women in NOW insisted that the organization take a stand on lesbian rights, "the most responsible lesbians didn't like it," she asserted. Friedan's fears of lesbianism were not just strategic: they were visceral and personal. Invoking the Cold War style conspiracies that had framed her young adulthood, in one essay she repeated an unsourced rumor that, as NOW struggled over the issue of sexuality in its first decade, unnamed lesbians had hoped to use her as a "straight front" to forward their minority agenda. They had even, she wrote, designated an agent "to 'seduce' me to insure my cooperation."[13]

Friedan may also have been throwing smoke to disguise the significant presence of lesbians in NOW from the very beginning. Her anxiety that their numbers would grow may have been partly motivated by her awareness that lesbians, many of whom had worked in the Civil Rights, anti-war, and homophile movements, saw themselves as central players in the gender equality and civil rights platform that NOW envisioned in the 1960s and enacted in subsequent decades. An early influence on Friedan, and eventual co-author of the NOW statement of purpose, was "an eminent black woman scholar at Yale," a veteran of the peace and Civil Rights movements, and a semi-closeted lesbian, Pauli Murray. Another "respectable" lesbian who was an early member of NOW, and a close advisor, was journalist Dolores Alexander, who became the organization's first Executive Director in 1969 and the co-owner of a famous restaurant, Mother Courage, where lesbian and straight feminists gathered nightly. Other prominent lesbians in NOW were Del Martin and Phyllis Lyon, the founders of the Daughters of Bilitis and the Alice B. Toklas Democratic Club in San Francisco; graphic artist Ivy Bottini, who designed the NOW logo still in use today; then-closeted scholar Catherine Stimpson; and New York politician Elizabeth Holtzman, who also remained closeted well into the 1990s.[14]

The internal upheaval over sexuality that pushed many lesbians, even politically moderate ones like Alexander, out of the organization was preceded by a series of mini-crises that caused other lesbians in the organization like Kate Millet, Rita Mae Brown, and Brenda Feigen Fastau to do their feminist work elsewhere. But many lesbians remained in NOW, and continued to join it over time, despite Friedan's homophobia. Outside of New York, as Stephanie Gilmore points out, "NOW was everything to everyone because it had to be." If lesbians in San Francisco, Chicago, Los Angeles, and New York could leave the organization and join a lesbian separatist group or the growing LGBT movement, women in smaller cities needed to work within the framework of NOW because it was the only feminist game in town. Conversely, small NOW chapters probably needed them. In every chapter, large or small, there were women who joined as lesbians and women who came out as lesbians as they moved towards feminism. Whether these women were out or closeted, it would be "unrealistic," Gilmore points out, to believe that as their feminism evolved within the framework of NOW "it obliterated their other concerns or disconnected them from contemporaneous social movements."[15]

While many lesbians devoted themselves to liberal reform and party politics through feminism and may have seen staying in the closet as a pragmatic choice, others drew on radical feminist and Gay Liberation Front ideology to declare their lesbianism as a vanguardist stance. Coming out was the ultimate radical act in a heteropatriarchal society, and a thumb in the eye of a society that wanted to simply "pretend that homosexuality does not exist."[16] Friedan was undoubtedly part of that society, but her disdain for the lesbians she caricatured is difficult to disaggregate from her scorn for a range of feminists, straight and gay, women who were too radical, too angry with men, and too lacking in respectability to be attractive to the mainstream Americans Friedan wished to attract to the cause of reform. New York's Redstockings came in for special criticism, as did the Women's International Terrorist Conspiracy from Hell (WITCH), a group that specialized in making its point through casting spells and loony street theater. But Friedan also displayed an unexpected awareness of the damage homophobia could cause the movement and sometimes refrained from trying to discipline lesbians. In an account of the Congress to Unite Women on May 1, 1970, written a full year before she retreated from her anti-lesbian stance at the 1977 International Women's Year Conference, Friedan omitted the lesbian action organized by Daughters of Bilitis veteran Martha Shelley, in which lesbians took the stage wearing tee shirts that said "Lavender Menace." Instead, she condemned an *ad hoc* women's militia who threatened a media figure and his male camera crew with karate kicks when they tried to report on an abortion workshop.[17]

Friedan was also not entirely wrong: lesbians represented a serious challenge to a broad-based acceptance of feminism as a liberal reform movement that could enhance the lives of men and create equality for women within heteronormative structures. One important point of agreement among white lesbians in the women's movement was that, although some found separatist practices to be "constraining and narrow," they didn't care about what happened to men.[18] In addition, many lesbians were still invested in a New Left-style revolution, one that fought homophobia, racism and class prejudice at the same time as it fought sexism, a stance that was often missing from radical, as well as liberal, feminist politics. Martha Shelley—a member of the New York chapter of the Daughters of Bilitis in 1967 and a co-founder of Gay Liberation Front in 1969—privately wrote a lengthy critique of Susan Brownmiller's 1970 article in the *New York Times* about Women's Liberation, complaining of Brownmiller's lack of attention to the movement's diversity, and particularly her "slurs to the gay sisters." Most lesbians had been "ardent feminists long before women's liberation," Shelley wrote, but had "worked in secret" to protect the feminist movement from homophobic attacks and to "not scare the shit out of you straights." What Shelley read as Brownmiller's dismissal of movement lesbians in the article caused her to be "pissed...as though you have to answer such charges as 'they're all lesbians.' If you are freaked out about lesbians, don't mention us." Shelley was sure that Brownmiller would "be able to sympathize with a sister who had to prostitute herself for a living, who was married to a sadist, who had three illegal abortions as a result of incestual rape, who was a welfare mother deserted by some guy." Why, then, the lack of attention to lesbians with whom Brownmiller worked every day? Shelley apologized grudgingly at the end of the letter, but explained that homophobia disseminated by feminists was a "personal concern for me." However, "sisterhood is not promoted, in my eyes, by airing our differences in public, under the sensationalist gaze of those who would prefer to continue our oppression."[19]

Perhaps remnants of her time in Daughters of Bilitis caused Shelley to choose the private airing of grievances rather than denouncing Brownmiller in public, as was not uncommon in the movement. However, in more public displays of resistance, lesbians (and radical feminists who looked like lesbians) insisted on embodying the greatest promise of, and the greatest fears about, the gender equity agenda in feminism's Second Wave. As feminist institutions made inroads into the mainstream, lesbian activists saw themselves as having inherited a counterculture spirit of women's liberation that liberal feminism was leaving behind. In 1974, *The Lesbian Tide* published an "inDYKEment" of *Ms.*, aimed at advertisements that were as heterosexually oriented and "looksist" as those critiqued in the magazine's famous "Click!" section. Under the inDYKEment, the two-year-old *Ms.*, and by extension, its radical feminist publisher Gloria Steinem, was charged with "gross neglect and psychic genocide against lesbian women; sexist and heterosexist representations of women; [and] perpetuating anti-feminist attitudes and politics: elitism, professionalism, classism, superstarism and dollarism." Acting on behalf of "the State of Lesbos," the anonymous authors drew on a close reading of the magazine to produce the following charges: that in its first twenty-four issues, only five out of 505 articles had been about lesbians; that fewer than 2% of published letters had been "by, for or about lesbians;" and that the magazine had had only one lesbian staffer ("not true," a grumpy Steinem penciled next to this one item).[20]

Betty Friedan's original insistence on an inclusive movement that brought men into the project of reforming workplaces and families, and the hope of radical women like Steinem that men could be radicalized too, was challenged forcefully by some lesbians' insistence that the "problems" of men, motherhood and marriage did not have to be solved. One could simply walk away, and choose other women. Art critic Jill Johnston, the author of *Lesbian Nation: the Feminist Solution* (1973), believed that feminist reform of the marriage institution was fundamentally wrong-headed because monogamy and child rearing hindered women's self-actualization. But Johnston also believed that marriage and heterosexual parenting in any form was damaging to *children*, hindered their independence, and reproduced sexism in the next generation. Johnston practiced what she preached, announcing to one group of admirers "that she had arranged for her twelve-year-old son to move into a collective of men who had developed a Men's Liberation group and were dedicated to working through incipient sexism in their own lives."[21]

Johnston's popular treatise promoted lesbian separatism, a minority position within a minority position, as radical vanguardism. This occurred at a moment when lesbians, and straight women who wanted to participate in a feminist sexual revolution, saw centering lesbian sexuality as a way to preserve the radical edge of a movement that was being absorbed into popular culture.[22] When activist and scholar Karla Jay, who had long suspected she was a lesbian, came out as "bisexual" in a Redstockings meeting, it positioned her as radical and immediately brought her "a few suitors." Straight women sometimes viewed lesbian sex as an act of radical solidarity, and "a cut above a relationship with the terrible enemy – men."[23]

From the consciousness raising groups where women debated orgasm, sexual violence and the frustrations of heterosexual intimacy, to the pages of early radical feminist blockbusters like Kate Millett's *Sexual Politics* (1970) and Shulamith Firestone's *The Dialectic of Sex* (1970), lesbians represented the danger and the promise of what women might choose in a society where they were truly free to refashion their own erotic and domestic lives. Lesbians were sometimes even the heroes of these books. In her analysis of Henry Miller, the only woman (other than Millett, the lesbian critic) who is able to triumph over Miller's misogyny is a mistress who turns out to be a lesbian, while Firestone saw lesbianism as a repudiation of heterosexual intercourse that more women would adopt absent "excessive pressure on them to conform."[24] By 1980, lesbianism was still highly visible in the movement as a revolutionary stance against misogyny, as well as an identity position defined by sexual desire. In a widely read woman of color anthology, African American poet and essayist Cheryl Clarke declared that "For a woman to be a lesbian in a male-supremacist, misogynist, racist, homophobic, imperialist culture, such as that of North America, is an act of resistance;" while Adrienne Rich articulated "lesbian existence" as an explicit rebuke to "compulsory heterosexuality."[25]

While coming out as a lesbian might have been an opportunity to embrace the physical pleasures of emotional intimacy in an activist framework, it could also trigger devastating loss as former lives, once chosen, dissolved.[26] Rich's deepening involvement with feminism, and her drift toward intimate relationships with women was a factor in the end of her decades-long marriage; new archives suggest that decision may have also led to her husband's suicide.[27] Such losses were deeply painful for women. Similarly, when civil rights and feminist activist Minnie Bruce Pratt, married and the mother of two children, saw two women "making out under a coffee table" at an all-women's party in the early 1970s, it sent her into an unexpected tailspin that upended her life. She remembered being simultaneously "repulsed and attracted." Recognition of her homophobia was quickly replaced by an understanding that being a lesbian was possible: "it wasn't like you were going to drop off the edge of the earth. It was a way to live. Social circles, intellectual life, political life." Yet that possibility was accompanied by impossibility; after her marriage dissolved, Pratt lost custody of her children, one of the most painful episodes of her life.[28]

Yet lesbian institutions, and lesbian communities, that were committed to feminist activism, offered women like Pratt the emotional support she had not found in her marriage, support she could draw on to make a life when feminist attorneys could not help her overcome the bigotry of the courts.[29] Some parts of the country, like Northampton, Massachusetts, became known for feminist political communities where lesbians dominated and helped to define feminist praxis. In 1985, a local historian in Western Massachusetts was able to identify 17 different feminist, women's, or lesbian initiatives that had been launched in the Northampton-Springfield area after 1971. Two women's colleges and a major state university became an anchor for a women's studies initiative in the region. The first openly lesbian groups were founded in Northampton in 1972; and that year Robin Morgan and Kate Millett, both of whom identified as bisexual at the time but soon came out as lesbians, were invited to speak at the University of Massachusetts, Amherst. By 1980, the Valley had become a hub of lesbian activity, with newsletters, centers, and organizations for lesbians alongside and overlapping with other women's and feminist causes.[30]

The emergence of such communities demonstrates the vibrant community and institution-building energy that lesbians brought to feminism. As Kristen Hogan points out, networks of feminist bookstores created a transnational feminist community linked by conferences and booklists, a community that saw creating anti-racist and anti-homophobic spaces as a critical mission. Largely run and staffed by lesbians, these bookstores emphasized coalitional work across differences. Similarly, although the history of the women's health movement is most frequently associated with maternal health, contraception, abortion, and reproductive rights—issues that were largely, although not exclusively associated with heterosexual women's bodies—the community-based centers that provided these services were a resource for a feminist gynecology practice that included discussions about sexual pleasure and preference. One early clinic at the Seattle YWCA made "sexual identity, lesbianism and gender identity" a topic for frequent rap sessions, led by a recently out transgender woman, part of a programming agenda that allowed women to explore how their sexuality defined their experience of oppression and inequality. Community-based feminist activists also did anti-homophobic consciousness raising in working class communities where grassroots organizations mobilized communities around neighborhood social justice issues.[31]

Although these feminist institutions that put lesbians at the center were hardly without conflict, they provide an important contrast to the idea that "differences"—race, class, and sexuality—were barriers to feminist projects and feminist practice, a perspective that has long been in need of correction. "The gay-straight split fragmented 'the sisterhood,'" Ruth Rosen writes in her comprehensive history of the feminist movement, "creating various kinds of hierarchies that excluded many women. The emphasis on sexual orientation scared away some women fearful of unfamiliar and unconventional relationships, as well as an alien alternative culture." Although Rosen goes on to acknowledge the enormous intellectual and organizing power of lesbians, the many grassroots projects that lesbians launched—battered women's shelters, rape crisis centers, and health clinics—also split the movement, in her view. "Heterosexual women," Rosen concludes, "frequently found it difficult to integrate this mushrooming culture into their jobs and families."[32]

Yet there is also ample evidence that this work not only knit lesbians together, it also promoted transformative feminist work for all women at the grassroots. It is difficult to find any account of Second-Wave Feminism that makes lesbianism as central a concern for the movement as it was to lesbians or that articulates lesbians themselves as primary agents within a feminist movement that by 1977, with Friedan's reluctant support, came to support lesbian rights as human rights. To Rosen, for example, feminism offered more to lesbians than it got in return. "The women's movement helped liberate two generations of women from the loneliness and isolation they suffered as they hid in closets or cruised bars," she writes: "To older lesbians, the movement offered the opportunity to embrace the identity of lesbian with pride and, if possible, to 'come out' to friends and family. For younger women, the sexual revolution provided a safe space in which to explore a different sexual preference." In contrast, in one of the earliest histories of the movement, Sara Evans, proposes a slightly different scenario: lesbian activists may have *chosen* feminism because it offered them freedom from the New Left's homophobia, and the possibility of attending to lesbian rights as civil rights. Evans— with whom Minnie Bruce Pratt was dancing when Pratt saw the lesbians making out under a coffee table—notes in a tantalizing citation that none of the New Left women she interviewed who were lesbians came out "until *after* the emergence of the women's movement."[33]

Far more work also needs to be done on issues of sexual orientation that were present, but often muted, among African American feminists.[34] Although analysis differed as to which of the many challenges facing black women and their communities often made it difficult to discuss lesbianism, much less free women to love each other, analysis of heterosexism did not occupy the central place that anti-racist thought did. For many within the many different organizations that made up the political network we might collectively call "black feminism," the Combahee River Collective statement, issued in 1977, may have been "the first time they were forced to recognize *publicly* black lesbian existence, the daily oppression black lesbians face, and the considerable sexual diversity within black communities." However, as Kimberly Springer notes, this crucial document also "neglected to specify the ways that black communities were complicit in perpetuating heterosexism."[35]

This absence exists in the context of a lack of attention to lesbian agency within feminism more generally, one that then fails to recognize the importance of feminism within the lesbian and gay activism that built a rights-based movement in parallel to organizations like NOW. However, radical feminism created a new model for inhabiting a lesbian identity in the 1970s. Gender radicalism overwhelmed and transformed the more genteel model of homophile activism pioneered by the DOB.[36] "What is a lesbian?" Radicalesbians had declared in "The Woman-Identified Woman" in 1970: "A lesbian is the rage of all women condensed to the point of explosion." But lesbians were also savvy organizers and coalition builders, politicians, and radical activists; above all, they increasingly organized as potentially rights-bearing subjects under the banner of a feminist movement that they also sought to transform. By focusing on feminism's homophobia, historians have missed the significance of lesbians as critical coalition builders within the movement. But by re-focusing on the centrality of lesbians to feminism, we can then also see the importance of feminism to the social movements—particularly AIDS activism—that extends Second-Wave Feminism into the 1990s. If we follow this thread, what also emerges is an important history of why committed feminists like Pratt chose to be lesbians, and why, despite many feminists' reluctance to grapple with homosexuality as a civil rights issue, lesbians identified with feminism and viewed it as a promising location for coalitional work.

Lesbian Rights, Women's Rights

Radical lesbians who had cut their teeth in other social movements understood the importance of coalition, particularly as the conservative revolution of the 1970s gathered momentum and threatened women's political achievements more generally. Speaking at a Women Against

Pornography rally in Times Square in 1979, human rights activist and former lesbian separatist Charlotte Bunche announced her belief that lesbians were a link between the gay and feminist movements; feminists and gays were both committed to sexual self-determination, freedom of expression and freedom from violence. "Last week at the National Gay Rights Rally in Washington," she declared, "over 100,000 people marched to demand better of our society. We demanded the right to control our bodies, including our sexuality, and we demanded an end to social degradation and violence against lesbians and gay men. Today, many lesbians are here marching again to demand that same right as women—to control our bodies and to protect all women from the violence of pornography." Labeling lesbians perverse, and criminalizing their sexuality, made them implicitly pornographic, Bunche argued, giving them a special stake in the feminist fight against the "woman-hating pornography" industry.[37]

It is ironic that the campaign against pornography, one of the most divisive moments in Second-Wave feminist history, was initially seen by this savvy organizer as an opportunity for lesbian and feminist coalition building. What Bunche spoke to more generally, however, was true: in the civil rights landscape of the 1970s, the interests of women and gays were converging. Because of feminist litigation, marriage and family began to undergo a seismic, legal redefinition from traditional, patriarchal models, setting the stage for lesbians and gays to win the right to cohabit, to parent children openly, to engage in intimate relations, and ultimately, to marry. At the same time, women were gaining the right to education, to credit, and to employment—rights that would also free them to live, and raise children, independently of men. From 1965 on, states gradually reformed divorce laws to eliminate adversarial proceedings, making it possible to dissolve marriages more easily, and without attaching legal fault to either party. Strengthening child support laws and moving toward joint custody, the courts laid the grounds for extended and blended families that defied the traditional links between monogamous marital domesticity and biological parenthood. In 1976, a landmark lawsuit established the possibility that cohabitation without marriage could create marriage-like obligations. The Lee Marvin "palimony" case signaled an end to the stigma of cohabitation and, in a precedent setting move of particular interests to gays and lesbians, "allowed the economic aspect of a cohabiting relationship to be recognized legally" even though the ruling recognized the relationship not as a marriage, but an "agreement between business."[38] Although marriage and legalized gay adoption were far in the future, between 1969 and 1985, lesbian mothers and gay fathers organized, both socially and politically, to build on these new definitions of domesticity. With the help of allies like the National Gay and Lesbian Task Force (NGLTF), NOW's Lesbian Rights Project, and the American Civil Liberties Union (ACLU), families characterized by two lesbian mothers began to emerge as a major political force pressing for the legalization of gay marriage.[39]

These developments relied on the emergence of lesbian political communities within feminism that imagined themselves as simultaneously distinct and as having common interests with heterosexual women and gay men. Persistent pressure on NOW from lesbians in the organization intensified after Friedan relinquished the presidency to Aileen Hernandez in 1970, and in 1971, the organization issued a statement recognizing lesbian rights as civil rights. In 1973, NOW established a Task Force on Sexuality and Lesbianism that acknowledged "the oppression of lesbians as a legitimate concern of feminism." At their sixth annual conference in the spring of 1973, NOW declared that women had "the basic right to develop their full human sexual potential," and that discrimination on the grounds of sexuality was counter to the feminist fight against oppression. As part of that effort, NOW declared its support for "civil rights legislation to end discrimination based on sexual orientation" as numerous lesbian and gay rights bills were making their way through local legislatures."[40]

Other forms of professional and political organizing nourished by feminism also provided support for lesbian equality within NOW, particularly within the academic women's studies movement. In 1978, Annette Van Dyke was gratified by the visible lesbian presence at the National Women's Studies Association (NWSA). An older graduate student and mother who had left her husband for a woman, Van Dyke recalled that Clare Bright, later a chair of NWSA's Lesbian Caucus, had reassured her that the organization was not homophobic. "At the time there was controversy over whether lesbians would be welcome in NOW, and since my partner and I were state NOW officers, this made Clare's assurances that NWSA would be different important," she remembered.[41]

By 1979, many feminists, lesbian and straight, understood the importance of coalition across differences in the face of strengthened conservative attempts to reverse the civil rights achievements of the movement's first decade. Conservative charges that the left, and feminism in particular, were sexually deviant, immoral and anti-family revived early movement warnings that the word "lesbian" was a weapon of intimidation against all women, straight or gay. But this time, straight feminists resisted. Recalling her participation in the March on Washington to demand the extension of the Equal Rights Amendment (ERA) ratification deadline, historian Eileen Boris noted that no feminist could separate any political issue from questions of sexuality and reproductive freedom, in part because the New Right had linked them. "The Eagle Forum's Phyllis Schlafly," Boris writes, "strategized her opposition to the constitutional amendment by invoking the collapse of gender norms." A post-ERA America, Schlafly had charged, would be overrun with "unisex bathrooms, lesbianism, 'homosexual' marriages, and women in combat."[42] Indeed, as lesbian and feminist Urvaishi Vaid would later recall, the worst was yet to come and the need for coalitional politics would intensify: "For lesbians, gay men, bisexuals and transgendered people, the Reagan-Bush years were the worst years of our lives."[43]

A new feminist history that recognizes the significance of Boris's insight might see particular lesbians like Vaid, a chair of the National Gay and Lesbian Task Force, and activist writer Sarah Schulman, as central figures in helping Second-Wave Feminism meet the challenges of conservative backlash. Arriving at the University of Chicago in 1976, Schulman had been expelled from her family at the age of 16 after having admitted to an affair with a classmate at Hunter High School. Joining the Women's Union, she became active in the Chicago feminist movement; upon her return to New York in 1979, she began to write for the feminist and the gay press, primarily *Womannews*, *Gay Community News*, and *The New York Native*. Although well aware of tensions between gay men's and lesbian politics, Schulman—like activists Maxine Wolf, Ann Northrup, Joan Gibbs, Jean Carlomusto and others—eventually came to understand her work in the 1990s for the AIDS Coalition to Unleash Power, a mixed-gender queer collective, as an extension of this lifetime commitment to lesbian and feminist activism. But, like the mainstream women's movement, ACT UP also served a second purpose: it was a larger vehicle for pursuing a lesbian agenda as the political space for social justice shrank in the 1980s. "For those of us from the feminist movement," Schulman recalled, "advocating for equal access to resources for women and people of color topped out list of priorities, even though we were involved in every aspect of policy and strategy development."[44]

ACT UP helps us see the plumb line between lesbian activism, as it was born in coalition with Second-Wave Feminism in the late 1960s, and lesbian activism as it developed politically in coalition with gay men 20 years later. Schulman's first action was on July 24, 1987, when the four-month-old direct action group founded by gay writer Larry Kramer staged its fifth major protest. At first glance, it would not have seemed like a feminist action. Dressed for the summer heat in tee shirts and shorts that sometimes revealed purplish-brown Kaposi's Sarcoma lesions, the mostly male protesters chanted and marched outside Memorial Sloan-Kettering Cancer Center on Manhattan's Upper East Side. Along with a few women, these men were demanding access to experimental treatment protocols similar to those that had always been available to cancer patients at this elite research institution. More than 6 years after AIDS had been identified by the United States Centers for Disease Control (CDC), and 4 years since the virus that caused immune system collapse had been identified, no new drug had been released to treat either the AIDS virus itself or the opportunistic infections that sickened and killed its victims. In March 1987, like the feminist activists of the women's health movement before them, gay men and lesbians began planning actions in weekly meetings of ACT UP, held at the Lesbian and Gay Community Services Center in Greenwich Village.[45]

Because ACT UP's leadership and core committees (for example, Treatment Action Group, or TAG) was predominantly white, bourgeois and male, the role of feminist, racial and class critique, as well as the role of lesbians steeped in the feminisms of the 1970s, has been partially concealed. The assumption that what would come to be the leading edge of a new politically radical LGBT movement had little to do with feminism has been exacerbated by the prolific writing and speaking of Kramer, also ACT UP's founder and most prominent member. Kramer consistently portrayed gay men as the most neglected victims of AIDS, and ACT UP itself as unique in the history of activism. This conceals many activists'—male and female—prior experience in feminism, as well as in the movements that preceded feminism: the peace, reproductive rights, and Civil Rights movements.[46] Activists of both genders brought strategies to ACT UP that had been devised in feminism and a feminist-inflected gay liberation politics. Lesbians, in particular, brought experience in creating theory that then shaped coalitions, political statements and direct action zaps. Born into the struggles for abortion and the ERA, and reaching adulthood in time for the sex wars of the 1980s, when they joined ACT UP, these women were imagining a more sexually explicit, rigorously class and race conscious, feminism for the 1990s.[47]

Lesbian hands that waved signs reading "Silence = Death" and "Silencio = Muerto" at Sloan-Kettering and subsequent demonstrations were also marching on behalf of women's civil rights agenda under siege by Ronald Reagan's conservative revolution; signs reading "ERA Now!" "Stop Rape!" and "Repeal All Abortion Laws!" were also common at ACT UP rallies. Ann Northrup, a lesbian journalist and educator who is pointedly ignored in Kramer's origin story, emerged as one of the four facilitators of ACT UP in its formative months. Like many feminists, Northrup's activism had begun in direct action protests against the Vietnam War. Drawn to feminism when Gloria Steinem spoke at her Vassar College graduation, she came out as a lesbian in 1971 while working as a writer on a feminist television news show and freelancing for *Ms*. Northrup had then participated in "a lot of demonstrations and actions" as radical feminism occupied the streets and the legislatures in the 1970s.[48]

In their accounts of ACT UP, lesbians make these direct connections between feminism and AIDS activism. One of the "dykes, drag queens lesbian and people with AIDS on the front lines" in front of Sloan-Kettering, Sarah Schulman, now a professor at City University of New York, and gay activist videographer Jim Hubbard have chronicled hundreds of ACT UP oral histories, many of which make this point. "When I came out in the 1970s," Schulman recalled in 1994, "I came out into a feminist movement of lesbians and heterosexual women working together for women's liberation. Abortion was legalized in this country in 1973 when I was 15 years old. And, my first real activist commitment was to keep abortion safe, legal and funded." Like many lesbians before her, the links between sexism and homophobia, between the devaluing of women's bodies and gay bodies by the Reagan administration and the escalation of homophobia, were intuitive and obvious.[49]

Collective action strategies, particularly those that emphasized dramatic public performances, in turn, became the basis for new feminist organizations and collectives springing out of ACT UP. In the context of the fight against AIDS, and a renewed attention to class and racial struggle, these lesbians launched some of the first radical feminist counter attacks against conservative policies that sought to retract rights which had been at the core of the women's liberation struggle. In 1989, the Women's Health Action and Mobilization (WHAM!) organized in response to the Supreme Court decision in *Webster v. Reproductive Health Services* that affirmed the right of states to defund reproductive choice, disrupting the confirmation hearings of George H.W. Bush's Supreme Court nominee David J. Souter. They joined with ACT UP in Stop the Church, an action in New York's St. Patrick's Cathedral that protested the Catholic Church's opposition to birth control, sex education, and condoms. WHAM! then produced two other direct action groups, New York Clinic Defense Task Force, which escorted women across anti-abortion picket lines, and Church Ladies for Choice. In 1992, a group of six lesbian feminists that included ACT UP veterans Schulman, Maxine Wolf, and Ann-Christine D'Adesky formed the Lesbians Avengers, whose protests made an impact through performances such as fire eating, an all-lesbian marching band, and handing out balloons with anti-homophobic slogans at public schools. In 1993, in coalition with the ACT UP Women's Network, the Avengers created New York's Dyke March, which still occurs the night before the Annual Pride March.

The history of grassroots lesbian organizations that brought a feminist analysis to a gay men's movement, and then returned that activism to a revitalized struggle for women's rights in the 1990s, is an opportunity to ask new questions about the feminist legacy that lesbians consciously brought to the fight against AIDS. Despite the "well-known lesbian purges" in liberal feminist organizations like NOW, activists like Sarah Schulman saw their feminism as inextricable from the lesbian identities that drew them into coalition with the gay men of ACT UP. "The version of feminism that I had inherited at the end of the 70s, and that many lesbians identified with," she recalled, "was a vibrant, activist movement engaged in re-evaluating and re-imagining every aspect of social life."[50]

It is not a new point that 1970s feminism foundered, to some degree, on its commitment to the myth of shared womanhood, and that lesbians persistently disrupted that dream. However, lesbians built on that dream too, crafting a coalitional style that built bridges between feminism and other movements. Sexual freedom, although it could be a source of discomfort, cliquishness and resentment within feminism, also created and empowered diverse political coalitions in ways that historians of women, gender and sexuality are only beginning to understand. What feminists came to call "body politics" was an activist stance that emphasized all women's right to reproductive freedom (including maternity); to sexual health and sexual self-expression; to freedom from violence; and to freedom from corporate and media driven standards of beauty. Because of this, the principles of Second-Wave grassroots feminism, often understood to have given way to the so-called Third Wave by the 1990s, continued to define lesbian activism and lesbian commitments to sexual justice into the twenty-first century.

NOTES

1. Jane Gerhard, *Desiring Revolution: Second Wave Feminism and the Rewriting of American Sexual Thought, 1920–1982* (New York: Columbia University Press, 2001), 3; Heather Love, "Gentle, Angry People: the Lesbian Culture Wars," *Transition* v. 9 no. 4 (2000), 98.
2. Radicalesbians, "The Woman-Identified Woman," 2; http://library.duke.edu/digitalcollections/wlmpc_wlmms01011/.
3. Nancy Hewitt has rightly noted that the "wave" metaphor, although it was widely used by feminists after 1965, "cannot fully capture these multiple and overlapping movements, chronologies, issues and sites." Yet, as she and the other authors in this collection imply, waves also allow us to characterize and generalize from distinct changes in the intellectual history and political conversation of feminism; see Nancy A Hewitt, ed. *No Permanent Waves: Recasting the Histories of U.S. Feminism* (New Brunswick: Rutgers University Press, 2009).
4. Kathy Davis, *The Making of Our Bodies, Ourselves: How Feminism Travels Across Borders* (Durham: Duke University Press, 2007), 27.
5. Joan Scott, *Only Paradoxes to Offer: French Feminists and the Rights of Man* (Cambridge: Harvard University Press, 1997).
6. See Alice Echols, "The Taming of the Id: Feminist Sexual Politics, 1968–1983," *Shaky Ground: The Sixties and Its Aftershocks* (New York: Columbia University Press, 2002), 109–128. Originally published in 1984; Lisa Duggan and Nan D. Hunter, *Sex Wars: Sexual Dissent and Political Culture* (New York: Rutledge, 1996); Carolyn Bronstein, *Battling Pornography: The American Feminist Anti-Pornography Movement, 1976–1986* (New York: Cambridge University Press, 2011), 279–308.
7. See Deborah B. Gould, *Moving Politics: Emotion and ACT-UP's Fight Against AIDS* (Chicago: University of Chicago Press, 2009); Jennifer Brier, *Infectious Ideas: U.S. Political Responses to the AIDS Crisis* (Chapel Hill: University of North Carolina Press, 2009); Tamar W. Carroll, *Mobilizing New York: AIDS, Antipoverty and Feminist Activism* (Chapel Hill: University of North Carolina Press, 2015). Katie P. Batza's book,

Before AIDS (forthcoming from the University of Pennsylvania Press), shows how gay men's clinics established in the 1970s drew on feminist community health models that laid a foundation for the response to the HIV virus.
8. See, for example, Gayle Rubin's running commentary on what she learned about lesbian politics and institution building from immersing herself in communities of gay men: see *Deviations: A Gayle Rubin Reader* (Durham: Duke University Press, 2011).
9. George Chauncey, *Why Marriage: the History Shaping Today's Debate Over Gay Equality* (New York: Basic Books, 2004), 30.
10. Betty Friedan, *It Changed My Life: Writings on the Women's Movement* (New York: Random House, 1976), 138–140, 175.
11. Katie King, *Theory in Its Feminist Travels: Conversations in U.S. Women's Movements* (Bloomington: Indiana University Press, 1994) 140; Becky Thompson, "Multiracial Feminism: Recasting the Chronology of Second Wave Feminism," *Feminist Studies* v. 28 no. 2 (2002), 336–360; Laurel A. Clark, "Beyond the Gay/Straight Split: Socialist Feminists in Baltimore," *NWSA Journal* v. 19 no. 2 (Summer 2007), 1–31.
12. Daniel Horowitz, *Betty Friedan and the Making of the Feminine Mystique: The American Left, the Cold War and Modern Feminism* (Amherst: University of Massachusetts Press, 2000), 11–12. For the effects of official homophobia on First-Wave feminist reform, see Estelle Freedman, *Maternal Justice: Miriam Van Wters and the Female Reform Tradition* (Chicago: University of Chicago Press, 1996).
13. Friedan, *It Changed My Life*, 141, 159; Horowitz, *Betty Friedan and the Making of the Feminine Mystique*, 15.
14. Friedan, *It Changed My Life*, 77, 179–181. Pauli Murray's account of her own life makes no reference to her sexuality; see *Pauli Murray, The Autobiography of a Black Activist, Feminist, Lawyer, Priest, and Poet* (Knoxville: University of Tennessee Press, 1987). Although Murray herself grew more comfortable with her lesbianism as she aged, knowledge about her sexuality was confined to a circle of friends for most of her life; it is possible that Friedan was not even aware of Murray's sexuality in the mid-1960s. Furthermore, as Glenda Gilmore notes, Murray's radical Christian faith, not her feminism, was her principle political impulse; see *Defying Dixie: The Radical Roots of Civil Rights, 1919–1950 (New York: W.W. Norton, 2009)*, 326.
15. Stephanie Gilmore, *Groundswell: Grassroots Feminist Activism in Postwar America* (New York: Routledge, 2013), 17, 23.
16. Karla Jay and Allan Young, eds., *Out of the Closets: Voices of Gay Liberation*, (New York: Douglas Book Corporation, 1972), 59.
17. Friedan, *It Changed My Life*, 77.

18. Kathy Rudy, "Radical Feminism, Lesbian Separatism, and Queer Theory," *Feminist Studies* v. 27 no. 1 (Spring 2007), 190–222.
19. Susan Brownmiller, "'Sisterhood is Powerful:' A Member of the Women's Liberation Movement Explains What It's All About," *New York Times*, March 1917; Martha Shelley to SB, March 16, 1970, folder 8, box 2, Susan Brownmiller Papers, Schlesinger Library, Harvard University.
20. The Lesbianation Supreme Court, For the State of Lesbos, "InDYKEment against *Ms.* Magazine," *The Lesbian Tide*, (August 1974), 5; Box 85, folder 1, Gloria Steinem Papers, Sophia Smith Collection, Smith College.
21. Jill Johnston, *Lesbian Nation: the Feminist Solution* (New York: 1973), 151–152; Deborah Goleman Wolf, *The Lesbian Community* (Berkeley: University of California Press, 1979), 157.
22. See Alice Echols, *Daring to Be Bad: Radical Feminism in America, 1967–1965* (Minneapolis: University of Minnesota Press, 1989;) Arlene Stein, *Sex and Sensibility: Stories of a Lesbian Generation* (Berkeley: University of California Press, 1997); Jane Gerhard, *The Dinner Party: Judy Chicago and the Power of Popular Feminism* (Athens: University of Georgia Press, 2013).
23. Karla Jay, *Tales of the Lavender Menace: A Memoir of Liberation* (New York: Basic Books, 1999), 66.
24. Kate Millett, *Sexual Politics* (Garden City, New York: Doubleday, 1970), 304; Shulamith Firestone, *The Dialectic of Sex: the Case for Feminist Revolution* (New York: William Morrow, 1970), 58.
25. Cheryl Clarke, "Lesbianism: An Act of Resistance," Cherrie Moraga and Gloria Anzaldua, eds., *This Bridge Called My Back (Ithaca, NY: Kitchen Table Woman of Color Press, 1983)* 128–137; Adrienne Rich, "Compulsory Heterosexuality and Lesbian Existence," *Signs* v. 5 no. 4 (Summer 1980), 631–660.
26. Estelle B. Freedman, *No Turning Back: The History of Feminism and the Future of Women* (New York: Ballantine Books, 2002), 265.
27. Michelle Dean, "The Wreck," *The New Republic*, April 3, 2015.
28. Oral history of Minnie Bruce Pratt by Kelly Anderson, March 16–17 2005, *Voices of Feminism Oral History Project*, Sophia Smith Collection, Smith College, 42. Pratt wrote about this custody battle in *Crimes Against Nature* (Ithaca, NY: Firebrand Books, 1989).
29. A. Finn Enke, *Finding the Movement: Sexuality, Contested Space and Feminist Activism* (Durham: Duke University Press, 2007).
30. Amy Silverstein and Diane Mueller-Klingspor, "An Updated Herstory of the Valley Women's Movement, 1978–1984" folder 12, box 11, Lesbian Calendar Records, Sophia Smith Collection of Women's History, Smith College Libraries.
31. Kristen Hogan, *The Feminist Bookstore Movement: Lesbian Antiracism and Feminist Accountability* (Durham: Duke University Press, 2016); Jennifer Nelson, *More Than Medicine: A History of the Feminist Women's*

Health Movement (New York: New York University Press, 2015), 92, 95–96; Carroll, *Mobilizing New York*, 114.

32. Ruth Rosen, *The World Split Open: How the Modern Women's Movement Changed America* (New York: Penguin Books, 2000), 174.
33. Rosen, *The World Split Open*, 164; Sara Evans, *Personal Politics: the Roots of Women's Liberation in the Civil Rights Movement and New Left* (New York: Vintage Books, 1979), 12.
34. Evelynn Hammonds, "Black (W)holes and the Geometry of Black Female Sexuality," *Differences* v. 6 no. 2–3 (Summer-Fall 1994).
35. Kimberly Springer, *Living for the Revolution: Black Feminist Organizations, 1968–1980* (Durham: Duke University Press, 2005), 108; 130–131.
36. Marcia Gallo, *Different Daughters: A History of the Daughters of Bilitis and the Rise of the Lesbian Rights Movement* (New York: Seal Press, 2007).
37. Charlotte Bunch, "Who Is Hurt?" in Laura Lederer, ed. *Take Back the Night: Women on Pornography* (New York: William Morrow and Company, 1980), 91–94; Claire Bond Potter, "Taking Back Times Square: Feminist Repertoires and the Transformation of Urban Space In Late Second Wave Feminism," *Radical History Review* no. 113 (Spring 2012).
38. Nancy Cott, *Public Vows: A History of Marriage and the Nation* (Cambridge: Harvard University Press, 2000), 206–208.
39. Daniel Rivers, "'In the Best Interests of the Child:' Lesbian and Gay Parenting Custody Cases, 1967–1985," *Journal of Social History* v. 43 no. 4 (Summer 2010), 917–943.
40. "The Vociferous Majority: the Future is NOW,'" *Ms.* (May 1973), 114; Rosen, *The World Split Open*, 83.
41. Annette Van Dyke, "Identity Politics in NWSA: Memoirs of a Lesbian Caucus Chair," v. 14 no. 1, *NWSA Journal* (Spring 2002), 51.
42. Eileen Boris, "A Memory of Struggle," *Women's Studies Quarterly*, v. 43 no. 3 & 4 (Fall/Winter 2015), 284.
43. Quoted in Sarah Schulman, *My American History: Lesbain and Gay Life During the Reagan/Bush Years* (New York: Rouledge, 1994), xi.
44. Schulman, *My American History*, 175.
45. Jennifer Nelson, *More Than Medicine: A History of the Feminist Women's Health Movement* (New York: New York University Press, 2015).
46. It is notable that in an extensive interview, Kramer never mentions the word feminism, and never speaks about the role of women in the organization. Larry Kramer, interviewed by Sarah Schulman, November 15, 2003; interview #35, ACT-UP Oral History Project, http://www.actuporalhistory.org. Kramer seems to have been more or less untouched by feminism: in collected essays from the period, *Notes from the Holocaust: the Story of an AIDS Activist* (New York: Continuum International Publishing Group, 1995), he cites only one feminist, Vivian Gornick, to support his own point about how

oppressed groups cannot necessarily be counted on to come together in a crisis (see 17).
47. Jennifer Brier, *Infectious Ideas: U.S. Political Responses to the AIDS Crisis* (Chapel Hill: University of North Carolina Press, 2009), 11–14.
48. Ann Northrup, interviewed by Sarah Schulman, May 28, 2003; interview #27, ACT-UP Oral History Project, http://www.actuporalhistory.org.
49. Schulman, *My American History*, 3.
50. Schulman, *My American History*, 1.

CHAPTER 10

Conclusion: Assessing Second-Wave Historiography

Lisa Corrigan

Abstract In her concluding chapter, Lisa Corrigan confirms the initial claim made by Sara M. Evans: that the wave metaphor should be replaced by a broader, more-inclusive history that accurately depicts the continuous and overlapping efforts of women activists. And our work is just beginning, notes Corrigan. Now, with the gift of hindsight and the awareness of the mistakes and the limitations of the Second Wave, is the time to reflect on the feminist cause in America and to chart its path forward.

From a contemporary perspective that has seen the Supreme Court uphold gay marriage, the popular culture embrace of the life stories of *trans women on television and in print journalism, and the high visibility of female #BlackLivesMatter activists disrupting presidential campaign events, this does seem like an opportune time to look backward to assess the trajectory of feminist politics in the twentieth century. As race, class, and sexual identity

---

The original version of the book was revised: Final corrections have been incorporated. The erratum to this chapter is available at
https://doi.org/10.1007/978-3-319-62117-3_11

L. Corrigan (✉)
University of Arkansas, Fayetteville, USA

© The Author(s) 2018
A. Maxwell and T. Shields (eds.), *The Legacy of Second-Wave Feminism in American Politics*, https://doi.org/10.1007/978-3-319-62117-3_10

have augmented identity politics while challenging the importance of feminist agitation, so too have they called into question white feminist assessments of the history of the movement. "Second-Wave" historiographies have demonstrated both the utility and the problems with the "wave" metaphor in evaluating the relationships among different periods of feminist activism. As Nancy Hewitt explains, "many feminists and scholars of feminism identified the first wave as comprising largely white, middle-class women focused on achieving narrowly defined political goals, most notably suffrage. In contrast, they claimed the Second Wave as more inclusive and transformative" (2). Certainly, the task of Second-Wave feminists was to document the oppression of women and theorize its history. Using biological, political, economic, and social frameworks, these feminists charted political disenfranchisement, economic deprivation, physical violence, social containment, and the failures of liberal "rights" frameworks. As Susan Carroll demonstrates in Chap. 6, Second-Wave feminists used the "gender gap" meme to help describe and impact the social and political oppression of women.

In assessing the scholarship (and the inclusivity and transformative potential of) Second-Wave feminist activism, it is clear that academics are nowhere near close to producing comprehensive histories of feminist history, politics, activism, or artistic production despite the rich contributions of this collection and the collaborations and interactions that propelled and constrained Second-Wave activists. Nonetheless, as Sara M. Evans contends in Chap. 2, establishing women's history and telling the stories of women continues to be a central preoccupation of feminist scholarship across disciplines as contemporary scholars work to center the feminist struggle in the contemporary milieu. New monographs examining the rich and diverse practices of feminist activists and intellectuals across the country demonstrate the complexity of feminist agitation during this period and document the persistent and pernicious barriers to equality for women in America. It is no longer controversial to assert the existence of multiple feminist micro-cohorts within this political generation that were being shaped and reshaped by internal and external pressures that created enduring boundaries among feminists.

This collection provides a rejoinder to those who want neat categories and linear narratives about the generational cohort commonly called "Second-Wave Feminism." Instead of reifying a bounded timeline, a series of "stars" leading the movement, or an account of movement activism focused on national organizations, this book provides a more textured account of the period to emphasize how variable and occasionally volatile coalitions marked the innovation of the movement. It provides multiple accounts of moments, activists, strategies, and tactics of the movement to prompt a contemporary conversation reassessing the goals of writing "Second-Wave" historiography. As many of the authors in this volume attest, Second Wave Feminism was characterized by intense opposition within feminist organizations as well as from those hostile to feminism more generally.

Still, as scholars continue to assess the distinctions that mark the "Second Wave" from the "Third Wave," attention must be paid to the creation of new forms of power, both individual and collective. For example, in her arguments about the dissimilarities between Second- and Third-Wave Feminism, Diane Elam has claimed:

> Feminism needs to take account of the fact that it does not simply stand outside of institutional power structures at the same time that it tries to imagine new ways of standing together. The problem with actually doing this seems to revolve around a lack of specifically feminist models of power and tradition. (64)

Collections like this that seek to trace the history of activist feminist traditions and strategies work to map the relationship between feminism and traditional models of power to showcase points of rupture, provocation, empowerment, and failure. In doing so, they chart the relationships among feminist activists and organizations.

As scholars continue to engage Second-Wave Feminism to challenge the essentialist or neat categories that early historiography has advanced, I want to suggest that two important threads for feminist scholars looking into and through the so-called Second-Wave generation. First, misogynist politics both propelled and constrained Second-Wave activism. Second, it is clear women of color have been a tremendous asset to feminist activism and have provided strategies and innovations that have become essential for feminist agitation and scholarship beyond the so-called Second Wave. These qualities of the Second Wave stand as important markers of this milieu and can help shape future scholarly investigation by highlighting complex factors that have influenced feminist politics then and now.

SECOND-WAVE FEMINISM: PROPULSION AND CONTAINMENT

From the contributions of this volume, it is clear that anti-feminist, anti-woman politics helped build momentum for the Second-Wave feminist movement even as it simultaneously undermined feminist activism. From the primary sources of this period of movement activism, we have treatises, memoirs, and debates that display a wide range of attitudes from overwhelming support to crippling ambivalence. As women's liberationists sought to distinguish their agenda from the splintering coalitions of the American left, they found tremendous opposition in the emergent right. As it became clear that most organizations in the US left would not accommodate feminist principles or strategies to identify ideologies of oppression that uniquely impacted women, let alone work to ameliorate sexist oppression, feminists worked diligently to build spaces for fully autonomous feminist praxis. Particularly as "the economy tightened in the early 1970s and the political climate became more conservative, social movement participants were unable to sustain their previous level of mobilization," changing both the nature of feminist participation as well as the political goals of new agitation in the Second Wave (Whittier 83).

Clearly, the recalibration of the Second Wave at the end of the 1970s was fueled by economic and political changes beyond the control of activists or the organizations and this impacted resource mobilization, an argument that Cecilia Conrad makes in Chap. 5. This was especially true as the GOP's loss of female supporters due to the party's antifeminism was dwarfed by massive gains "among white men. Many traditionally Democratic men who felt alienated by their party's embrace of women and minority concerns were switching parties" (Rymph 123). Rymph adds that even at the end of the 1970s,

> women across the political spectrum … could understand themselves to be part of one feminist movement, even when they were of different political parties, and even disagreed about the meaning of feminism itself. Twenty-five years after Reagan's election, feminism itself has ceased to be a broad social movement as it was during its seventies' heyday (236).

This assessment suggests that the identity politics that emerged in Second-Wave Feminism eroded the broad support for the movement even as more groups and ideological perspectives had seats at the table.

With political initiatives like the Equal Rights Amendment, Title IX, and the National Women's Political Caucus, cultural interventions like *Ms.* magazine, the birth of women's studies, black studies, and Chicana studies in the academy, the rising importance of female religious leaders (as Laura Foxworth demonstrates in this volume), the proliferation of consciousness-raising groups and organizations, and the "sex wars" over radical lesbian politics, many Second-Wave feminists pursued a liberal agenda that sought to improve the lives of women across the country even as socialist and radical feminists were introducing more complicated gender frames for understanding social oppression and resistance. However, while they worked to create new spaces to organize, new tools to examine oppression, and new models of building coalitions, feminists of all stripes met increasingly intense opposition by both conservatives and liberals.

From the right, as Marjorie Spruill notes in Chap. 3, opposition groups, rallying around what they called "family values" as opposed to women's rights, challenged feminists. Although some conservative politicians supported the ERA and although Republican presidents from Eisenhower to Ford supported abortion rights, conservative women provided a springboard for the mass opposition of feminist politics from the right. As Ronnee Schreiber has argued, "the advocacy of conservative women has been premised on the idea that feminism is too radical and threatens their preferred gendered order of social relations" and "[m]ore current advocates also claim that feminists have strayed too far from the goal of promoting equality" (18). Beyond these claims were conservatives that "often spoke of feminism as a great evil rooted in secular humanism and advocating great sins, including abortion and homosexuality. It was common to link feminism with Communism and to insist that it would weaken the traditional family, the bulwark of a free America, and replace the care and influence of parents with federally run child care beyond parental control" (80). The pendulum swung back harshly against lesbian activists, in particular, with popular voices of the movement even turning against the "lavender menace." As Claire Potter demonstrates in Chap. 9, scholars too have failed to recognize not only the important feminist activism of the lesbian community, but also the theoretical and conceptual contribution they made to envisioning a feminine sexual, economic, and political reality wholly separate from men. Rather, they became the scapegoat by which feminism was attacked.

The Reagan administration made the demonization of feminists a top priority as it opposed the ERA, pushed a federal Family Protection Act, demonized what Reagan dubbed "welfare queens," sought a constitutional amendment to ban abortion, and announced its intention to only appoint anti-abortion judges to the federal bench. Zillah Eisenstein's research reminds us that "the right-wing policies of the first term of the Reagan administration as centered on a series of anti-feminist, anti-egalitarian strategies which attempt to reconstitute the patriarchal basis of the state and society" (236). In the early years of the administration, STOP ERA, Phyllis Schlafly's Eagle Forum, and Beverly LeHaye's Concerned Women for America pushed back against liberal support for

NOW and NARAL as the "leadership of the right identified the responsible male as the missing ingredient in the traditional family formula" (Hardisty 93). This assertion of a "traditional" patriarchal family structure drove the opposition to feminist organizing inside of the right as well as outside. GOP feminists (and at the end of the 1970s, there were *many* Republican Party women who identified as feminist) were marginalized within the party and many succumbed to neoconservative backlash, undermining their voices in the GOP. These shifts *within* the GOP eroded possibilities for bipartisan support for feminist initiatives, undermining cross-party solidarity and resource mobilization while calcifying the "family values" meme that characterized "neocon" rhetoric. Feminists among the multiple camps were forced to reckon with these challenges and recalibrate accordingly as the 1980s began.

Among feminist activists and organizations, defections, expulsions, and schisms precipitated by both internal and external forces shaped the Second Wave. It is precisely this dynamic environment that both propelled and contained feminist activism even as antifeminism began to shape national politics so clearly.

SECOND-WAVE FEMINISM: RESISTING WHITENESS

Beyond the conservatism that found federal support in the Reagan administration, feminist agitation was also shaped by the racial politics of the era, which saw the Civil Rights and Black Power movement making substantial contributions to social movement activism, generally, and the women's movement, in particular. This was particularly true after 1968, when President Lyndon Johnson announced his decision not to seek reelection, Martin Luther King, Jr. was assassinated, Attorney General Bobby Kennedy was assassinated, and Richard Nixon heralded the political shift to conservatism. Desegregation, voting rights, political representation, busing, and economic justice were just a few issues that created the backdrop for new black intellectual production that helped drive innovations in feminist agitation as well as in the feminist canon. The black arts movement also helped to birth and shape feminists of color working to build a cultural framework for social transformation.

Instead of collapsing Second-Wave Feminism into the framework of whiteness, this collection has worked to challenge the hegemony of white feminists, resisting the model of collections that often focus on white leaders and organizations at the expense of non-white organizers and organizations. As Benita Roth has remarked, "previous pictures of Second Wave feminism have erased the early and substantial activism of feminisms of color … and scholarship has generally failed to capture the genuine complexity of feminist mobilizations in this era" (2). Like Roth, Anna Valk is rightly critical of scholarship that "often perpetuates a declension narrative that correlates the birth of feminism with the dissolution of other left movements and stresses the decline of radical feminism in the mid-1970s, as the push for commonality gave way to cultural feminism" (4). Rather, Valk suggests that black liberation campaigns inspired feminist agitation and support for explicitly feminist organizations. While scholarship now tends to acknowledge this observation as an accurate assessment of early Second-Wave scholarship, too often scholars today fail to describe and analyze the complexities that marked this multiracial, cross-class, gender queer series of feminisms. As Roth contends, "the Second Wave has to be understood as a group of feminism, movements made by activist women that were largely organizationally distinct from one another, and from the beginning, largely organized along racial/ethnic lines" (2–3).

Still, the Second Wave of feminism was also intensely shaped by feminist approaches and strategies initiated by women of color. Manifestos like those written by the "Combahee River Collective," organizations like the National Black Feminist Organization (NBFO), symposiums like the First National Chicana Conference, and leaders like Dolores Huerta and Barbara Smith helped shape Second-Wave Feminism in a myriad of ways that still need excavation. As black and Chicana women chose to be identified as *feminists*, they often risked disapproval from men and women in their communities of practice, particularly as they began to theorize the multiplicity of oppressions that buttressed white supremacy, patriarchy, and class divisions. Certainly, the canon could benefit from more studies that trace the intellectual influence of feminisms of color on movement strategies within the feminist movement and outside of it. As Christina E. Bejarano and Valerie Martinez have demonstrated in Chap. 7 feminists of color manifested tremendous political mobilization even as the state worked intensely against feminist agitation through the end of the 1970s and early 1980s.

Particularly in theorizing intersectionality, Second-Wave black and Chicana feminists worked through the mutually reinforcing oppressions of gender, ethnicity/race, and class. In the Second Wave, "[f]eminists of color constructed intersectional theory on the basis of their lived experiences and embodied knowledge. Their theories were oriented toward guiding their activism; in a continuing process, theory and activism constructed further definitions of what constituted a feminist agenda" (Roth 13). Feminists of color helped to drive the internal conversations within the movement about issues ranging from economic policy to violence to reproductive justice.

Feminists of color transformed activist language and practice in the Second Wave with their contributions to Critical Race Theory that moved beyond the strategies and rhetorical choices employed by the early southern Civil Rights Movement: "Virtually all Critical Race Theory is marked by deep discontent with liberalism, a system of civil rights litigation and activism characterized by incrementalism, faith in the legal system, and hope for progress" (Delgado and Stefancic 2). The use of intersectionality along with Critical Race Theory helped to transform the identity politics of feminist activists across the country because they revealed the betrayals of (white) liberals while introducing new vocabulary and theoretical apparatuses that shifted activist energy away from small, short-term bureaucratic changes toward long-term consciousness-raising that put white supremacy in conversation with gender politics. These ideological shifts (and others like them) made tremendous impacts on Second-Wave activism (as Nadia Brown, et al. document in Chap. 9) by shaping the participants active in feminist organizations and cohorts that have built, maintained, and lost political power. These changes have also helped shape contemporary movements, as the #BlackLivesMatter movement suggests.

Conclusion

While the essays in this collection chart important moments, readings, and figures in Second-Wave history and thought, sadly, the persistence of popular pronouncements of the death or end of feminism demonstrate the disappointing continuity of gender inequity. As the popular press continues to declare feminism obsolete with a co-option of "postfeminism," scholars need to take seriously the popular historiography of feminist activism and the identity politics privileged by scholars. Scholars need to be diligent that they are not writing their own political ideology into assessments of feminist activism, particularly around race and sexuality.

As scholarship about feminism in this period continues to assess the strategies and legacies of the Second Wave, this collection suggests scholars should train their attention to alternative models for charting the centrality of non-white, non-American, non-Western ideologies on feminist activism; feminist collaboration and confrontation; the role of oppositional groups in shaping and reshaping feminist organization and strategy; and the different goals motivating structural political change versus those pushing for tactics that transformed individual consciousness.

But even as feminist organizing was influenced from outside, so, too, was that outside influence problematic for women's liberationists. As Christine Stansell writes in a section that bears lengthy quotation:

> Women's liberation retained the male left's habits of sweeping indictment, the heavy-handed Marxist-Leninist theorizing, the scorn for compromise, the insistence that life was lived in blacks and whites and not in grays, the penchant for histrionic displays of outrage and suffering, the faith that sheer will could bring about a perfect—or near-perfect—society purged of wrongs, and the scorn for liberalism, electoral politics, and government. The impulse to make a clean sweep, to scour society of every vestige of sexism, came from faith in the powers of a revolution that would clean the Augean stables of exploitation (230).

As feminists mobilized the rhetorical and political habits of the male left (in many of its incarnations), they occasionally worked against the explicit interests of their movement, compromised their values, made political blunders, and calcified ideological precepts that made future organizing more difficult. These missteps formed the critical edge of radical and socialist feminist activism, enabling a creative tension to drive feminist praxis.

Still, the political and rhetorical baggage of the male left seems especially important for historiographers of the feminist movement to document, particularly in the Second Wave. Too often, because the political stakes are so high, scholars seem reluctant to criticize the tactics and strategies of feminist activists or organizations when they appropriated sexist and racist ideology, undermined short-term success, endangered long-term movement viability, or destabilized strategic coalitions. With the enduring importance of organization and agitation in a neoliberal, late capitalist society, scholars must be vigilant in pointing to and charting the opportunities and costs of strategic choices in feminist activism across time, taking care to assess those places where feminist activists missed opportunities, sabotaged collaboration, or committed tactical errors. Only when historiographers can document *both* the successes and the failures of feminist activists can we truly have a more robust account of activism in the Second Wave.

REFERENCES

Delgado, Richard, and Jean Stefancic. 2000. *Critical Race Theory: The Cutting Edge*, 2nd ed. Philadelphia, PA: Temple University Press.

Eisenstein, Zillah. 1987. Liberalism, Feminism and the Reagan State: The Neoconservative Assault on (Sexual) Equality. In *Socialist Register*, vol. 23, eds. Ralph Miliband, John Saville, and Leo Panitch, 236–262.

Elam, Diane. 1997. Sisters Are Doing It to Themselves. In *Generations: Academic Feminists in Dialogue*, eds. Devonay Loosner and E. Ann Kaplan. Minneapolis: University of Minnesota Press.

Hardisty, Jean. 2000. *Mobilizing Resentment: Conservative Resurgence from the John Birch Society to the Promise Keepers*. Boston, MA: Beacon Press.

Hewitt, Nancy A. 2010. Introduction. In *No Permanent Waves: Recasting Histories of U.S. Feminism*, ed. Nancy A. Hewitt. New Brunswick, NJ: Rutgers University Press.

Roth, Benita. 2003. *Separate Roads to Feminism: Black, Chicana, and White Feminist Movement in America's Second Wave*. Cambridge: Cambridge University Press.

Rymph, Catherine. 2006. *Republican Women: Feminism and Conservatism from Suffrage Through the Rise of the New Right*. Chapel Hill: University of North Carolina Press.

Schreiber, Ronnee. 2012. *Righting Feminism: Conservative Women and American Politics*. Oxford: Oxford University Press.

Spruill, Marjorie. 2008. Gender and America's Right Turn. In *Rightward Bound: Making America Conservative in the 1970s*, edited by Bruce J. Schulman and Julian E. Zelizer. Cambridge, MA: Harvard University Press, 71–89.

Stansell, Christine. 2010. *The Feminist Promise: 1972–The Present*. New York: Random House.

Valk, Anne M. 2010. *Radical Sisters: Second-Wave Feminism and Black Liberation in Washington*. Urbana: University of Illinois Press.

Whittier, Nancy. 1995. *Feminist Generations: The Persistence of the Racial Women's Movement*. Philadelphia, PA: Temple University Press.

Erratum to: The Legacy of Second-Wave Feminism in American Politics

Angie Maxwell and Todd Shields

Erratum to:
A. Maxwell and T. Shields (eds.), *The Legacy of Second-Wave Feminism in American Politics*, https://doi.org/10.1007/978-3-319-62117-3

The original version of the book was inadvertently published prematurely before incorporating the final corrections due to an error in the production process. The version supplied here has been corrected and approved by the author [authors].

The updated online version of this book can be found at
https://doi.org/10.1007/978-3-319-62117-3_1
https://doi.org/10.1007/978-3-319-62117-3_2
https://doi.org/10.1007/978-3-319-62117-3_3
https://doi.org/10.1007/978-3-319-62117-3_4
https://doi.org/10.1007/978-3-319-62117-3_5
https://doi.org/10.1007/978-3-319-62117-3_6
https://doi.org/10.1007/978-3-319-62117-3_7
https://doi.org/10.1007/978-3-319-62117-3_8
https://doi.org/10.1007/978-3-319-62117-3_9
https://doi.org/10.1007/978-3-319-62117-3_10 and
https://doi.org/10.1007/978-3-319-62117-3

© The Author(s) 2018
A. Maxwell and T. Shields (eds.), *The Legacy of Second-Wave Feminism in American Politics*, https://doi.org/10.1007/978-3-319-62117-3_11

The manufacturer's authorised representative in the EU is Springer Nature Customer Service Centre GmbH, Europaplatz 3, 69115 Heidelberg, Germany. If you have any concerns regarding our products, please contact ProductSafety@springernature.com

Printed and bound by CPI Group (UK) Ltd, Croydon, CR0 4YY

23/03/2026

02076666-0009